SON OF
A POACHER

SON OF
A POACHER

WYOMING WARDEN IN THE MAKING

SCOTT C. WERBELOW

To order additional copies of this book, contact:
Xlibris
844-714-8691
www.Xlibris.com
Orders@Xlibris.com
822392

CONTENTS

Dedication

This book is dedicated to the most wonderful man I have ever met in my life: my stepfather, Martin R. Mayland. Thank you so much Martin for shaping my early childhood life and making me the man I am today. You gave me huge responsibilities as a young child and trusted me every step of the way. You never doubted me no matter the task. You taught me to be confident and responsible at a young age. You always led by example in how you treated others. You are a very kind, patient, and soft-spoken man. All the hard work and long hours working in the fields at Bear Creek Ranch. All the time spent working with and drinking coffee with various sheepherders shaped my early life. I will always remember a few of your quotes from a young age: "Treat others the way you would like to be treated" and "Never burn a bridge with anyone in life as you never know when you might need that person for help someday." I will always love you, Martin R. Mayland, with the bottom of my heart! Sorry for leaving you in the bar that one night!

(Martin R. Mayland)

A special thanks to my mother, Diana J. Mayland, for all her love and support along the bumpy road we all call life! She has always been there for me and taught me many valuable lessons in life. She taught me how to work hard to earn the things I wanted out of life. She sat through hours of wrestling matches and football games over the years supporting me in sports. She provided hundreds of memories of our life at Bear Creek Ranch, some of which are written in this book. Thank you for always being my mom. Love you much, DJ!

I would also like to thank my brother Wade for being at my side through many tough and fun times! We talk on the phone nearly every day and the stories past and future will never end! Thank you, Brother Wade, for always being there for me, I love you!

To my father, William C. Werbelow (August 7, 1945–September 15, 1985) at age forty. You inspired me to write this book, and I know you have been with me every step of the way on my incredible journey. Rest in peace, Dad. Love you forever!

My life has been blessed. I have got to experience things that few people could even imagine! My journey in life started early and would carry through twenty-five-plus years working for the Wyoming Game & Fish Department. I would like to thank Bob Trebelcock of Lander, Wyoming, for all the great memories working together in our younger days and going to bat for me to get hired permanently with the Wyoming Game & Fish Department. I would also like to thank Terry Cleveland and Jay Lawson for all their help and support along the way! Everyone needs great mentors in their life to succeed, and I had them along the way!

I would have never written this book without the encouragement and support from my awesome friend and neighbor Marge Hall. She was by my side editing every chapter and providing words of encouragement to keep me focused at every step in developing the book! Thank you, Marge Hall, for your contribution toward getting this book published and all your love and support along the way. Love you, Mario!

I would like to thank my beautiful wife, Kim Werbelow, for all her help and support while writing this book. She encouraged me to keep writing, even though there were many days and nights we visited little because I was busy writing and sometimes just thinking! Thanks for being patient with me every day! I love you, honey!

And last, I would like to thank Jo Jean Thomas DeHony from Cody, Wyoming, for encouraging and referring me to Xlibris Publishing Company. Without her and all her pieces of advice, I would have never pursued getting a book published. And it all started from a conversation we had in her yard one winter day about a sheep wagon she was trying to sell.

About the Author

I feel like I have been on a blessed journey my entire life. Sometimes I felt I had a clear purpose and was on a path in the right direction, but then there were times when life took a turn, and I wasn't sure I had a purpose at all. In the end, those unanswered prayers turned out to be miracles. I just didn't know it at the time.

The first five years of my life were spent in Emblem, Wyoming, population, 10. My father worked hard to pay the bills, and we lived paycheck to paycheck. My dad was an alcoholic, and my parents divorced when I was five years old. My mother remarried my stepfather, Martin Mayland, who owned a large ranch on which I grew up enjoying hunting and fishing; but more importantly, I worked hard, cared for land and livestock, and assumed responsibility beyond my years. My parents instilled self-confidence and a strong work ethic in me from a very young age.

It was my dream to become a Wyoming Game Warden someday. The thought of wearing that red shirt and enforcing wildlife regulation was all I thought about. Except I wasn't good at school. I acted out when I was bored and spent the majority of many school days being disciplined for poor behavior. I just didn't apply myself because I hated it. I did graduate high school, but I had no thoughts of college. My brother, Wade, talked me into playing football at Chadron College in Nebraska after high school. Since I had to enroll in courses to play on the football team, I ended up with a BS degree in industrial technology.

I always wanted to be a game warden, but my college advisor talked me out of it because there were few permanent jobs at that time. I worked as a substitute teacher upon graduation from college; but when a job opportunity came open in the Game and Fish Department, I jumped at the chance. It was an uphill battle, to say the least. I eventually got hired by the Wyoming Game & Fish Department and spent the next twenty-five-plus years living a life that many couldn't even comprehend. After twenty-five-plus years of experience and stories with the Wyoming Game & Fish Department, I was inspired to write a book explaining my journey starting from childhood to the point of finally getting hired as a game warden.

All the stories in this book are true—at least the way I remembered them back then anyways! This book will tell you my early journey of what I went through to finally become a Wyoming game warden. I would much like to continue writing true stories of a Wyoming game warden as I have twenty-five-plus years of wild and crazy stories stored in my head I feel like I have lived a very blessed life with many crazy adventures and stories. Now it's time for me to share some of them!

Chapter 1

First Memories

The date was February 14, 1968. I remembered having a difficult time breathing, and my whole body felt like it was being stuffed into a small sock! I could hear a woman screaming. That screaming was coming from my mother! I was having a tough time opening my eyes. The room was extremely blurry! I could barely make out the face of a man wearing a white mask and wearing round wire glasses. This person was dressed in blue, wearing a weird hat and white booties. There were other people dressed in blue rushing around the room. Suddenly, the pressure released, but I still couldn't breathe!

I was quickly held upside down and slapped on my rear by the man in the white mask and glasses. I cried; and thankfully, I could slowly breathe again. I heard the man wearing blue say, "It's 1:40 p.m., and we have a healthy baby boy. Congratulations, Mom!" I started screaming because I was hungry and cold. The next thing I remember was me suckling on my mother's breast, and all was good again! Actually, I remember none of that happening, but that was the day I arrived in this world, the day that my incredible journey would begin! My parents later named me Scott Carsten Werbelow.

My first memories were living in a small white house in a tiny town called Emblem. There wasn't really a town, just a post office sitting along a highway with a sign that read Emblem, population 10. This population sign was shown on the Johnny Carson show in the 1970s as the smallest populated town in the United States. People who lived in this small community were primarily farmers. My dad spent time working on the railroad and stacking bags of bentonite at a local bentonite plant north of a small town called Greybull. My dad, William Carsten Werbelow, also known as Bill, also did some farming on his forty acres in Emblem.

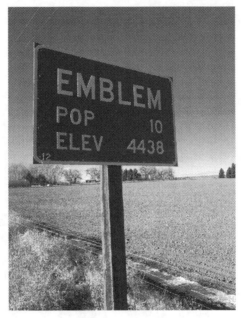

My home town

My dad was tall, handsome, and athletic. People who knew him well said he was the strongest man they had ever met. He was an exceptional wrestler because of his strength and played defensive end for the Greybull Buffs football team. My dad played on one of the only state championship teams that the Greybull Buffs ever won! Because he was such a handsome and strong athlete, he met one of the prettiest women in high school; and they dated. They soon fell in love and married at a young age and moved to Emblem. This woman had beautiful blue eyes, blonde hair, and a very nice figure! This beautiful woman later became my mother, Diana Jean Werbelow, also known as DJ.

My Dad Bill Werbelow, in his glory days!

My mom was beautiful and energetic. She liked nice things, and it was important for her to have a pretty yard and clean house. The house we lived in was small and well kept. The yard was well kept with a fence around it and pretty purple lilac bushes on two sides of the fence. In the front of the house were various beautiful flowers that my mother planted and cared for. My mother had planted hollyhock flowers that grew over five feet tall and grew up the side of the house. My dad's parents lived across the pasture to the west in a larger white house with a big yard and lots of pretty flowers. They raised farm animals, mostly chickens and cows. My grandpa Lester farmed approximately 160 acres, and my grandma Helen

Grandparents house in Emblem WY

3

prided herself on the huge garden of fresh vegetables she produced each year.

My grandparents were very hardworking people who lived very simple lives, but they always seemed happy! My grandpa drove to Greybull every Tuesday night during the winter months to bowl at the local bowling alley. He became a very good bowler and had a large glass display case full of his bowling trophies he was very proud of. My grandmother, who was a very sweet lady, played bridge with her friends every Thursday afternoon during the winter months. My grandpa loved to hunt, fish, trap, and collect guns. My grandpa was a large and very strong man. He talked little, but when he did, you better listen! My grandma raised over one hundred chickens and milked her favorite cow Daisy twice a day. She was constantly washing eggs, straining the cream off the milk, and preparing both eggs and milk to sell to local markets for extra money.

I never observed my grandma wear anything but knee-high nylon stockings with flowered house dresses or skirts. She always wore lace-up old lady shoes. She would go out to milk Daisy with a red scarf around her head, a heavy yellow jacket, and her short skirt with nylons and lace-up shoes. She made a stool to sit on while milking that consisted of a small board nailed to a piece of firewood. Grandpa Lester was probably mad at her for taking that piece of wood out of the pile to build a stool because the wood was scarce and was the only source to heat the large house they lived in.

My mother became pregnant with my older brother, Wade William Werbelow, while living in Emblem. She wanted to have kids but wasn't sure just how many. After I was born a year and a half later, she was sure she only wanted two. She did have a third baby boy named Anthony J. Werbelow (Tony) who was born on April 22, 1970, and died of complications after living only one day! This was very tough on my mother to bury that baby boy in the Emblem cemetery. My older brother and I were too young to remember the loss of our baby brother. My brother and I grew up in a small house in Emblem. To say we were hell on wheels is probably an understatement! How my mother ever lived through those years of the two of us growing up is simply a miracle! We were just very curious young boys with a high energy level! When you combine curious with high energy and then add the little-boy factor, it would have sucked to be my mother or our occasional babysitter who never returned after one session of not watching us but chasing us!

I did learn the law of electricity at a very young age. My mother was busy sewing, and I was crawling on the floor underneath her electric sewing machine when I came across a pair of scissors. I knew the scissors were meant for cutting, so I searched for something to cut. I cut the electrical sewing cord plugged into the wall. All I remembered was a loud explosion with a bright flash and the sounds of my mother screaming, similar to when she gave birth! The electrical shock blew the scissors in half and even melted some of the metal portions of the sharp blades. My little two-year-old hands were burnt and colored black because I had to use both hands to apply enough pressure to cut the thick electrical cord in half. My mother said a few choice words I had never heard before. This might have been the first time that the spankings began! I could never smell electricity before, but I have never forgotten that smell since!

I don't recall seeing my dad around much in my younger years. His work with the railroad kept him away from home on many nights. I remember having to do the chores when he was gone. My brother and I would have to feed the pigs. We would fill up an old cream can with water and tap the lid on with a rock. We would then both carry or drag the cream can full of water for approximately four hundred yards to where the pigpen was located north of the house. I'm sure the can of water weighed more than both of us! We would then have to take a five-gallon bucket and climb a ladder into the back of a grain truck and fill with corn and haul that about one hundred yards to feed the pigs. It was all we could do to accomplish these tasks each morning when my father was gone, but we made sure it got done, or there would be a butt whooping when my father returned home if the chores weren't done! We were both scared to death of the pigs because both my parents told us they would eat us alive if we ever got in the pen with them! My dad would feed the pigs antelope meat he had poached out of season, and I think they got a taste of raw meat and loved the taste of it!

The worst butt whooping I ever received from my father was the day a neighbor friend and I crawled up on my grandma Helen's chicken coop and tore all the shingles off the roof. It started with me throwing the loose shingles like a Frisbee, and then my friend and I got in a contest to see who could throw the shingles the furthest. Quickly, we had stripped the entire roof off the chicken coop! My grandma Helen came out and looked up at me as I was throwing the last shingle off the roof and said, "Scotty, what are you doing?"

I responded, "Nothing, Grandma, just playing."

Grandma crawled up the ladder and noticed all the shingles had been torn off the roof. She said nothing, but she told my mom; and when I got home, my mom said, "You wait until your father gets home!"

Grandma Helen's chicken coop

When my father got home, he took me outside underneath the chokecherry tree. He took his belt off and hanged me upside down by one leg and spanked my butt until it was raw. When he was done, he scolded me for what I had done and told me I would have to sleep in that chicken coop with no roof over my head with the chickens! I never forgot those words because I was scared to death of those damn chickens! The last thing I wanted to do was spend the night with them! I didn't care about sleeping in with no roof over my head, but I was traumatized about the thought of sleeping with the chickens!

The other spanking I remember crystal clear was the day that Wade and I were playing with fireworks in Grandma Helen's orchard. I thought it was a great idea to place a firecracker in the straw stack because you could shove them between the bales of straw and then light them. Quickly, smoke came out of the straw stack, and it broke out into flames! I got scared and ran to Grandma's house in a panic.

When I got into the kitchen, I yelled, "GRANDMA, GRANDMA, someone started your straw stack on fire!"

Grandma responded, "Gee, I wonder who could have done that?" She quickly ran out the door and threw buckets of water on the fire until it was out. She again never scolded me but told my mother about the incident, and again, my mother said, "You wait until your father gets home!" I hated those words because I never knew when my father would be home, and I would sit and worry about my ass-whooping sometimes for several days!

I never remember playing with my dad as a child. The only day I remember playing with my dad, he was standing in our fenced yard throwing car tires at my brother and me as we ran in circles around him! Thank god, he never hit one of us! We would yell and scream and run as fast as we could while dodging flying car tires above our heads! Sometimes Dad would take my brother and me for a ride with him on the tractor as he plowed up the dirt. Mom would always come out and feed us a tuna sandwich and a soda pop for lunch. When Mom would show up, Dad would throw us off into the soft dirt and tell us to go home with our mother.

My mother had her hands full trying to raise us boys without a father figure around much. My dad could usually be found at the Burlington Bar! My brother and I spent a great deal of time with my grandparents across the pasture because Mom would usually have a second job driving a sugar beet truck in the fall. My grandma Helen spoiled me to death! I would show up at the house, and she would ask me if I wanted a sandwich. I would tell her no, and she would smile and say, "Scotty, would you like some chocolate no-bake cookies for lunch then?" I lived on no-bake cookies at Grandma's house for many years to come. My brother, Wade, and I made so many trips over to Grandma's house we wore a path in the grass across the pasture.

We only had a few obstacles to deal with, and that was two irrigation ditches to cross and two electric fences next to each irrigation ditch. I *again* gained respect for electricity one blue-sky day when I was swimming in the irrigation ditch with nothing on but my cutoff jeans. I had forgotten about the electric fence that crossed over the corner of the swim hole. I stood up while standing in the water and leaned most of my back up against the electric fence! It zapped and burned me so badly that my mother could hear me screaming clear across the pasture! I ran all the way home and never even took a breath of air, just one solid scream at the top of my lungs! My mother just knew my brother had shot me or something out of the ordinary that day.

As my brother and I got a little older, we were seeing less of my parents and spending more time with both sets of grandparents. My mother's parents lived in Greybull located about twenty-five miles east of Emblem. My grandpa Lyle was a very hardworking and kind man. My grandma Peggy stayed at home and kept a clean house and yard. She loved us grandkids to death, but we better not eat our small bowl of Cheetos off the little rug she placed us on and we better never sit on the couch with the plastic cover! Nobody—and I mean nobody—may sit on that couch! If the president of the United States showed up at Grandma Peggy's house, he *might* get to sit on the plastic for a moment, but nobody ever sits on the couch material uncovered—ever!

My grandpa Lyle spent most of his life installing heaters and air-conditioning units in homes. He had his little shop in downtown Greybull where he made all the ductwork and proper fittings for heating units in his shop out of sheet metal. My grandpa Lyle could build almost anything out of sheet metal. His shop was connected to the bowling alley; so as a young boy, I could sometimes visit my grandpa Lester while he was bowling and slip over and see my grandpa Lyle while he was working in his shop. My grandpa Lyle was a very patient man and would allow me as a young boy to build things out of about anything in his shop. He would even let me use his tools to cut and bend metal. I would usually spend all day building some large contraption that resembled nothing you had ever seen before in your life. My grandpa would come over and say, "Man, that looks nice. I wish I was as talented as you are!" I'm sure that he was always relieved that I had blown nothing up or cut off any body parts while building all my masterpieces over the years!

My parents never had much money and lived paycheck to paycheck. My brother and I shared a small bedroom in the corner of our house in Emblem. I had a bunk bed, and Wade had a small twin bed. We had a large plywood toy box that my grandpa Lester built for us seated against the far wall next to a small dresser we shared. Wade got the top drawers because he was taller, and I got the three bottom drawers. The house was built out of red clay blocks. The blocks were hollow in the middle and stuck with cement. The inside and outside walls were covered with a thin layer of cement and painted. There was absolutely no insulation in the walls or ceiling of this house!

During a winter snowstorm, if the wind blew hard, my brother and I would wake up with a snowdrift on the floor between our beds. The walls and windows would be coated with a thin layer of frost. My brother and I would get so cold we would wake up in the night and grab our blanket and lay it out in the living room in front of the propane heater. The heater had a fan and would blow warm air out the bottom. My brother and I would fight for position on who sat closest to the furnace to stay the warmest. My brother would generally win, so I learned how to attach the blanket to the stove above where the warm heat would come out and the warm air would blow underneath our blankets. The only problem with this setup is my dad had little money to spend on propane, so he would turn the thermostat down to fifty degrees at night while we were sleeping so the stove wouldn't run all night. The furnace would only turn on for a short time and turn off. My brother and I learned at a very young age where the thermostat was located and how it worked! If you simply turned it up to ninety degrees, it would run all night; and you no longer needed a blanket because sweat would be pouring off your body in just a few hours!

My dad heard us fighting over blankets one night and woke up and found my brother and myself lying in front of the heater. He yelled, "Who turned the thermostat up to ninety degrees?"

I said, "WADE DID!"

He grabbed us both and beat our asses! He said, "I better not ever catch either one of you touching that thermostat again, or I WILL BEAT YOUR ASSES!"

My dad went outside the next morning and discovered that the propane tank he had just filled was nearly empty, and it needed to last us through the entire winter. He came back in the house, yelled at us, and beat our asses again! As the nights drew colder and my brother and I lay in our beds shaking, we knew we could never get caught walking in front of my dad's open bedroom door to turn up the thermostat. If we got caught, it would not be pretty!

We soon learned to crawl through a small hole in the wall underneath my brother's bed. We would simply remove the metal heat register cover and crawl through the small hole! This would put us in the dining room corner behind the gun cabinet. Simply slide the heavy gun cabinet over and squeak out into the dining room, low crawl to the living room around the corner to the thermostat, and click it to ninety degrees! We would then take turns turning the thermostat up and down so the furnace wouldn't run nonstop and wake my dad. The tricky part was not to fall asleep and be found in the morning with the thermostat on ninety degrees!

One night my brother and I were fighting over the blanket, and we heard my dad, Bill, wake up! I whispered to my brother, "OH SHIT! HERE

HE COMES." We jumped up in the dark, turned down the thermostat, and hauled ass to the dining room and through the small hole behind the gun cabinet and landed back in our cold beds within seconds! My dad checked the thermostat setting, poked his head into our bedroom, and went back to bed. I only remember doing this for about two years, and then my dad heated the house with a wood stove probably because he could no longer afford propane because of my brother and me trying to stay warm.

I remember many nights hearing my dad and mom having arguments late at night. I'm not sure what they were arguing about, but I remember hearing my mother yell, "Bill, you need to stop drinking. We can't go on this way anymore!" I remember hearing other comments from my mother, "Bill, where have you been? Were you at the bar all night again?" It was becoming apparent to my brother and me that our parents weren't getting along well anymore and that maybe our father had a drinking problem! My brother and I spent many hours sitting in our father's car while it was parked out in front of the Burlington Bar. My dad would say, "You kids wait here and don't get out of the car until I return." He would then give us a salted nut roll or Snickers candy bar. We were plumb content sitting in the car as long as we had a candy bar or sometimes two depending on how long my dad would be in the bar.

My mother would get upset and call the bars, and sometimes she would even come looking for my dad if she didn't believe the bartender's response telling her he hadn't seen Bill all day. One evening my dad came running out of the bar and jumped into his truck. He said, "SHIT, your mother is on her way. We need to get the HELL OUT OF HERE!" He fired up the truck and peeled out squealing his tires as we hit the pavement. It was nearly dark, and he was headed toward home just as fast as that old Ford would go when I heard him say, "Shit, there she is!" I looked up over the dash because he had told me to lie down on the seat; so if we passed my mother on the highway, she wouldn't know that I was with him at the bar. He quickly whipped the truck hard to the right, and we slid sideways onto a gravel county road headed due east.

This is when I learned that my ole man could drive with the best of them. He romped on the throttle of that old 1970s green-and-white Ford F-250 and drove it like it was stolen! I looked in the passenger-side mirror and could see the grill of my mother's purple 1967 Pontiac Bonneville with my pissed-off mother at the wheel! She was on our ass and gaining when my dad said, "HOLD ON, SON, THIS IS GOING TO BE A REAL

TANK SLAPPER!" I think *tank slapper* referred to water splashing out of container being hauled in the back of your truck because things were about to get rough. Whatever I knew, it would not be good; and I held on for dear life! We didn't wear seatbelts back then. Some vehicles didn't even have them!

I remained lying on the bench seat of the old Ford when I felt the truck go sideways to the left, and it felt like the truck had possibly become airborne for just a short time! We nearly rolled, the truck landed hard, and we were now headed south on a rough two-track road. By now, it was dark. My father romped on the throttle again, went a short distance, and turned off his lights while slamming on the brakes almost simultaneously! He looked in the rearview mirror as a 1967 Pontiac Bonneville went racing by traveling at a high rate of speed. My dad had just successfully ditched my mother. He looked in his rearview mirror and said, "WHEW, THAT WAS CLOSE!" We then turned around and hauled ass in the opposite direction and traveled home fast. He looked at me and said, "Don't ever say a word about this to your mother. You were not with me tonight. Tell her I picked you up at your Grandma Helen's house and gave you a ride home."

Not sure how all that ended for my dad, but I never heard a word from my mother regarding that incident. I recall another incident late at night when my mother discovered my dad was at the Burlington Bar with us kids. She jumped out of the shower in her pink see-through robe, hair in rollers, and piled in the 1967 purple Pontiac Bonneville to head for the bar. She made it about one mile short of the bar and ran out of gas. A highway patrolman arrived and questioned her about why she was out strolling around during the night with nothing on but her pink robe.

Dad later wrecked that purple '67 Bonneville on a trip between Shell and Greybull. He was headed home late one night after a night of drinking. He looked up, and six horses were crossing the highway in front of him. He mashed on the brakes and collided with all six horses, killing them all! One horse went through the front window of the car and died in the backseat of the car. Dad pulled the car off the side of the road, parked it, and walked to a nearby house to get some help. The car was totaled, and Dad walked away from the accident with only a few minor cuts and scratches. I only pray that when my dad locked my mother in the truck of this car that it was before the horses were killed and one lay in the backseat of that car for years!

1967 Pontiac Bonneville after killing 6 horses on the highway

Once my brother and I grew tall enough to see over the top of a pool table, my dad would bring us to the bar with him; and we could play bumper pool. We actually became good at the game over time intoxicated adults would come ask us to play for a drink. If we lost the game, we would tell Dad he owed them a drink; if we won the game, we would order a Roy Rogers. This was Coke with a cherry stuck through a toothpick and placed on top of the drink. I remember loving the taste of those damn cherries!

While in the bar, my brother and I witnessed many fights, and they often involved my old man! Dad was tough, and we had never seen him lose a fight. Most of his fights involved migrant workers. Not sure why they would get in a fistfight, but it happened often, and Dad would even take on more than one at a time! I recall a time when my dad took a man outside the bar and nearly beat him to death. The only thing that saved the man was his pregnant wife begging my dad not to kill him. I remember hearing the lady scream, "Please, Billy, don't kill him!" My brother and I grew up tough. We decided at a young age we shouldn't take shit from anyone. We later grew up to be excellent pool shooters, probably because of all the practice we had before we were old enough to enter the bars legally.

The fighting between my parents continued nightly. One night, my mother got mad at my dad and locked him out of the house. She wanted to know what time he would be sneaking into the house when he returned from the bar. She left the small bathroom window open and filled the bathtub plumb full of cold water and ice. She knew when he got home from the bar after closing hours, he would try and enter the house through the window rather than kick down the locked door. She was right. One night, as I was lying in bed, I heard this horrible thump. That was the sound of my dad slipping in the bathtub full of cold water and hitting his head on the edge of the tub as he went down. Shortly after that, I heard loud screaming coming from my parents in the back bathroom. Well, she discovered what time he got home all right, and the screaming match began. My dad got so mad he dragged my mother out of the house and locked her in the trunk of the purple Pontiac so she could "cool down" for a while. I'm not sure how long she was in the trunk of that car. I never witnessed this event. I only heard my mother talk about it years later.

The next thing I remember was riding in the back of an early seventies brown Lincoln Continental car with my brother, and we were leaving Emblem, heading to Billings, Montana. My mother had had it with my father, and she was leaving him to attend beauty school. I was too young to understand what was going on with my parents. I just remember fighting with my brother over who got to play with the rusty paddle lock we found on the floorboard of the Lincoln. Once in Billings, my mother stopped at K-Mart and parked the big ole boat of a car. She locked all the doors and slammed the driver's side door shut. The only problem with this was my small little hand and four fingers were slammed in the door!

I screamed at the top of my lungs because it hurt so badly. My mother screamed, "OH MY GOD, I HAVE LOCKED THE KEYS IN MY CAR!" She yelled, "SOMEBODY, PLEASE, PLEASE HELP ME!" Not only were the keys locked in the car, but my hand was also slammed in the door. I remember screaming for a short time, and a man came running over with a pry bar and opened the door enough for me to pull my hand out of the closed door. Mom told me to quit my damn whining, or she would give me something to cry about. We then went into K-Mart, and I got separated from my mother as I was looking for a new paddle lock to play with. The next thing I remember I felt lost and that my mother might have left me forever with no plan of ever returning. I screamed bloody murder, running around the store, frantically looking for my mother. I remember several ladies grabbing me and saying, "Oh my god! Look at that poor child's hand!"

My mother finally came running and told the women I was fine, that she had recently slammed my hand in the car door and locked her keys in the car when doing so. The women looked at my mother like "Oh my god, who is this woman?"

This is the first time I had ever been in the "big city." My mother took my brother and me out to Shakey's Pizza for dinner. I remember little about the pizza, but they gave us balloons filled with helium. My brother, Wade, pulled me under the table and said, "Here, take a big breath of this air." I took a deep breath, and my brother told me to yell as loud as I could. I yelled something, and my voice was so screwed up that my brother laughed so hard he pissed his pants. Quickly, we were both lying on the floor under the table in the restaurant taking hits of helium. We both laughed so hard that I even pissed my pants! Mother was not impressed with us, and I remember her dragging me by the collar out the front door and me screaming, "I WANT MORE BALLONS!" We later ate lunch at McDonald's, and I got to meet Ronald McDonald in person. That guy scared the shit out of me, and I have never liked him since.

I remember little about spending time in Billings while my mother attended beauty school. I do remember living in the upstairs of a small green house that sat next to a busy street. The house was on Grand Avenue. I also remember going to day care and having to lie on a thin mat on the floor and take a nap daily. I hated taking naps. The babysitter would walk around all the kids as they were napping to make sure that everyone was sleeping. If you didn't go to sleep, you were spanked and not allowed to join the other kids during fun time. I never went to sleep. I always faked it; and when the babysitter would walk by, I would quickly close my eyes and pretend to snore!

One day, the babysitter walked next to me and accidentally stepped on my finger. I screamed ouch, and she said, "What is wrong with you?"

I said, "You stepped on my finger. Look at the white spot on my fingernail from you smashing my finger with your boot."

She said, "I did not step on your finger. That white spot is just toothpaste from this morning." She did step on my little finger, and the white spot was not toothpaste! It was from her boot smashing my fragile little finger.

I hated taking naps when I was young. I sure wish I had to take a nap every day now that I'm older.

The next thing I remember was my mother had graduated from beauty school, and she set up a house trailer in the front yard of our Emblem home. She operated her beauty salon out of that trailer, and she would have little old ladies showing up at all hours of the day to get their hair done. I never understood this. The little ladies walked in there looking old, and they left looking old with their hair combed. They were always happy and paid my mother to talk to them and have her comb their hair. I didn't understand why she had to go to school to learn how to comb hair. She combed my hair every morning before she went to school. She even learned to lick her fingers with spit so she could wipe Grandma Helen's no-bake cookies off my lips and cheeks. She would pinch my cheeks with one hand and rub my entire face with a napkin she spat on until my face was bright red. I would squirm around, and my mother would say, "DAMMIT, hold still. Your face is dirty enough to plant a garden on!"

My mother would always yell at my brother and me when we entered her shop. She would yell, "You boys go out and play right now and quit bothering my customers!" So one day, we did just that. We went out in the pasture and caught my dad's horse named Paint. My brother threw a rope around his neck and told me to hold him while he finds a box. My brother came back shortly and proudly laid a cardboard box on the ground next to Paint. I said, "Well, go ahead and jump on him!" So he crawled up on the box and grabbed a handful of Paint's mane and swung a leg over to ride him. This is when I realized that maybe ole Paint had never been ridden before! Just when my brother Wade was onboard, ole Paint grabbed his ass and headed for an open gate at the other end of the pasture.

The open gate's electric fence was strung about seven feet high, so the horses could go through the gate and utilize both pastures. There was also an irrigation ditch that ran across the open gate. Ole Paint was running like he was about to win the Triple Crown Derby when he made a jump to clear the irrigation ditch and touched the tip of his ears on the electric fence. My brother maintained balance with two fists full of Paint's mane and was still onboard until this happened. Ole Paint went into a buck; and all I heard was loud farts coming from ole Paint's rear end as my brother, Wade, hit the ground flat on his butt—right in a fresh pile of green cow manure! He was wearing only cutoff jeans and a tank top when he graciously slid through the cow manure.

He was covered from head to toe in cow manure. The fall had scared him, so he cried. He then learned that his nose was bleeding, and he was sure that he was close to death, so he ran and screamed toward the house. He met up with me on the way back to the house, and I said, "Are you all right? Hey, look at this guarder snake I just caught!" He didn't stop to look at the snake and continued running and screaming to my mother's beauty salon. He blew through the front door screaming and covered in wet green cow manure with a bloody nose. There was a little old lady sitting in a chair with a plastic bowl over her head (I think they called it a dryer). My mom screamed, "OH MY GOD, WHAT HAVE YOU DONE?"

He replied, "MOMMY, MOMMY, PAINT BUCKED ME OFF!"

About that time, I came screeching through the door, yelling "MOM, MOM, LOOK AT THE PRETTY SNAKE I JUST CAUGHT!"

The little old lady under the hair dryer fainted. Thank god, she didn't have a heart attack and died! My mother beat both of our butts and told us to never come in her beauty salon again or she would kill both of us. I'm not sure if the little old lady ever returned.

My mother always did her best to raise us boys, but it was a challenge. One day, my mother was burning weeds in the irrigation ditch next to the house. She filled a plastic Kool-Aid pitcher full of gas to start the fire and left the half-full pitcher of gas next to the ditch bank. I was playing nearby when

Paint the horse with my dad packing out an elk. Who needs a pack saddle?

I observed the pitcher of what I thought was Kool-Aid sitting next to the ditch bank. I picked up the pitcher of gasoline and took a huge drink. I gulped so much of it I couldn't breathe and gasped for air!

My mother finally heard me trying to scream, and she came running over to see what had happened. Once she figured out that I had swallowed much gasoline, she picked me up and put me under one arm and ran for the house as fast as she could. I remember not breathing and the sound of my mother screaming, "OH MY GOD, OH MY GOD!!" She called 911 and talked with a doctor. He told her to mix up a raw egg with milk and get me to drink it so I would throw up! I clenched my teeth and would not open my mouth. My mother forced her fingers down my throat to get my mouth open, and I finally breathed again. The doctor told her she probably saved my life by holding me so tight when she ran to the house that I could not take a breath of air, allowing the fumes to escape before I breathed them down my lungs. If she hadn't done that, I might have passed out from lack of oxygen and possibly died.

My grandpa Lester was a large strong man. He never said much, but you listened when he talked. My grandpa loved us grandkids to death but never knew how to show love. In all the years around my grandparents, I had never seen them kiss or hug or show any signs of affection. If my grandpa swatted my grandma on the butt, that meant he loved her! One day, my grandpa swooped me up and threw me into the air above his head. He caught me and said, "How are you doing, Biz Bag?" My grandpa always called me Biz Bag because I was always so dirty from playing outside and my grandma would have to wash my clothes with a laundry detergent called "BIZ." Grandpa didn't realize I had a mouthful of peanuts when he threw me in the air and caught me. I sucked a peanut down my throat and coughed. I was not old enough to talk, and nobody ever knew what happened.

I became very sick over six weeks. My mother could hear me breathe at night clear across the house. My breath made a deep wheezing sound! She took me to six doctors, and nobody could figure out what was wrong with me. I finally got so sick I got pneumonia and could hardly breathe. My mother rushed me to a specialist doctor in Billings, and he X-rayed my lungs. The doctor discovered that I had a collapsed lung. He also discovered that I had a peanut lodged in my lung. The lung became infected, and they needed to perform surgery immediately. My mother called my father and grandparents, and they drove approximately 150 miles to be there for my surgery.

My father sat in the waiting room with his legs crossed and tears streaming down his cheeks and told my mother he couldn't stand the thought of having to bury another child. This was the only time my mother had ever seen my father cry. The surgery went well, and I remember spending many days in the hospital underneath a plastic tent that provided oxygen. I had been sick for almost two months and had lost twelve pounds.

My mother was sure I would die. She saved that small piece of peanut and placed it in a small pill jar and still has it today.

After my mother had operated her beauty salon for a few years at home in Emblem, things seemed to worsen between her and my father. They continued to fight, and my father continued to drink even more. One day, my mother was upset, and she loaded Wade and me into the seventies Lincoln Continental car and was headed out the driveway at our home in Emblem.

My father was coming down the drive as we were headed out. I'm not sure if my father had been drinking or where we were headed that day with my mother. My father blocked the road so we couldn't leave or get around him. There was an irrigation ditch and fence on each side of the road. My mother said to us boys as she stopped the car in the road, "STAY IN THE CAR, LOCK THE DOORS, AND DON'T LET YOUR FATHER IN!" They got into an argument, and I could see them yelling at each other as I sat in the backseat of the car. Quickly, my father ran over and tried to open the door on the car and discovered that it was locked. He moved to the passenger seat of the car and banged on the window, yelling at me, "OPEN THE DAMN DOOR!" I was scared to death, so I opened the door.

My father jumped in the front seat, put the car in gear, and mashed the throttle down headed for his pickup parked in front of us. As he was about to hit the pickup head-on, he jerked the car to the left, went through the electric fence, and jumped the irrigation ditch in the Lincoln Continental. He went around the pickup; jumped another irrigation ditch; and blasted through the highway right-of-way fence, down through the barrow pit, and up on the highway, sliding sideways. This scene could have come straight out of the movie *Dukes of Hazzard*—Mother screaming in the background and the sounds of rubber doing a burn out on the highway. My brother and I lay down on the floor in the backseat,. Our mother had taught us this drill to be safe whenever Dad was driving like an asshole.

We headed for Greybull, and the speedometer was buried past 120 miles per hour! We flew over the hill headed down into Dry Creek, and my dad mashed on the brakes because a beet truck traveled at a slow rate in front of us as we popped over the hill. I heard my dad say, "SHIT, HANG ON!" He couldn't pass the truck because another vehicle was coming toward us, and we would have hit them head-on. He mashed on the brakes and slit the hood of that Hot Rod Lincoln underneath the bed of that beet truck. I remember hearing tires squealing and the smell of rubber burning.

The front of the car almost touched the rear wheels of that truck. Just before we made contact, my father swerved hard to the left and barely missed the oncoming car and blew past the beet truck. My father romped on the throttle, and away we went to town. To this day, I don't remember where we went that night. My dad had told my mother he was taking us boys to the drive-in movie theater in Basin.

The next thing I remember my mother saying was "Boys, I'm sorry, but we are moving to Greybull without your father." At that age, I still didn't understand what that meant or what a divorce even was. All I knew is I would get to see more of my other grandparents Lyle and Peggy, and I would be starting first grade in Greybull Elementary School. I would miss going to kindergarten in Otto, and I would miss my school friends. The year was 1973. My brother, Wade, went to first grade in the old school house in Emblem. He would now go to school in Greybull as well and start third grade.

Emblem School

Chapter 2

THE DIVORCE

The next thing I knew, we were living in a small blue house two blocks south of Main Street in Greybull. The house was small but seemed spacious because it had a downstairs with a bathroom, two bedrooms, and a playroom. My brother, Wade, and I still shared a bedroom, and we ended up with an old hand-me-down record player we placed between our beds on a nightstand. I think we had only one record, and it played "Monster Mash." I still remember that song, "He did the mash. He did the MONSTER MASH!"

The playroom was filled with mostly junk and a few pieces of exercise equipment. I remember there was this one exercise machine you would wrap a six-inch-wide belt around your midsection and turn on the power. This machine would shake the belt and your belly so hard that you would bite your tongue and eventually fall down, only hoping that you could unplug from the wall before it wrapped you up in the strap and killed you! My brother and I feared it at first, but we later would have contests to see who could stand up the longest. We would get to laughing so hard at each other jiggling all over the place we eventually peed our pants from laughing so hard. My brother would put the strap around his waist and lean into the belt while it jiggled and try to sing Johnny Cash songs, which always made me pee my pants. I'm not sure how this contraption was supposed to make you any skinnier short of shaking the fat right off your stomach or butt.

Over time, my mother turned part of the upstairs into a hair salon, and she operated her business from home. The house had two rotary-dial telephones actually connected to the wall. One phone was in her salon and the other in the hall downstairs. My brother and I learned that we could listen to my mother talk on the phone if we snuck downstairs and picked the phone up off the receiver quietly. Sometimes we heard things we shouldn't have heard; and other times, we would laugh so hard that my mother would hear us on the other end and yell at us to get off the damn phone.

Living in town was fun because we had more friends to play with. We would ride our bikes and play in the nearby park almost every summer night until nine. Our curfew was to be home once the streetlights turned on each night. My grandpa Lyle and grandma Peggy lived three blocks to the east of us, making it easy to walk or ride our bikes to their house daily. My brother, Wade, and I were close to both sets of grandparents. My grandpa Lyle was a hardworking man but always found time on weekends to take us kids fishing or hiking, looking for arrowheads in the Bighorn Mountains. I actually found my first arrowhead in the Bighorn Mountains at six while hiking with my grandparents near Snowshoe Pass. My grandma almost fainted when I showed her the perfect arrowhead I had found. She told me to give it to her so I wouldn't lose it. I gave it to her and never saw it again until almost twenty years later!

Once my parents separated, there was a period that my brother and I would stay with our grandparents overnight often. The divorce was difficult for either of my parents. The fighting, drinking, and screaming continued as my dad would either call my mother or just show up unannounced. If he showed up at my mother's house, there was always a fight! One night, my father showed up at the house in Greybull, and he had been drinking heavily. He and my mother got into a fight, and my mother got scared and called my Grandpa Lyle. She screamed on the phone, "PLEASE COME QUICK BEFORE HE KILLS ME!" The phone went dead on the other end, and I remember hearing my grandpa say, "DIANA, DIANA, are you all right?"

I heard my grandpa tell my grandma, "Billy is back in town. I must go help Diana right now." Grandpa blew out of the house and headed west to my mother's house. When he arrived at the house, the door was locked; but he could hear screaming going on inside the house. My grandpa kicked the door open and rushed into the house to find my dad in the bedroom choking my mother half to death. My grandpa rushed into the bedroom and put my dad, Bill, in a chokehold as he was choking my mother. My grandpa was hanging from my father's neck with a chokehold, and his feet were off the ground. He squeezed and squeezed, making the chokehold tighter and tighter; and then all at once, my father passed out and fell over backward onto my grandpa.

My mother coughed and cried, and my grandpa yelled, "CALL 911. I can only hold him so long!" My grandpa would not let go of his chokehold until my father was in handcuffs and backup was present. My grandpa knew that if my father gained consciousness, he would kill both. My father was a very strong and young person at this time. How my grandpa was able to overcome him that night was a miracle. My grandpa was half his size and didn't have near the strength of my father. My mother called 911. My father would be arrested and transported to jail a short time later!

This was the last episode they had before the divorce was final. Eventually, my mother dated men occasionally. My brother and I were always observant when my mother would cut men's hair. We were sure every single guy in town wanted a date with our mother!. I'm sure my mother went on a few dates and never told us boys Sometimes we would have some cute little girl show up to babysit us for the night. We never knew where Mom was, but we were sure happy to have a babysitter because we knew we could get away with just about anything with a babysitter. It seemed they would only offer to watch us one time, and we would never hear from them again.

One night for dinner, the babysitter served us Kraft macaroni and cheese and green Jell-O for dessert. My brother and I had a macaroni-and-cheese eating contest to see who could eat the most in the shortest time. I won the contest and ate so much so fast I puked macaroni and cheese all over the table and across the kitchen floor while running to the garbage can! I then sat back at the table and leaned back in my chair to drink some green Kool-Aid out of the pitcher when I suddenly went over backward in my chair and dumped approximately one gallon of green Kool-Aid over my face and into my eyes and nose! I was lying on my back on the kitchen floor soaked in Kool-Aid and trying to breathe when my brother, Wade, leaned over me with a full mouth of green-colored Jell-O and slapped both his cheeks with both hands, causing the Jell-O to spew all over my face at a high rate of speed.

I couldn't catch my breath because I was choking on Kool-Aid juice and Jell-O plus my nose was still full of macaroni-and-cheese mixed puke. My brother laughed so hard he peed his pants, and we both got our first official spanking with a wooden spoon from the babysitter. We later told

Mother not to hire that babysitter again because she smoked cigarettes and had boys coming and going from the house at all hours of the night. We never saw her again.

My dad kept in touch with us boys as much as he could. He did love us despite his drinking problems and the divorce. I remember him sending gifts for Christmas and birthdays, and I even remember getting a giant plastic blow-up Easter bunny from my father the year of the divorce. I remember missing my dad on Easter and wondering how he delivered me an Easter bunny. My dad was a lot like his father. He loved us kids to death. He just didn't know how to show it. My brother, Wade, was close to my dad and loved him dearly even through all the tough times with my mother.

One year, my dad bought me a Big Wheel for my birthday. This was the best gift I had ever received! The Big Wheel had three wheels: one big wheel in the front and two small wheels in the rear. It was made to sit on with an adjustable seat and handlebars to steer. You would pedal it with your legs, and it sat low to the ground. My Big Wheel was red, blue, and yellow; and it even had a lunchbox behind the seat.

I would ride my Big Wheel all over town, up and down main street, and over to Grandpa Lyle and Grandma Peggy's house. My grandpa Lyle was worried that someday somebody would run over me with a vehicle because I sat so low to the ground, so he made me a flag pole about ten feet tall with a bright-orange flag attached to the top so motorists could see me coming. He made a bracket and zipped some sheet metal screws through the frame of my Big Wheel to mount the flag. Off I went like a streak of lightning headed down town to jump off the three-foot-high curb in front of Probst Western Store on the corner next to the only stoplight in Greybull.

I remember being possibly the coolest person in the world ripping around town with my sexy flag mounted to the back of my Big Wheel. My brother, Wade, laughed at it, and I calmly said, "Shut up. Chicks dig it!" I rode that toy so much that eventually I wore through the heavy plastic on the front tire and literally broke the tire down to the point it wouldn't go anymore.

My mother struggled raising us boys without a father figure. She worked hard at her beauty salon to earn enough money to feed us. If we wanted something for ourselves, my mother would say, "Go get a job, and then you can buy whatever you want!" She used to leave my brother and me a list of things to do to help her out around the house. She told us that if we completed everything on the list by Friday, she would give us $1 per week for our allowance. This all sounded good until further inspection of the list. She would hang our list on the refrigerator door, and it would take up all the room on the door because it was so long. My list alone would include cleaning the entire house until it was spotless, vacuuming and mopping the entire house, dusting the entire house, watering the plants, doing the dishes, taking out trash, cleaning toilets, and washing the car. Christ, by the time I had my list completed, I was too tired to spend my dollar. And if something wasn't done right, my mother would give me half my allowance or $0.50 for the week.

Once my brother and I received our allowance, we would ride our bikes down to the five-and-dime store on Main Street in Greybull. That store had the best collection of Matchbox toy cars you have ever seen in your life. I would stand in front of that glass display for hours trying to decide which Matchbox car I would purchase with my hard-earned $1 weekly allowance. Back then, you could buy one of those toy cars for just under a dollar. We would then go next door to Dunning's Department Store and look at all their cool toys for sale. We had no money left by the time we went to Dunning's, so we bought nothing from that store.

One day, I came home; and my brother, Wade, was playing with a brand-new slinky. I asked my brother where he had got the slinky, and he said, "At Dunning's Department Store."

I said, "How did you pay for it? I know you don't have any money. You spent it all last week with me at the five-and-dime store."

He quietly said, "I stole it."

I said, "YOU DID WHAT?"

"Yeah, I stole it," he replied. He then said, "Yeah, it's easy. Just go into the store and look around. When nobody is looking, just put whatever you want in your pocket and get the HELL out of there!"

This seemed exciting because I had been eyeing some Silly Putty down there for some time and could never afford to buy it. I told my brother he should come with me and show me how it's done. He said, "Nah, you can do it. Just get on down there and don't get caught!" I grabbed my green heavy winter jacket with the fur on the hood and jumped on my bike and headed for Dunning's Department Store.

Minutes later, I arrived at the store and walked through the front door and headed straight for the rack that displayed the Silly Putty. An older gentleman said, "May I help you with something?"

I said, "No, thank you, just looking around!" I stood over and stared at the Silly Putty hanging on the display rack for about ten minutes. I had my hands in the pockets of my big heavy green coat, and I had my hood on with the fur around the brim. I was very nervous and kept looking around to see where the owner of the store was. The owner of the store asked me at least three times if he could help me, and I just kept saying, "No thanks, just looking around!"

I must have been in that store for what seemed like an hour. I finally grabbed the Silly Putty quickly and stuck it in my coat pocket. I turned and headed out the front door with my hands in my pocket and hood up. Just as I was about to exit the front door, I felt a tug on my hood, and I heard a voice say, "Stop right there!" The store owner had grabbed the fur on my hood and pulled me backward a few steps. He said, "Come over here to the front counter, young man, and empty your pockets out." I was scared, and I reached in my pocket and pulled out the Silly Putty and laid it on his countertop.

He said, "What is your mother's name, and what is her phone number?" I told him my mother's name and her phone number. He reached down and dialed a phone located underneath his desk top and said, "Hello is this Diana? Yes, I have your son down here at my store at Dunning's Department Store, and I have just caught your son shoplifting from my store."

At that very moment, my life flashed in front of me. I knew without uncertainty I was going to jail for the rest of my life, and that's if my mother didn't kill me first. All I could hear was the sound of my mother yelling on the other end of the line. I did hear her say, "Keep him there, and I will be down in a minute!" I didn't say a word, and neither did the store owner. It seemed like the longest ten minutes of my life.

Minutes later, I was expecting my mother to come through the front door, and I wasn't sure how she would kill me, but I knew it would not be pretty. About that time, I looked up and here was my mother busting through the front door of the department store. Not only was she coming at a fast pace with a pissed-off look on her face, but two police officers also came through the door right behind her. I was scolded and interrogated for the next twenty minutes from my mother, the police officers, and the store owner.

I cried, saying, "I'm SORRY!" The police officers asked my mother if she wanted me to go to jail.

She replied, "How long will he be in jail?"

The officer said, "He could be in jail for up to ten years for an offense this serious, ma'am!"

My mother pleaded and begged the officers not to arrest me and take me to jail for the rest of my childhood years. She said, "Please just let me take him home and have his father discipline him." I hadn't thought about that just yet. I would rather spend ten years in jail than have my father pull his belt off and give me a whooping like he had done before when I misbehaved.

The officers finally agreed that my mom could take me home if I was disciplined properly and if I apologized to the store owner for stealing his merchandise.

I apologized to the store owner and shook his hand. My mother grabbed me by the fur on my hood and dragged me out of the store, repeatedly saying, "Wait until your father hears about this!" I was very embarrassed and scared for my life. I just wanted to go home and kick my brother's ass for telling me to do this. "Go ahead. It will be easy," he said. No, it wasn't easy, and now I'm a hardened criminal with a record for the rest of my life. I eventually got through this, and yes, my ole man whooped my butt when he heard about this. I was grounded for weeks, and my weekly allowance went away even though I was still doing all the chores.

Looking back on this, I'm proud my mother handled this situation the way that she did. She called the police and told them to come down to that department store and scare the shit out of me. And that's what she needed to do because I learned a very valuable lesson that day and swore I would never shoplift again. My brother still laughs about that incident today; and every time he brings up the story, he just laughs and says, "You big dumbass!"

My mother continued cutting hair from the small blue house she had rented in Greybull. There were always people coming and going, and my mother would make them look beautiful. Most of her clients were elderly ladies. Back in those days, there were a million weight loss programs out there, and I'm sure my mother tried them all. I remember a program that my mom tried that involved wrapping your entire body in Saran wrap. The younger ladies would show up at the salon and get almost naked and tightly wrap their bodies in Saran wrap. To this day, I'm not sure how they were supposed to lose any weight by doing this. Hell, even the exercise machine downstairs couldn't shake the fat off you when it's wrapped in Saran wrap. Maybe it just compressed all their fat so they could wear tighter-fitting clothes. Hell, I don't know. I never did understand that one. All I remember is when my brother and I would see chubby girls running around the salon half naked wrapped in Saran wrap, we would laugh our asses off. Most of the time, my mother would yell at us, "You boys knock it off and get your butts downstairs for a while!"

Over time, a man showed up at the house. Most of the time, he was just stopping by the salon to visit my mother. I remember he wore a gray cowboy hat and cowboy boots and had long side burns along his cheeks. He was a very pleasant and handsome man. I remember he was always very nice to my mother, and he smiled and laughed a lot. My mother always seemed happy when he would come around. He was always nice to my brother and me.

One winter day, he showed up at our house in Greybull with a green international pickup and a snow machine in the back of the pickup. I think it was around Christmastime. He came into the house, and my mother said, "Boys, come over here. I want you to meet someone." We ran into the living room, and here stood this handsome cowboy with long sideburns. She said, "Boys, this is Martin. He is my friend."

Martin said hi and shook both our hands as he introduced himself. He seemed nice. Mother was always happy when he was around. He asked us boys if we had ever ridden a snow machine. We replied no.

Martin and his green international pickup with my brother, Wade, and me.

He said, "Well let's get you boys dressed up in some warm clothing and go take my snow machine for a ride!" We were excited. Nobody had ever offered to do something fun with us, and we were dying to try out his snow machine. Wade and I loaded up in his green 1970s international pickup and headed east out of Greybull. We turned right and backed into a steep hill on what the locals called the Greybull Bluffs. We helped Martin pull the snow machine out of the back of the truck. He turned the key on, flipped the kill switch, and gave it a squirt of starting fluid and pulled the rip cord on the right side of the engine. The machine fired right up, and man did it sound loud. I remember saying to myself, *I bet this thing hauls ass.*

Martin showed us how to make it go by squeezing the plastic throttle handle on the right-side handlebar. He yelled over the sound of the engine, "That's how you make it go! The handle on the left is your brake for stopping!" He then yelled, "Who wants to ride it first?"

I happily screamed, "I do!"

He said, "OK, well, don't go too fast and stay close to the truck!"

I don't know how many hours my brother and I drove that damn snow machine around that day. I don't think there was even that much snow, but we sure had fun.

My brother and I decided that day this Martin fella was a cool dude. We might get along with this guy just fine. We finally ran the snow machine out of fuel. It was getting late in the day. Martin said, "I better get you boys home and let you get dried out a bit." I was so in love with the snow machine I asked Martin, "So what kind of snow machine is that?"

He replied, "It's a 1969 Arctic Cat Puma 440."

From that day on, I wanted a snow machine so bad I could taste it. But how would I ever afford one with my $1-a-week allowance?

Wade and I started school in Greybull that year, and my first-grade teacher was named Mrs. Dentley. She was a sweet and loving lady I just adored. After school, we would often ride our bikes or walk down to Grandma Peggy's house. Just about every time we would go see Grandma Peggy, she would say, "Oh, before you boys take your shoes off, could please run down town and pick up a prescription for me?"

"Sure, Grandma," and out the door we would go!

Once we returned to the house, she would say, "Oh, I forgot. I'm running out of milk. Would you boys run down to Safeway and pick me up a quart of milk?"

"Sure, Grandma."

Then she would say, "OK, thank you, and here is a little extra money to buy yourself a treat!" She would generally give us about $0.50 to buy a couple of candy bars.

My grandma loved us boys to death; but the older I got, the more I realized why she sent us downtown several times every time we came to see her. My brother and I drove her crazy, and that was her way to get us out of the house for a while. Grandma Peggy's house was always clean. Rough housing was never allowed. We were to sit on a rug or blanket and eat our after- school snacks, which were usually a small bowl of pretzels or Cheetos. If we spent the night there, we had to take a bath every night before bedtime. I used to love sleeping with my grandparents. Their bed always smelled so fresh and clean, and I loved both to death. My grandma was always taking prescription pills. She would take one pill to fix one aliment and take several other pills to address the side effects of the first pill. My mother would always say, "Christ, Mother, you take more pills than Carter has peanuts."

Grandma would reply, "Oh, Diana, you don't know your ass from a hole in the ground."

Both my grandparents smoked heavily. My grandma smoked Carlton 100s. My grandpa Lyle rolled his cigarettes with Prince Albert tobacco. My grandpa could drive and roll a cigarette with one hand. It was the most amazing thing I have ever seen. He would hold the little paper square in his right hand and remove his can of tobacco out of his right shirt pocket with the same hand. He would then open the can of tobacco and pour the tobacco into a small piece of cigarette paper, then fold the cigarette paper over, and lick the paper with his tongue and roll the cigarette with one hand. He would then place the tobacco back in his shirt pocket, place the cigarette in his mouth, and pull out an old-style metal lighter with a flip lid and light the cigarette. I swear, the whole process took him less than five seconds. He was also a master at blowing smoke rings. I can remember I loved the smell of his hand-rolled cigarettes.

My grandma Peggy was always trying to quit smoking. She eventually tried the all-new nicotine patch. My grandma was wearing the patch one day and smoking a cigarette. I asked her how she was doing with quitting her smoking habit. She replied, "I think I'm addicted to both of them now."

It soon became apparent that my mother was dating this guy named Martin. Wade and I were seeing more of him around the house, and Mother was hiring more babysitters to watch us during nighttime hours. Martin owned a ranch called Bear Creek Ranch. That ranch kept him very busy with work, so we didn't really ever get to see much of him. I really hoped that someday I would get to see his ranch and what he did for a living. I remember having a cute babysitter come over and watch my brother and me right before Christmas. She said she knew what Santa Claus was bringing me for Christmas. I begged her to tell me. After some real sweet talk, I finally got her to tell me that Santa was bringing me a new Arctic Cat snowmobile suit. I thought, why would I ever need a snowmobile suit unless someday I might have a new snowmobile? I was so excited I couldn't sleep that night.

The next day, my brother called me out to the front porch of our house. He said, "Guess what I just found out."

I said, "WHAT?"

He said, "Go ahead and look in that upright freezer right there!"

I opened the door of the freezer and was expecting to see frozen food. That day I will never forget! This freezer was not plugged in, and my mother had been using it for storage. The freezer was full of Christmas presents from top to bottom. I read the names on the packages, and they read to Scott from Santa, to Wade from Santa, to Scott and Wade from Santa. My heart sank. I thought to myself, *How can Santa be real if these presents are in our freezer right now? Santa comes on Christmas Eve, and we are several days from that. Santa comes down the chimney and eats cookies and drinks milk. What in the hell is going on here?*

My brother looked over at me with squinty little eyes and said, "I smell a rat! Santa is not real, and these are presents that our mom has bought us!" I was devastated. Santa is not real!

I looked at my brother and whispered, "You want to open them up and see what's inside them boxes?"

My brother whispered, "Yeah, we can play with them and then rewrap them back up, and nobody will ever know!"

We found a pair of scissors and delicately opened all the packages without tearing the wrapping paper. I opened the first present and couldn't believe my eyes. In that box lay a brand-new Arctic Cat snowmobile suit with purple-and-white stripes. Shortly after that, Wade opened a package, and he also had a brand-new Arctic Cat snowmobile suit. We were so excited we tried them on, and I yelled at Wade, "Let's go outside and play in the snow and see how warm they are!" We took off from the house and headed over to the community center building across the street to the north. This building was probably twenty to thirty feet tall. I looked up. One side of the building had these huge icicles hanging down from the eaves on the building. Some icicles were probably six to eight feet long and over fifteen inches in diameter.

I told Wade, "Holy cow, look at the size of those icicles!" Wade came over to where I was standing and looked up to see the huge icicles. About that time, one of the huge icicles broke loose from the roof and came sailing down toward us faster than a bullet. I yelled at Wade, "RUN!" Wade ran and that icicle not only hit him in the top of the head but it stuck about two inches into the top of his skull.

My brother hit the ground and was unconscious. There was blood going everywhere including all over his new snowmobile suit we would have to clean and rewrap into a present. I quickly grabbed a handful of snow and cleaned the blood away from the wound to assess just how bad my poor brother was hurt. The tip of the icicle was stuck in my brother's head about two inches deep and had broken off. As soon as my brother woke up, I explained to him what had happened. He was covered in blood, and he cried. I told him, "It's okay. It's only stuck in there a bit!" I said, "Hurry up and take your snowmobile suit off and go tell Mom what happened. I will clean your new snowmobile suit and hide it until we can put it back in the freezer."

Brother Wade took off like a bullet screaming for home with his hand on the top of his head to try to slow the bleeding. When he entered the house, my mother had been cutting someone's hair. She heard Wade screaming and met him at the front door. When my mother saw the wound, she almost passed out. She yelled, "What in the hell have you been doing?"

My brother said, "We were just playing, and an icicle fell off the building and hit me in the head."

My mother yelled, "For Christ's sake, you could have been killed!" To this day, I'm not sure how she got that icicle out of my brother's head. Maybe the ice just eventually melted. I don't know. But I can tell you it left a large hole in the top of my brother's head for nearly two years.

His hair wouldn't grow in that spot for almost two years. A class picture of my brother somewhere shows that huge hole in his head with no hair growing. It was a miracle that my brother wasn't killed that day. I did some handy work on cleaning the snowmobile suit, and we successfully got them packed back up and rewrapped for Christmas morning. I told my brother, "Just don't forget to act excited when you open your presents on Christmas morning!"

Christmas morning came and went. Even though I got a new snowmobile suit for Christmas, Santa did not bring me a new snowmobile. Maybe Santa thought I was a naughty boy and didn't deserve a new snow machine. I didn't care. Santa was not real anyways.

Chapter 3

BEAR CREEK RANCH

One Sunday during the spring, my mother loaded up my brother and me into her 1970s Lincoln Continental car. She said, "Load up, boys. We're going for a drive!"

I said, "Where are we going, Mom?"

She said, "I'm taking you boys up to Bear Creek Ranch to spend a few days with Martin."

We were very excited as we had not been to Martin's ranch yet. It seemed we drove forever before we finally hit a rough dirt road. We made so many turns I didn't know where I was at anymore. As we went up the rough dirt road, the road kept getting rougher, and quickly it rained. I think we had a cloud burst, and it rained hard for a short period. The road became very muddy. Mother was struggling to keep the boat of a car on the road. The car would slide to the right and almost go off the road, and then we would slide to the left and go sideways across the road. I looked at my mother, and her knuckles were white from holding on to the steering wheel so tight. She was nervous, and this was not a time for my brother and me to be playing grab ass in the car. She yelled, "YOU KIDS HANG ON. IF WE RUN OFF THE ROAD OUT HERE, WE ARE GOING TO BE STUCK FOR A LONG DAMN TIME!"

Sometimes the car would fall into deep ruts and get high centered. Mother would give it the onion, and that ole car just kept digging and digging, slowly moving forward. In time, she might have dragged her exhaust system off in the mud and ruts because the car got much louder and sounded like a demolition derby car. I looked over the backseat out the front window and could see smoke and steam boiling out of the cracks in the hood. We started up a steep hill, and Mom had to give it the onion, or we would get stuck! I looked up, and I could see an archway over the road, and it read Bear Creek Ranch.

I was so excited and knew we were getting close when suddenly the car slid off the right side of the road. I heard my mother yell, "OH SHIT, HANG ON, BOYS!" She gave it the onion, and off the road we went. There we sat stuck in the mud right underneath the Bear Creek Ranch sign. My mother was very upset she didn't know what to do. We were stuck, and she didn't have a shovel, and we were still about two miles from the ranch house. She said, "Martin is going to be so upset with me. You boys stay put, and I will go for help and return shortly."

We were just fine in the car. My dad had trained us well for sitting in the car while he was at the bar over the years. A short time later, Mom returned with Martin in his four-wheel-drive ranch truck. Martin just laughed as he hooked up the chain on the front bumper of the hot-rod Lincoln. He said, "Get in and give it some gas when I start to pull you!" Martin tried to ease into the chain without jerking the front bumper off the

car, but he could not move the big ole boat of a car. Finally, he got about ten feet of slack in the chain and leaned out the window of his truck and yelled at Mom, "When the chain gets tight, GIVE IT THE ONION!" He hit the end of that chain, and all I remember was lots of mud hitting the front window of the car from Martin spinning in the mud, trying to pull Mother out. He finally got us up on the road, and we made it the rest of the way into the ranch without getting stuck.

When we rolled into the ranch house yard, that ole Lincoln had smoke rolling out of its hood and was covered in mud with the front bumper

Wade and I at Bear Creek Ranch with the hot-rod Lincoln in the background

slightly bent and the exhaust system dragging on the ground. Other than that, she was cherry.

I remember the ranch yard being beautiful. The yard was huge and lined with huge cottonwood trees. The yard had a wooden fence built around it that was painted white. Next to the front gate was a beautiful yellow rose bush that climbed up the white fence. In the front yard, there was an apple tree and several large weeping willow trees. Old wooden wagon wheels leaned against the trees and the front yard fence painted red with white spokes.

Wade and I enjoyed having some real space for once to play. We ran around the yard for several hours and climbed trees. Martin came out of the house yelling my name. I finally answered, "I'm up here!" I had climbed to the very top of a huge cottonwood tree.

Martin looked up and yelled, "You better get down from that tree before you fall and break your damn neck!" He then ran into the house and got my mother and brought her outside. He said, "Do you know where your son is right now?"

She said "No. Why?"

Martin said "Look up there. He's clear to the top of that damn tree, and he's going to kill himself if he falls!"

I just laughed and was not afraid. I loved to climb trees!

The house was white with red-painted trim and a red asphalt shingle roof. There were plenty of large windows on the south side of the house that gave you a nice view when you were inside the house. We finally entered the house after playing in the yard for several hours. My mother showed me my bedroom when we would be staying there. It was upstairs and had two large windows on the north side of the house with large weeping willow trees right next to the windows. I was so excited. I finally got my own bedroom!

Wade's bedroom was downstairs, and I remember the basement had flooded, and all the carpet was wet because the cistern in the backyard had run over and drained into the basement of the house. The downstairs was very dark and smelled of mildew. It had a tiny bedroom in the corner with an accordion-style door that slid on a rail. The other room had a washer, dryer, upright freezer, and small shower in the corner. There were also two brace poles in the room that supported the upstairs ceiling. There were absolutely no lights in the basement except a lamp in my brother's room. I remember walking through the laundry room often in the night and running into those damn support beams because it was darker than the inside of a cow down there. My brother seemed to like it down there because for once he had his privacy and could listen to his music without me interrupting him all the time.

The first Saturday we stayed at the ranch, Martin asked me if I wanted to go help him irrigate. I was excited because that meant I got to ride on the back of his Suzuki 90 motorcycle he took to irrigate. It was a blue fat tired motorcycle with a shovel holder made out of PVC pipe attached to the frame of the bike with two hose clamps. The exhaust pipe had burned through the plastic pipe of the shovel holder and made it a custom fit against the exhaust pipe. I just loved to ride on the back of that bike and go working with Martin.

Once we got several miles from the house, we drove out into an alfalfa field and drove over to a very large four-wheel-drive International tractor. Martin asked me if I could drive that tractor home for him. I responded, "Yup, I think so."

He said, "Well, crawl on up there, and I will show you how to operate this tractor."

I couldn't believe it. I was only about six or seven years old, and Martin trusted me to operate a $50,000 tractor. He showed me how to start it, how to shift it, and how to stop it. He said, "Don't forget you're pulling a large disc behind you, so be careful going through the cattle guards and gates on the way home. Here is the throttle and make sure you keep it in low gear."

I couldn't believe that Martin was doing this as I sat in the large captain chair of that tractor watching Martin drive off on his motorcycle headed for home.

I was too small to sit in the chair and run the pedals on the floor. The pedals were the clutch and the brakes. So I stood up and grabbed the steering wheel, throttled the tractor up, pushed in the clutch, put it in low gear, and slowly let the clutch out. The big ole tractor lunged forward and almost stalled. Quickly, I could see black smoke rolling out of the tractor's exhaust, and it acted like it was working way too hard to move forward. Suddenly, I looked back and forgot to raise the disc before moving. Martin had said nothing about raising the disk. I'm glad I noticed it, or I may have disked up the entire road all the way home. I quickly pushed in the clutch and mashed the brake pedals to stop the tractor. I put the tractor in neutral and played with all the fancy levers until I found one that raised the disc up. *YEAH, I FOUND IT,* I said to myself. *Let's try this again.*

I repeated all the steps, and that ole tractor and I were headed for home! I finally reached the house and was approaching a narrow gate with a cattle guard right in front of the house. I throttled the tractor way down and inched my way through the gate. I remember standing up looking on both sides of the tractor as I went through the gate. I had cleared the fence posts on both sides of the gate by less than two inches with the tractor and the disc. As I drove into the ranch yard, I'll never forget the look on my mother's face as she stood by the front gate watching me drive by the house headed for the shop. She yelled at Martin standing next to her, smiling, "What in the hell are you doing letting Scotty drive that big tractor?"

Martin replied, "He'll be just fine!"

This was a huge turning point for me with Martin. Nobody had ever trusted me before to give that much responsibility to me as a child. This told me that Martin not only trusted me but also loved me like a son. He never treated me like a child; he trusted me and treated me like an adult. This would be the start of a life lesson that taught me so many things in life and gave me the confidence I could do anything that I put my mind to and nobody would ever tell me anything different. I started to love this fine man and hoped he would be my stepfather someday.

Bear Creek Ranch was in a very secluded area about thirty-five miles north of Greybull at the base of the Bighorn Mountains. The last ten miles of the road was a dirt two-track rough in places and very muddy when it rained. If you slid off the road, you would be stuck until someone may come along someday and pull you out. A lot of the soil consisted of alkali and bentonite and became very slick when wet. We had no phones at Bear Creek Ranch, only a two-way radio system with a dispatcher who would place calls for you and give someone a message. Back then, there were no bag phones or cell phones. If you broke down or got stuck, you were often stranded for a long period or had to walk many miles for help.

I didn't know the details at the time; but the more I got to know Martin, the more I understood just how busy of a man he was. He and his brother Wally owned a large International Implement Store in Greybull and Worland, where they sold heavy farm equipment, mostly tractors. They also owned an Arctic Cat snowmobile dealership and sold snow machines and winter clothing such as helmets, winter boots, winter gloves, and snowmobile suits. Martin and his brother Wally were in business together and owned or leased at least four ranches or farms. There was Bear Creek Ranch, Beaver Creek Ranch, White Creek Ranch, Nickolson Place, and a bunch of farmgrounds in Emblem where Martin's mother, Polly, and father, Martin Sr., lived.

I'm not sure just how many sheep and cattle they ran together on the ranches, but I think it was around three to five thousand sheep and several hundred cattle. Martin and Wally also had a great deal of property in the Bighorn Mountains. They owned at least six homesteader cabins with property from Bald Mountain south to the Trapper Creek area. They had a small homesteader cabin at Bald Mountain, Jack Creek, Johnny Creek, Anthony Timber, Snowshoe Pass, and Bob's Timber. If they didn't own the ground, they had grazing leases for the cattle and sheep. They ran a huge operation and ran it well.

Wally also lived in a house below our house at Bear Creek Ranch with his wife, Dorlene. I later learned that Martin had just been divorced; and he had three kids from his first marriage: two girls and a boy, who were named Lisa, Laurie, and Larry. I never got to see Martin's kids much at a young age although I did meet them and later would work with his son Larry on Bear Creek and Beaver Creek Ranches. All of Martin's kids were five to ten years older than I.

The more that I got to know Martin, the more I learned that he worked ten to fourteen hours a day seven days a week. He was always busy irrigating, farming, moving sheep, lambing sheep, tending sheep camp, and taking care of all his sheepherders. They had hired other people to run the implement store and Arctic Cat dealership but still spent much of their time tending to business. Bear Creek Ranch was an awesome setup to run many sheep but also a huge amount of work. The ranch had two reservoirs above the headquarters near the base of the Bighorn Mountains that would store water from spring run-off. Once the reservoirs were full, Martin would take his motorcycle up there to open the head gate and send water to the ranch located five to six miles away. This water was used to irrigate all the meadows south of the ranch house.

They primarily raised alfalfa and corn. The irrigation system was very complicated and some years water was short because of limited run-off from snowmelt. The ranch also had a deep artesian well that produced a great amount of water. The water was ninety-eight degrees when it came out of the ground. This water was used to water sheep down at the sheep sheds about two miles away. The sheep sheds were well built and elaborate.

They had alleyways with hundreds of separate pens to mother sheep and their babies up shortly after birth. They also had both indoor and outdoor drop lots where many sheep could have their baby lambs and later dragged into a large building with small "jugs" to mother the babies up with their mom. This also allowed sheepherders to doctor any lambs and make sure they were sucking properly and being healthy before taking them to the outdoor sheep pens and alleyways.

Each alleyway was labeled *A–F*, and each pen had its number on the front gate. That way, you could keep track of which pens needed to doc lambs or which pens needed to doctor lambs. For example, Martin would say, "There is a sick ewe with twins in pen A-9"; and you knew exactly where to go. Or Martin may say, "We are going to doc all the lambs in row B," and that meant you would doc all the lambs in all the pens in row B. To doc a lamb meant to castrate the males. This was done by setting the lamb up on the fence with its rear legs spread open. The sack of the lamb's testicles would be cut open, and the testicles would then be pulled out with either your teeth or a pair of pliers—whatever you preferred to use! The male lambs would get their right ear clipped off at the end, so that when you would sort sheep, you could tell the males from the females quickly. The lambs would also get a painted brand on their side and doctored for the scours. All lambs would get their tail cut off. Females would have a shorter tail than males so males could breed the females easier with the tail out of the way.

The sheep would be trailed from the mountains to Bear Creek Ranch in the fall of the year. The sheepherders would come down and stay in their sheep wagons at the sheep shed. The sheep would be fed daily and later lambed in the spring of the year. Once lambs were old enough to travel and grass grew, the sheep would be trailed to their summer range; and sheepherders would watch over them daily all summer long. The sheepherders were unique characters, and I spent many days as a young child tending sheep camp and

Scott as a young boy helping Martin feed sheep in the mornings

drinking coffee with the herders for many years. Some herders were wanted by the law, and they hid out in the mountains tending sheep. Some herders had spent time in prison and took up herding sheep later in life. Some herders couldn't speak English, and some herders hardly spoke. Some herders had very hot tempers, and some had very laid-back personalities with a great sense of humor. Spending time with all the sheepherders as a young boy also played a huge role in shaping me for the person I later became.

The year was about 1977 when my mother purchased a large building on Main Street in Greybull for $32,000 so she could have her business as a beautician. At this time, we were still living in the little blue house in Greybull but traveling back and forth to the ranch regularly. The building was white in color and was previously a doctor's office. One side of the building could be used for cutting hair, and the other side of the building could be a separate business or rental to live in. My mother named her business Diana's Pink Slipper. The building needed to be revamped into a hair salon, so many needed repairs needed to take place. My grandpa Lyle could fix or build anything. I remember my grandpa spending many hours at night after work helping my mom get her shop ready for business. My grandpa had to run all-new plumbing. He set up three hair stations in the front room and another in the back room. My mom now had four functional hair booths in her shop and three dryers. She even purchased a tanning bed and a pop machine for the salon. She later rented out the other hair stations to other beauticians to help pay the mortgage each month.

That summer Martin took me under his wing, I was his right-hand man as a very young boy. He taught me how to drive trucks, rake hay, and operate tractors, performing various jobs. Martin always chewed Copenhagen chewing tobacco. Just about every time I had seen him, he would be putting in a large three-finger dip of chewing tobacco into his lower lip. I also noticed all the hired hands and sheepherders chewed tobacco. I decided if I would work like a man and have all these responsibilities as a young child, maybe I better act the part and take up chewing.

One hot sunny summer day, I was raking hay with a small three-wheeled tractor when Martin pulled up next to me on his Suzuki motorcycle to bring me lunch. He took a big ole dip of chew in front of me. I asked him if I could try a pinch. He smiled and laughed and said, "Sure, go ahead!" as he handed me the can of chew. I would not be outdone by Martin, so I buried my three fingers into that can and put a chew in my lower lip that made my lower lip look like I was sucking on a super ball. Martin smiled, winked at me, and drove off on his motorcycle. I had eaten a handful of grapes for lunch just before taking that dip of tobacco. I fired up the tractor and went back to raking hay.

Within about five minutes, sweat dripped off my head; and I became very dizzy. Suddenly, I had this strong urge to puke—and *puke* I did all over the front of my shirt and the tractor. I was so sick I lay facedown in the hay field for about twenty minutes. I was sure that I had food poisoning from those damn grapes. I hiked across several fields to find Martin irrigating. Once I reached him, I was as pale as a paper plate. I told Martin I wasn't feeling so well and I thought it was those damn grapes I had ate for lunch. He looked at the puke on the front of my T-shirt, smiled, and said, "I don't think it had anything to do with those damn grapes. It was probably the Copenhagen!" He was right. It was the Copenhagen. I just kept chewing until I quit puking, but I finally felt like a man because I could chew with the rest of them now.

So here I was in the third grade headed down to Safeway to buy myself some Copenhagen. They actually sold it because I told them it was for my dad, and a boy my age wouldn't be chewing Copenhagen. I paid $0.25 for my first can of chew when I was nine years old. I later bought a can of Happy Days chewing tobacco and talked my brother, Wade, into trying it. He didn't want to, but I said, "Try it, you PUSSY. It won't make you sick!" So brother Wade stuck a big ole dip in his lower lip as we were headed to Bear Creek Ranch in the back of the hot-rod Lincoln. Quickly, he yelled at Mom and said, "MOM, pull over. I'm carsick and need to puke!" Mom pulled over, and Wade puked in the borrow pit for some time. When he got back in the car, he was very pale and shaking. He looked at me with an evil eye and whispered, "You ASSHOLE!" All I could do was laugh because I knew he would puke his guts out. I felt like we were even now after he talked me into stealing that damn Silly Putty.

About this time, my mother had paid someone dearly to shampoo her white carpet in the blue house in Greybull. I came home from school that day and walked through the front door when my mother yelled at me, "TAKE YOUR DAMN SHOES OFF. I JUST HAD THE CARPET PROFESSIONALLY SHAMPOOED!" I stopped at the door and took my shoes off. I took my light coat off and spun it around in the air to hang on the wall. I heard a noise that sounded like something landing on the floor from my coat pocket. It was at that precise moment I observed the most amazing thing I had ever seen in my life.

My can of Copenhagen had flown out of my coat pocket and landed on the newly shampooed white carpet and begun to roll at a high rate of speed across the carpet. Suddenly, the goddamn lid came off the can, and the can of chew went completely across the living room and into the kitchen, spewing a trail of moist black nicotine all the way across the living room carpet. Also, at that precise moment, my mother walked through the kitchen to the living room; and the can of Copenhagen came to a rest at her feet. She looked down at the trail of Copenhagen that ran all the way across the living room floor on the newly shampooed carpet and let out a scream I had never heard before in my life. I'm sure I had never seen my mother this mad ever. Somewhere in the scream, I heard something that sounded like "YOU DIRTY, ROTTEN LITTLE F——!"

I knew I was dead, and I needed to escape ASAP. But I had just taken my shoes off and didn't want to run down the street with no shoes on because my mother would have chased me in the car for miles until she could run over me several times with the hot-rod Lincoln! I quickly decided to try to dart past her and get to my bedroom where I could lock the door and possibly save my life. As I went by her, she grabbed an electric vacuum cleaner attachment that weighed about twenty pounds and swung it at me. I zigged, zagged and ducked and missed the first two swings, but the next swing caught me square over the top of the head as I was running down the stairs to lock myself in the bedroom.

My mother resembled a lumberjack in a wood-splitting contest as she ran down the stairs behind, me swinging that vacuum cleaner attachment over the top of my head. She nearly beat me half to death before I crawled into my bedroom and locked the door while being smashed with the attachment. I think she would have kicked the door down, but she was too tired from beating my ass with the heavy vacuum cleaner attachment. The moist path of chew had stained the carpet all the way across, and my mother had to call the carpet shampoo guy to come back and clean again.

When my mother got mad, you better run because she would whip your butt with whatever she could grab quickly. We just hoped it wasn't something big enough to kill us. Her favorite kid-beating tool over the years was one of those orange plastic Hot Wheels tracks that were thin plastic and about four feet long. Man, that would sting and leave a welt on your ass for days and sometimes weeks! I was stupid enough to get a Hot Wheels racing track for Christmas one year and had it lying all over the floor. My mother asked me to pick it up and put it away, and I regretfully lipped off to her, and that's when the beating with the Hot Wheels track all began.

My mother learned that it was an effective kid beater, so she learned to hide it in her closet and only use on special occasions. It was light and easy to swing unlike the vacuum cleaner attachment. She would always aim for our ass first; but if we covered our butts with our hands, she would yell, "MOVE YOUR DAMN HANDS, OR I'M GOING TO HIT YOU IN THE FACE!" So we would try to time our mother's swing, and our hands would go from our butts to our face, butts to our face, and so on. One day my mother asked me to take out the garbage and burn it. I had the best idea of my life that day: get that damn Hot Wheels track out of her closet and burn the damn thing. And I did. That was the end of the beatings—at least with the Hot Wheels track.

I worked for Martin all of that summer in the fields and learned a great deal about operating equipment. I soon became attached to Martin at a young age because I had never had someone in my life who trusted me and gave me responsibility like he did. I would do anything for that man. I enjoyed working seven days a week along his side! During that summer, he let me ride his Trail 90 Honda irrigating bike. The bike was too big for me, and it didn't go fast, but I loved riding that bike. I worked for Martin all summer; and one day, as we were going down the road in his 1977 white Chevy pickup, Martin said, "Thanks for all your help this summer. I can't afford to pay you but would like to give you that ole Trail 90 Honda motorcycle for all your help." Man, was I excited I finally got my motorcycle! Now my mind was spinning. Man, if I got a job and earned money, maybe someday I could buy a pickup truck.

As that thought went through my mind, I asked Martin, "Hey, how much did you have to pay for this new '77 Chevy pickup?"

Martin replied, "About $4,800."

I remember getting quiet and thinking to myself, *How in the hell will I ever afford a brand-new pickup truck for that kind of money?*

The old Trail 90 Honda motorcycle was about a 1972 model. It was yellow and had a rack on the back to carry your dog or girlfriend, or I guess whoever would ride with you. It had a piece of white PVC pipe mounted to the right side so you could carry your irrigating shovel. To be honest with you, it was an ugly bike: faded yellow paint, small dents with rust in them and overall just kind of an ugly design for a motorcycle. It kind of looked like a girl's bike because the frame dipped down in front of you to allow easier access for getting on and off the bike. But this was a work bike and not a play bike. I noticed it had a lever by the left-side foot peg that would allow you to put it in high or low gear. I don't think Martin wanted me to find this lever, or maybe he didn't even know it had one because of all the mud caked up under the bike's frame from years of plowing through mud while irrigating. Nonetheless, I found that the lever was in low gear. I switched it to high gear, not even knowing what the lever was for. Figured I'd fire the bike up and see if it made a difference.

Now, you don't just fire this bike up with an electric starter or kick-starter, not that this bike didn't have those options but the battery was dead and the kick starter was busted off. You needed to put the bike in high gear and push it later until you nearly puked from breathing so hard. Once you were lightheaded and out of breath, the bike would generally fire unless you forgot to turn the key and the kill switch on. Once the bike fired, you better get on her quick because you were generally in third or fourth gear when the bike takes off at a high rate of speed. I would sometimes resemble Superman while trying to mount this bike—both hands on the handlebars and feet dangling in the air behind me—until I could sit back down on the seat with no cushion.

Sometimes I would push that bike so far down the road, and it wouldn't start, so I would just leave it there for another day when I got my strength and wind back. Martin would come home from work and say, "Why is your motorcycle down by the haystack? Did it die on you?"

I would say, "Hell no, I never got it started in the first place!" But by god, I got her started that day. I switched the lever to high gear, and I soon discovered just how fast that ole bike would go. I went ripping and tearing all over the ranch at a high rate of speed. I jumped the cattle guard and laid the bike on its side while I spun a doughnut in the dirt road. I left cookies all up and down the road with black marks from my tire burning into the dirt. I looked over and saw about a five-foot-high embankment and thought to myself, *Man, that would be fun to jump and see how much air I can catch!* I wheeled the bike around and hit the loud lever throttle) and gave her the onion.

I was having visions of me racing in the world motocross championship. I was in first place with someone right on my tail about to cross the finish line. Suddenly, I hit that jump, and that ole Trail 90 and I caught some serious air. I flew so high it took my breath away. I even landed on both tires simultaneously. That bike had absolutely no suspension. I landed so hard that I bent the handlebars and broke four bolts off that held the foot pegs on. My testicles hit the girly frame of that bike so hard that it pitched me over the handlebars and onto my head. I skipped about three times on top of my head and came to a rest lying next to my treasured Trail 90. By god, she was still running!

I gathered up the foot pegs and pushed her to the garage for needed repairs. The four bolts had busted off, and I couldn't get them out, so I just welded the foot pegs to the frame because I didn't want that to happen again. I then fired up the oxyacetylene torch with the rosebud tip and heated the metal on the handlebars and bent them back into their proper position. Other than some black burn marks on the chrome, she was cherry.

Oh, by the way, did I tell you that Martin also taught me how to weld at a young age? That was a necessity because when you broke something on the ranch, there was no taking it to town for repairs as I didn't have money to pay for repairs and town was a long ways. Martin got home from irrigating that night and pulled up to the shop as I was finishing my repair work. He said, "Goddamn, what did you do to that bike to make it go so fast? I see burn-out marks and cookies all up and down the road!"

I just smiled and said, "I flipped the magic lever under the foot pegs."

That winter Martin asked me if I could come out to the shop. He wanted to show me something. We went into the back room of the shop, and there sat the 1969 Puma 440 snowmobile I so vividly remembered riding for one day the previous winter around Christmastime. He said, "Do you remember this machine?"

I said, "OH MAN, do I remember that machine."

He said, "I would like to give you this machine for Christmas."

Man, that was one of the happiest days of my life! I thanked him, hugged him, and took it for a ride around the ranch.

The Puma machine had a faded hood and gas tank and was missing decals. The skies were faded black with rust, and the front bumper was made of heavy steel with a large dent indicating someone had run into something very solid at one point. The track had metal cleats that ran across the track about every six inches to give it traction on the ice. This machine was loud and ran well. I sat in the garage, admiring my new machine, and decided I could "fix it up." I repainted the hood, skis, and gas tank and put new decals on the side of the hood and top of the gas tank. Man, this machine looked brand-new now. I couldn't believe it was mine!

Just before Christmas, my mother wanted to take the snow machines up to the base of the Bighorn Mountains and cut a Christmas tree. This would involve us leaving from the house at Bear Creek with snowmobiles and traveling about five miles to the base of the mountain. I was so excited. This would be my first official snowmobile trip with Martin, Wade, and my mother. Wade and I rode double on the Puma 440, and Martin and my mother each had their machine. Martin was riding a Panther 440, and mother was riding a Panther 5000—both new machines. Martin climbed a steep hill; and my brother and I waited at the bottom of the hill, wondering if we should try to climb the hill or not. The hill was very steep; and if we didn't make it, we may have a wreck or get stuck in the hill. I looked up at Martin, and he was waving me to climb the hill. I told Wade to hang on. We took off, and I mashed the throttle as hard as it would go. I didn't dare let off the throttle and not make the hill, or we may both have been injured or even killed.

As I got near the top of the hill, apparently, Martin was motioning me to turn to the right. But I did not notice the hand gesture as Martin was taking a pee while he was motioning me. I hit the top of the hill going wide open and remember feeling this sensation we were flying. It was not a sensation! We were actually flying through the air, and I looked down to see open water in the reservoir below. We had just jumped the dike of the reservoir, flew plumb over the dike, and were headed for open water. I yelled at Wade and said, "JUMP!" We both flew off the machine and landed on the dry ground only to watch the Puma 440 have an undisturbed launch into the open water of the reservoir. I remember watching my prized machine slowly sink in the water until only the windshield was sticking up above the water.

Martin quickly jumped in the lake and grabbed the rear bumper of the machine, saving it from sinking to the bottom of the reservoir. Nobody was injured, and my brother and I stayed dry. Martin was soaked and not very happy with me. He said, "Why didn't you follow my hand signal and turn right at the top of the hill?"

I replied, "Because you had a hold of your wanker when you gave me the hand gesture!"

He just laughed and said, "I'm sorry!"

The machine fired right up after draining all the water out of it, and we continued to the base of the mountain to search for the "perfect" Christmas tree. We hiked straight up the mountain and must have passed up at least fifteen trees that all looked good to me but not to my mother, DJ. She had to have the "perfect tree," which meant something out of the movies in a love scene next to a fireplace. There couldn't be a single needle or branch out of place, and it needed to be the perfect shape of a Christmas tree with no holes or broken branches. After hiking nearly ten miles, we all looked at a tree on the ridge line above us. It looked like it had a halo of bright light around it. Was this the perfect Christmas tree? Yes, it was. My mother fell in love with it, and we chopped it down and dragged it down the steep mountainside to our snow machines.

Martin hooked a rope around the base of the tree and hooked the other end of the rope to his Panther 440 and took off headed for home like he was in a cross-country snowmobile race. Wade and I tried to keep up with him. As we would get closer to him, all we could see through the blowing snow kicking up from behind his machine was a flying Christmas tree. The tree would fly up about five feet in the air and then slam on the ground. I swear Martin never let off the throttle for five miles, and that tree only touched the ground for about half the trip home. When Martin and the Christmas tree arrived at the house, the tree was packed full of snow, and there wasn't a single pine needle left on the tree. The tree probably weighed about three hundred pounds because it was packed with snow. There was no green color left in the tree, just brown branches with no pine needles. This perfect tree turned into a Charlie Brown tree on the ride home.

I'll never forget the look on my mother's face when she finally arrived home and saw the pathetic tree lying on the ground behind Martin's snowmobile. She said, "Martin, WHAT THE F——CK DID YOU DO TO THAT TREE?"

Martin just laughed and said, "I don't know, honey. What's wrong with it?"

She said, "YOU GET YOUR ASS BACK ON THAT SNOW MACHINE BECAUSE WE ARE HEADED BACK TO THE MOUNTAIN TO GET ANOTHER ONE!"

And that was what we did! I don't know how many miles we walked that day, but I'm sure I lost about ten pounds. We did find another "almost perfect" tree except for this time we wrapped it in a blue plastic tarp and my mother dragged it home carefully behind her snowmobile.

**Family trip to the mountains on Arctic Cat snow
machines, 1969 Puma 440 in the background**

Chapter 4

WORK ON THE RANCH

My second summer at Bear Creek Ranch was full of many life experiences that helped change and shape my life forever. Martin again utilized me to the fullest extent and had me working long hours in the fields seven days a week. This work included raking hay and irrigating alfalfa and corn fields both with gated pipe and setting dams. Back then, we "cubed" hay and put hay up with a loafer. The loafer resembled a huge loaf of bread. The machine would pick the hay up out of the field in a windrow and shoot it into a large hopper that resembled a large loaf of bread. Once the hopper was full, you would simply take your load to the hay storage yard and push the stack of loose hay out of the wagon and onto the ground. Once on the ground, it resembled a large loaf of bread. You would then use a tractor to pick bucketloads of hay out of the stack and put the hay into a grinder that would grind the hay and feed out the side of the machine into feed bunks or simply a windrow of hay on the ground for sheep or cattle to eat in the winter months. This machine was pulled with a tractor. We hired a man to do nothing except feed sheep all day long during the winter months.

The cube machine was large. It picked the hay up out of the field in the windrows and ran the loose hay through the machine and turned the hay into small cubes. The cubes of hay resembled large sticks of butter you bought at the grocery store. The machine would shoot the hay cubes into a large storage bin pulled behind the machine that made the cubes. Once the storage bin was full, the operator of the cube machine would stop and turn on an amber light. This amber light was to let the truck drivers know that they were full and it's time for the hay cubes to be dumped into the cube truck and hauled to the hay storage yard.

Trucks would dump loads of cubes into a large hopper with an elevator that would carry the cubes up and drop them into a large pile. The elevator allowed you to make bigger and taller piles of cubes. Some cube piles would be over thirty feet high once completed. In the winter months, you would use a tractor with a bucket to scoop up the cubes and dump them into the feed wagon. The feed wagon would go along feeding troughs of the sheep and shoot the cubes of hay. We had miles of feed troughs to feed three to five thousand sheep each winter.

We also had a corn chopper that would cut the corn and grind it up into silage. Again, the hopper would get full of chopped corn and signal to a truck driver with amber light. The truck driver would pull alongside the corn chopper. The corn chopper would dump the ground-up corn into the truck. The truck driver would haul the ground-up corn to the hay yard and dump it in piles. There would be another tractor operator who pushed the ground-up corn into a large pile. Over time, this pile would get higher and higher, and the tractor operator would drive back and forth on top of the corn to make it compact. Once the corn was turned into compact in the pile, it would sit all summer and into the fall and ferment. Once it was fermented, it was officially called silage and used for feed in the winter.

These piles of silage would be higher than the wires on a telephone pole and be about thirty yards wide and sixty yards long. My job in the summer months was cutting hay with a swather, raking hay, driving a cube truck, and compacting silage with a large four-wheel-drive tractor. As a young boy of about ten, it was very rewarding to help Martin and work with other adults. I felt like I had a purpose in life and was learning new things every day. I felt like a grown-up and was treated like one even though I was a young boy. Martin trusted me to do about anything, and I could operate any equipment on the ranch. This gave me confidence as a young boy to know that I could do anything if I put my mind to it. If someone ever said, "You can't do that!" I would say, "Watch me!"

I can tell you learning how to run this equipment did not always go perfect. I went through some serious life lessons that could have injured or killed me or my brother. I remember my brother, Wade, taking me out in the field for the first time to show me how to drive a three-wheeled tractor and rake hay. Once we got out in the field, my brother told me to get in the driver's seat of the tractor and he would show me how to run the tractor and rake hay. He was sitting on the fender of the tractor next to me when he said, "Idle it up and slowly let the clutch out." I put the tractor in low gear, idled it up, and apparently failed to let the clutch out slowly.

The tractor had a very touchy clutch; and as soon as I let the clutch out, the tractor lunged forward, popping a wheelie! My brother shot off the fender and went off the back of the tractor right into the hay rake. By the time I got the tractor stopped, it had lunged forward enough to run my brother, Wade, through the hay rake! The rake spit him out to my left as I was driving the tractor. I remember thinking, *OH MY GOD, I HAVE JUST KILLED MY BROTHER!* Wade quickly jumped up with blood running down both arms and his face and yelled, "I TOLD YOU NOT TO POP THE DAMN CLUTCH!" Wade was all right and not very happy with me; but by god, the next time I let the clutch out, he was damn sure hanging on.

He actually got even with me for that one a few days later. We were both out in a large alfalfa field, driving a cube truck. I was parked in front of Wade's large truck, waiting for him to go get a load of cubes. The cube machine made a loud pop and had sheared a pin, so the operator of the machine stopped the machine. I walked over to the machine to help them repair it. Wade saw that the machine was stopped, so he thought they had a load of cubes to dump. Wade backed the large truck up to get turned around as I was walking toward the cube machine with my back toward him.

Suddenly, I felt something hit me from behind my head, and I did a quick face plant in the alfalfa field. My eyesight became blurry. I realized that Wade had just backed into me with the large cube truck. Wade continued backing up, not knowing he had run over me. I put my hands over my head and felt the hot exhaust of the truck scrape over my back as he traveled in reverse. Luckily, I was centered with the truck's large tires and never got run over.

When I popped up to see what was going on, Wade was still backing the truck up, looking into the mirror. I thought to myself, *What a dumbass. He just ran over me and doesn't even know it.* I jumped up and ran up to his driver's side door and jumped up on the footstep and banged repeatedly as hard as I could on the door of the truck. This scared the shit out of Wade, so he suddenly slammed on his brakes and killed the truck's engine. He looked down at me with a scared look on his face and yelled, "WHAT THE HELL DID YOU DO THAT FOR?"

I said, "You just ran over me, you dumbass!"

He said, "I did not. That's a damn lie, and you know it!"

To this day, I have never convinced my brother, Wade, he did run over me that day.

Another time, Martin asked me if I could drive this old three-wheeled farmhand tractor over to Beaver Creek Ranch from Bear Creek Ranch. Beaver Creek Ranch was about six miles east of Bear Creek Ranch. Martin said once I got to the ranch, he would pick me up, and we needed to go work on a hay swather at the Nicholson Place located about three miles southeast of Beaver Creek Ranch. Martin set me up on the tractor and told me to use only low gear. He said, "Just take your time and keep it in low gear!" Martin drove off in his pickup; and I popped the clutch on that ole tractor, pulled a small wheelie, and was headed for Beaver Creek Ranch at about a top speed of two miles per hour. This lasted for a few miles; and once I was on the county road, I thought to myself, *This is bullshit. This tractor can go faster than this.*

I shifted gears in the tractor, and quickly, I was in third gear and throttled up. Fourth gear was high, and I could only get it going if we were going downhill. I finally found a downhill slope, idled the tractor wide open, and slammed it in fourth gear. I had never seen a tractor travel that fast in all my life. The tractor made a *put, put, put* sound; and black smoke rolled out of the smokestack. Quickly, I'm sure that ole tractor and I were moving down the county road at about forty miles per hour. I had enough momentum I made it up and over a small but steep hill. As I crested the hill, the tractor picked up speed; and now we were sailing along!

Suddenly, I looked down; and there was a huge aluminum gate closed at the bottom of the hill quickly approaching. I put the clutch in and mashed on the brakes. Guess what? There were no brakes. I yelled "OH SHIT!" and grabbed the hydraulic lever to lower the forks mounted on the front of the tractor. The head lowered, and all I heard was *bam*. I blew right through that gate and pitched the gate about twenty feet in the air and off to the left-hand side of the road.

Now I understood why Martin told me to keep the tractor in low gear. Why didn't he just tell me the damn brakes didn't work? I never even stopped the tractor to pick up the gate. I just kept on trucking to Beaver Creek Ranch. I arrived at Beaver Creek Ranch, and Martin asked me how it went. I said, "Oh, just fine, but those brakes could use adjusted a bit!"

He said, "Did you get shut down for the gate?"

I said, "Nope."

He said, "I figured. That's why I wanted you to stay in low gear!"

Truth be known, Martin had probably done the same thing before.

Martin said "Load up. We need to go over to the Nicholson Place and fix a swather!" The hired hand, who was an attractive lady named Levi, had gotten word to Martin that the swather was broken down, and it was stuck in gear. Levi was an attractive lady who worked harder than most men. She had long black hair, a cute smile, and a nice figure. My mother was always a bit jealous of Levi because she got to work alongside Martin seven days a week.

Martin jumped on the hydrostatic swather and tried to put it in neutral. Levi and I were standing behind the swather when Martin turned on the key to start the machine. The swather fired up, and black smoke shot out of the smokestack. It started, but there was a small problem: the swather was stuck in gear and took off spinning in circles! I looked up and saw the rear tire of the swather headed toward me at a high rate.

I had no time to get out of the way. The rear tire hit me hard and knocked me to the ground. I hit the ground so hard that it knocked me unconscious. The swather came around a second time and would run over me when Levi quickly grabbed me and pulled me out of the way. Martin finally got the swather shut down and realized that he had run over me. Levi was slapping my face and yelling, "SCOTT, SCOTT, CAN YOU HEAR ME?" I finally came to, and they both got me stood up. Martin asked me how I was feeling, and I told him I was feeling a little tired. He told me to go lie in the back of his truck and get some rest. I walked over to the truck and lay down in the bed of the truck and fell asleep. Martin continued working on the swather and even finished cutting the field while I peacefully napped in the hot sun. When Martin was done with the field, he jumped in the truck; and we drove back to Bear Creek Ranch with me still sleeping in the bed of that '77 Chevy. I look back on that incident, and I'm sure I was in shock and could have possibly died that day.

It's a wonder that one of us didn't die out on the ranch with all the work we did on heavy equipment. There were so many close calls over the years! One day, Martin had broken down out in the middle of a large field. He was by himself, and he was pulling a disk when one disk broke off. He jacked up the heavy piece of equipment with a handyman jack and crawled underneath to change the broken disk. The jack slipped as Martin was under the attachment; and the disk quickly dropped on Martin's head, pinning him to the ground. A piece of sharp metal had struck Martin in the head and had Martin pinned to the ground.

Levi was out irrigating and saw that Martin had stopped the tractor in the field. She figured that he was broken down, so she jumped on her motorcycle and headed over to check on him. When she arrived, she observed Martin pinned to the ground underneath the heavy piece of equipment. She screamed, "OH MY GOD, MARTIN, ARE YOU ALL RIGHT?" Martin had blood pouring out of his head and couldn't move. Levi grabbed ahold of that heavy piece of equipment and picked it up with her bare hands. She yelled at Martin, "GET OUT OF THE WAY!"

Martin moved his head; and she dropped the disk to the ground, narrowly missing his head again. Levi got her truck and loaded Martin up and took him to the hospital fifty miles away to get his head stitched up. Martin later told me he couldn't believe that Levi had lifted that heavy piece of equipment off him that day. He said she had inhuman strength that day and that ten men couldn't have lifted that piece of equipment off his head. Looking back, maybe Levi was our guardian angel as she also saved me from Martin running over me a second time with the out-of-control swather.

Martin and his International tractor

That summer Martin gave me the job of packing silage with a large four-wheel-drive International tractor. My job was to push the new loads of ground-up corn into a large pile and drive back and forth all day long, compacting the ground-up corn. The pile eventually grew higher than the telephone lines located next to me. It was a very scary job because you would have to compact the edges of the silage pile, which means you would have to have the large tractor right on the edge of a material that wasn't very solid. If you got too far over, the tractor would slide off the edge of the silage pile and roll down to the ground. Some of these piles were twenty to thirty feet high.

One day, I slid off the edge of the silage pile and nearly rolled the tractor. I was so scared I put the tractor in gear and shut it off and never moved an inch in my seat because I was that close to rolling over. I nervously sat there until Martin's son Larry brought another truckload of ground-up corn to dump. Larry saw me and the look on my face and yelled, "DON'T MOVE! I'LL BE RIGHT THERE!" Larry found another tractor and a long chain and pulled me sideways back up onto the pile. I went back and forth in that tractor for hours all day long. When I would get to the top of the pile, I was always scared that the tractor might not stop and I would go over the edge of the pile front first for twenty to thirty feet straight down!

This scared me badly, and I remember having nightmares. I would dream I was going over the top of the pile and I couldn't find reverse. It got so bad I would be sitting on the edge of my bed at night driving that damn tractor. I could hear that tractor running, and I couldn't find reverse. I would sit on the edge of the bed with my eyes open, yelling and trying to find reverse all night long. It was weird because I was awake but still having nightmares. I finally had to tell Martin I didn't think that was such a good job for me anymore, and he put me to work driving a truck instead.

At the end of the summer Martin and I were driving down the road one day. Martin looked at me and said, "Scott, I want to thank you for all your hard work this summer!" He handed me a check made out to me for $500. I almost fainted. Do you realize how much money this was to a young boy used to getting a $1-a-week allowance? I asked Martin if it would be okay for me to trade that old Trail 90 motorcycle for a new dirt bike. He said, "I think that would be a good idea. We should go look for a new bike for you!" I was so excited I couldn't sleep at night thinking about that brand-new dirt bike I would own someday.

One day, we loaded up the ole Trail 90 and hauled it to the motorcycle shop in Greybull. I looked at all the new dirt bikes on the showroom floor and fell in love with a 1978 Honda XR-80. The price tag read $550, and I only had $500. There was an elderly gentleman named Bob who owned the store. I asked him what he would trade for that old Trail 90. He said, "Which bike are you interested in, and how much money do you have?"

I said, "I really like that Red Honda 80 over there in the corner, and I have $500."

He said, "I'll tell ya what, young man, I'll give you $50 trade for that Trail 90, and you give me that $500 in your hand, and you can take that bike home with you!"

This was probably without a doubt the most exciting day of my life. I had actually worked my butt off and earned enough money to buy something that I wanted. We loaded that bike in the back of Martin's truck, and I was so excited I sat on the back of the bike all the way home to Bear Creek

Ranch. I couldn't wait to actually start it and see just how fast it would go. Every corner we went around, I sat on that bike and pretended that I was racing and going over jumps and around sharp corners headed for a first-place finish with the second-place rider right on my tail.

Winter came that year, and I was always busy working down at the sheep sheds. I got to the point where I enjoyed visiting with sheepherders and watching them work. Martin taught me how to draft a dead lamb to get a ewe that had lost her lamb to take another lamb belonging to a ewe that had died. My job was to skin the dead lambs and take the hide and put it on a bum lamb and then place that lamb with a ewe and see if she would take the bum lamb because it smelled like her lamb that had died. This worked well. I was proud of

**My brand-new Honda
XR-80 motorcycle**

myself that I could operate a sharp knife and do a good job skinning the dead lambs out. I also got to run the skid-steer loader. My job was to pick up any dead ewes or lambs daily and haul them to the dump located a short distance to the north of the main sheep shed. I loved running that skid steer.

If we ever had a ewe that needed a lamb pulled, Martin would ask me to do it because my hands and arms were smaller than anybody else's. I thought it was gross at first to put my entire arm up the end of a sheep and feel around for a lamb in her womb. Over time, I got good at it; and it was always rewarding to pull a healthy live lamb out and remove the sack off its nose and see it take its first breath of air and later stand up and suck on his mother's teats. The worst part is when I would have to pull a lamb dead or rotten in the womb, and often it would come out in pieces and have a horrible smell! Again, Martin made me feel very responsible by allowing me to do these things and trust I would do it correctly without killing the lamb or even the ewe.

In the spring, we would hire a large sheep-shearing crew who would come to the ranch and set up for about a week. The crew came from

Australia, and man, could they shear sheep. We would run several thousand sheep through their shearing trailer in a matter of days. They would run the sheep through a large enclosed trailer with stalls or bunks on each side of the main alleyway. There were about four to five sheep shearers on each side of the main alleyway. They would reach out in the main alleyway and grab a ewe by the head and pull them into a small pen and shear them. Each sheep took less than three minutes to shear, and they would kick them out a side door of the trailer into a large corral once the ewes were sheared.

The sheep shearers would all have a rope tied around their waist with a large weight hanging from a pulley system above their head. This rope and weight would help them raise and lower their back so they could continue to shear all day without severe back pain. They would wrap the bundles of wool with a brown cardboard-looking string that was very durable. Other workers would gather the bundles of wool and haul them over to the wool compacter.

They had a lady who operated that machine, which consisted of shoving the wool into large wool bags that looked like huge gunny sacks. The wool compactor had a large round disk on the end that would push the wool into the sacks and compact it until the wool sacks were full and tight. Once done, the wool sacks would stand about six feet high and be about three feet in diameter. The sacks of wool would weigh from three hundred to six hundred pounds depending on how much wool was compacted into each bag.

My job was to load the semi-trucks with the wool sacks, using the skid-steer loader. I would raise a sack of wool high on the trailer and rest the forks of the skid steer on top of another bag of wool. I would then have to get off the skid steer and manhandle the bag of wool to pull it around and stack it neatly on the truck. The load on the truck would get so high that my skid steer couldn't raise its forks any higher and there was no room to dump the sack onto the truck. So I would have to rest the forks of the skid steer on the top layer of wool sacks and get off the skid steer, climb to the top of the wool stacks, and manhandle the bags of wool to get them properly stacked.

One day, as I was on top of the stacked wool, I pulled a bag of wool off the forks; and my skid steer took off, rolling backward toward a large canal ditch. I could not get to it quick enough to stop it because I was on top of the semi-loaded about eight rows high of wool sacks. The skid steer went into the canal backward and almost tipped over before it came to a rest. This scared me badly. I soon learned to put a large rock behind the tire to prevent the skid steer from rolling once the weight was off the forks unloading wool sacks. I never did tell Martin about that little episode as no damage was done to the skid steer.

The wool would then be hauled to Greybull and stored in a large storage building next to the railroad tracks. Each bag of wool would be manhandled with a dolly to weigh them and stack them on end in the storage facility. Once the room was full, the bags of wool would be loaded onto freight cars and shipped off to sale. Some year's wool was worth a great deal of money; and sheep operators were even offered a "wool incentive," which also paid producers based on the total weight of wool sold. Some years the wool incentive was worth more to the producers than what they would get to sell their lambs. So the sheep business was lucrative when each ewe generally had twin lambs and the producers could fatten the lambs up in the summer months and sell them in the fall and sell their wool and collect the wool incentive. Years later, the market became flooded with wool; and it got to where sheep producers couldn't even give away their wool each year.

Ranching was a tough business back in those days because everyone needed bank loans to provide operating monies to maintain and operate equipment, purchase fuel, seed, and feed plus the cost of purchasing heavy equipment to farm the ground and harvest the crops. Most ranchers back then worked hard all year just to pay off the interest payment they owed on the bank loans because interest rates were running high between 10 and 14 percent. There was a saying back then that read, "Every successful rancher is married to a woman with a real job." My mother carried Martin through some tough times with her income as a beautician. Often, her income provided for food on the table for us kids.

Chapter 5

Hunting, Fishing, and Trapping on Bear Creek Ranch

I finally made it home and got to ride my brand-new red Honda XR-80 motorcycle. Man, did I love that bike! I ventured around the ranch, taking two-track roads, cattle and sheep trails, and just about everywhere I could get that bike I went. It wasn't real fast but started easy and was dependable and never left me stranded somewhere in the middle of nowhere. I used to love to ride that bike out in the alfalfa fields in the summer months. The fields would be full of large buck mule deer and hundreds of sage grouse.

Martin even gave me my first dog that summer. It was an Australian shepherd/border collie cross. Martin thought it would be a great dog to have around sheep and help him move sheep when needed. He told me to take my motorcycle down to his brother Wally's house and pick out a puppy. I looked at a litter of eight puppies and picked the cutest one of the bunch. It was a male blue in color and had large black patches of hair on its body with a white stripe that ran down its nose. His one eye was blue, and the other eye was white. Wally said, "Which one do you want?"

I said, "I believe I'll take that blue-colored one with the white eye."

He said, "All right, hold him up here, and we will bob his tail for you." I didn't know what bob his tail meant, but I soon discovered.

Wally took his pocket knife and cut the dog's tail off, so it was only about three inches long. That puppy yowled and screamed. I thought it would die right in my arms! Blood shot everywhere Wally said, "You'll have to pinch down on the end of his tail until the bleeding stops." I was never sure why they bobbed the tail of a dog, but I guess that is what you are supposed to do when you get a new puppy? I named that puppy Blue, and he went everywhere with me. He even learned to ride on the seat of my motorcycle. He would sit in front of me and put his paws on the gas tank. I could drive fast and hit small jumps, and he never fell off.

I was still working for Martin that summer, and he agreed to pay me $10 a day. I couldn't believe how rich I would be by the end of the summer. If I worked every day of the month, hell, I could earn up to $300 per month. I would put a little X on the calendar for each day I worked so I could keep track of my time. I remember working nearly every day of the month during the summer months. I got to where I would ride my new motorcycle from Bear Creek to Beaver Creek to help with work in the fields. It always felt so refreshing after a long hot day working in the hot sun to jump on that motorcycle and feel the fresh evening air blow through my hair on the way home each night with my favorite dog Blue between my legs.

One Sunday afternoon, Martin took some time off work, and he took my mother and brother and me for a picnic lunch on Beaver Creek. After we got done eating a hotdog, we had roasted over an open fire, and Martin said, "Come on, boys, let's do some fishing!" Martin pulled out a fishing pole from behind the seat of his '77 Chevy pickup and showed us boys how to tie on a hook and bait it with a worm. Once we had the hook baited, he said, "Toss your line in that hole, and when you feel a bite, set your hook." He showed us how to do it by catching the first cutthroat trout. Then it was my turn, and I rebaited the hook and tossed the line in the same hole. Within minutes, I felt a bite on my line so I set the hook. I set the hook so hard that the poor fish came hurling out of the water straight over my head and hung from a tree branch in a nearby tree behind us. Martin said, "YEAH, just like that!"

It was at that very moment I became addicted to fishing. My brother and I grabbed the can of worms, and off we went to catch more fish. The fish in this creek were amazing and beautiful native cutthroat trout. The average fish was about twelve to fourteen inches long but we also caught some that were six to eight inches and even some that were eighteen to twenty-two inches in length. I soon became addicted to fishing and would ride my motorcycle from Bear Creek Ranch to Beaver Creek Ranch every chance I had to go fishing. I never remember there being a limit on fish back in those days, but I'm sure there was, and I was probably over my legal limit of fish most of the time.

A few weeks later, Martin took my brother and me up to the head gate on Beaver Creek located about two miles north of the Beaver Creek Ranch house. This stretch of creek was much better than the one we fished before. This stretch of creek had beaver dams that created large pools of water that also created great fish habitat. We soon learned that the fish in this stretch of the creek were much more abundant and larger in size. While Martin was adjusting the head gate to get more irrigation water to the fields on the ranch Wade and I were fishing, man, did we catch a mess of beautiful cutthroat trout! A couple of large very deep holes held a ton of fish in them. We could catch a fish just about every cast.

Our yard at Bear Creek Ranch was lined with huge cottonwood trees, and the leaves would fall off in the fall, lining a nearby irrigation ditch with dead leaves. The irrigation ditch was fueled with warm water from the artesian well located nearby. This created the best worm digging in the world. You could dig up one or two shovel scoops of dirt and collect enough angle worms to fill an ice cream bucket. This is where we gathered our worms for fishing bait.

One Monday morning I wasn't feeling like going to school. Our bus stop was about six to seven miles of rough gravel road, and we needed to be on the bus every morning by six thirty. So we had to get up early every morning during the school year and have Mom take us to the bus stop on the days she didn't work at her beauty salon in Greybull. That morning I played sick and told my mother I felt terrible. She told me to stay in bed and get some rest. She soon left the house to go to work and take Wade to school, and Martin left the house for the day to work on one ranch. As soon as everyone was gone, I jumped out of bed, got dressed, and decided I was going fishing over at Beaver Creek that day. I dug worms, placed them in a one-gallon ice cream bucket, grabbed my pole and my little red motorcycle, and headed for Beaver Creek, which was about seven miles away.

I hiked up the creek from the head gate for about one mile and found the most beautiful fishing hole I had ever seen. The beavers had made a dam across the creek and backed the water up into a huge pond surrounded by willow trees. A large cottonwood tree had fallen from the bank of the creek and into the pond. I crawled out on the large cottonwood tree and fish out in the deep pond without getting wet. The first fish I caught was over twenty inches long and probably weighed about four pounds. I had an old bamboo fishing creel with a small hole on top of it to shove fish into once caught. This fish wouldn't even fit through the hole in the basket, so I had to open the whole top half of the basket to shove him in there. The fish barely fit in the basket. I continued fishing most of the day and honestly didn't know how many fish I caught, but they were huge fish and fun to catch. I filled my bamboo creel with cutthroat trout and decided I better get headed home before Mom and Martin returned from work.

I jumped on my little red motorcycle and hauled ass back to Bear Creek Ranch with my fishing pole, creel full of fish, and ice cream bucket now empty of worms. Just before I got to the house, I looked over my shoulder to see if I could see the plume of dust that my mother's Suburban would make as she headed up and down the dirt road to work each day. I turned around to see that my mother was right behind me and almost home! I thought, *OH NO! My mother will catch me playing hooky from school and beat my ass!* I gave that little red motorcycle all the throttle I could, and away we went headed for home only about one mile in front of my mother. I was going so fast when I crossed the cattle guard in front of our house I wrecked my motorcycle bad. My front tire hit a rut in front of the metal cattle guard. It caused my front tire to turn sideways, which ejected the rear end of my bike, pitching me over the handlebars of the motorcycle. I heard a loud bang; and the next thing I remember, I was skipping down the gravel road on top of my head. When the dust settled, I had dead fish lying everywhere, a broken fishing pole, and a smashed ice cream bucket. I quickly leaned my bike up against the front-yard fence, gathered up dead fish scattered everywhere, and shoved them in my creel and made a run for the house. I threw the fish into the chest freezer downstairs and ran up to the bathroom upstairs to look at myself in the mirror.

The top of my head was bleeding, and I had a green grass stain that ran along the right side of my head. I also had small pieces of gravel stuck in my scalp with small trickles of blood coming out of the wounds. I washed my face, combed my hair over the wounds, and dove in bed just to hear my mother coming through the front door. She came into the bedroom to check on me, and I pulled the covers over my head. She said, "Hi, Scotty, I'm home. How are you feeling?"

I said, "Not very good. My head hurts." At least, I wasn't lying.

She brought me some aspirin and a glass of water and told me to get more rest. My mother never knew what happened that day, and I'm surprised that no one ever asked me about all the fish in the freezer and the broken fishing rod lying out in the parking lot I had forgotten to pick up.

It seemed my brother and I always had a BB gun or a pellet gun when we were young, and we grew up trying to shoot about anything that moved. We shot mice, sparrows, chipmunks, bluebirds, yellow canaries, barn swallows, cliff swallows, garden snakes, rattlesnakes, etc. Each animal was worth so many points, and we would take off hunting for a few hours and bring back whatever we had killed. I remember everything was worth one or two points; but the yellow canary, bluebird, and chipmunk were worth like ten points apiece! At that age, we didn't realize that they were protected or illegal to shoot. We just saw them as good target practice. We actually never hit many small birds. That's why they were considered ten points, and the chipmunks were always so fast you rarely got a good clean standing shot at them.

My dad, Bill, gave Wade a brand-new bolt-action single-shot .22-caliber Savage for his birthday, and I inherited a bolt-action Marlin .22 rifle from Martin's father. The .22 had a tube you could fill with 22-caliber shells—I think it held about fifteen shells—so I could shoot faster than Wade because he had to load his gun one bullet at a time, and I had to only run my bolt action to load each time. The gun I had was very old and missing the trigger guard, which made the gun very unsafe to shoot because nothing was there to protect the trigger from hanging up on something and causing the gun to accidentally fire.

My brother and I became very good shots with our .22-caliber rifles, and we practiced a lot. We spent a great deal of time hunting cottontail rabbits, jackrabbits, and rock chucks. Martin would take us boys up to the cabins in the Bighorns, and we would spend the weekend shooting rock chucks. They were a very destructive varmint that dug large holes everywhere including underneath the cabins. Martin wanted us to kill everyone we saw. Just about every Friday afternoon, my brother and I would stop by a store in Greybull named Coast to Coast and buy hundreds of .22-caliber shells. Back then, you could buy one hundred shells per container for about $1.

I nearly killed my brother one day with my unsafe .22 rifle. We were out rabbit hunting, and my brother was walking in front of me. A jackrabbit jumped up and ran in front of us. I loaded a shell and raised my gun to shoot at the rabbit when suddenly, my trigger hung up on my coat pocket as I was raising the gun to aim at the rabbit. For whatever reason, Wade, walking in front of me, suddenly dropped down to one knee just as the gun went off. My gun was pointed right at the back of my brother's head when it went off, and my brother kneeled down to his knee a millisecond before the gun fired. It scared me to death. My brother had no idea that the gun was aimed at the back of his head when he dropped to one knee. He yelled, "WHAT THE HELL ARE YOU DOING?" I told him I was aiming at the rabbit when the trigger caught on my coat pocket and caused the gun to fire. I asked him why he kneeled down so quickly even though his back was to me. He said, "I don't know. Something just told me to drop to my knee quickly." I told him if he hadn't done that, I would have shot him right in the back of the head. Someone was watching over us again that day.

Martin would tend sheep camp weekly, so it was normal for Martin to have a bunch of groceries in front of his pickup truck ready to haul to the sheepherders early each morning. Martin would park his truck in the shop at night with the windows rolled up to protect the groceries. One morning, Martin went out to the shop and discovered that a raccoon had gotten into the groceries because he left his passenger-side window down on the truck. The raccoon made a terrible mess and ate bread, jelly-filled doughnuts, eggs, bacon, and whatever else he could find in the grocery bags. The raccoon left tracks on the front window, indicating that it was a very large adult raccoon. Martin told my brother and me about the incident and asked us if we would set traps in the shop to catch the raccoon, so we gathered up all the traps we could find and went to setting traps.

The set involved me setting three coil spring traps and one jump trap on the cement floor in the shop. I wired off the traps to the leg on the workbench, so if I caught him, he wouldn't steal my trap! I had never trapped before and knew absolutely nothing about catching raccoons. I knew raccoons liked dog food, so I sprinkled dog food on the floor around the traps and placed dog food on the pan of the trap with a hair trigger. The next morning, I just knew I would have a raccoon in my traps. I headed out to the garage to check them and found that the raccoon had visited that night and ate all the dog food and left all four traps still set on the floor. I decided that didn't work well, so I rigged up a fishing pole and laid it on the workbench and hooked an ear of fresh corn on the cob to my hook so the corn was hanging about three feet above the four set traps. The raccoon would have to stand on his hind legs to reach the ear of corn; and when he came down, I would catch one of his front legs in a trap.

The next morning, I went out to check my traps and discovered that my fishing pole and ear of corn were gone! All the traps were still set on the floor, and my pole was gone. He must have got ahold of the ear of corn and dragged it off somewhere to eat it, but it was hooked to my fishing pole. I never did find that fishing pole, so I'm not about to be outdone by a smart raccoon. I asked an elderly sheepherder how to best catch a coon. He told me to take an Alka-Seltzer bottle and wire it to the leg off the workbench and place peanut butter in the bottom of the bottle and lay the bottle next to the set traps.

I tried that. The next morning, I discovered that the coon had eaten all the peanut butter out of the small glass bottle, but the traps were still set. By now, I'm getting obsessed with catching this coon. I just wanted to at least see what a smart coon looked like in real life. I met up with another sheepherder for his trapping advice. He told me to take peanut butter and put it on the pan of the trap and set a hair trigger. We also noticed that our garden had damage to the sweet corn that looked like maybe a coon was responsible for, so Wade and I set a trap in the garden and several in the shop baited with peanut butter on the pan of the traps.

About ten that night, as we were lying in bed, my mother yelled, "Scotty, did you guys check your traps tonight? I hear something screaming out there. Sounds like a pig screaming!" I jumped, threw on my clothes, and ran downstairs to wake Wade up. I said, "WADE, WADE, WAKE UP! I think we caught the coon!"

Wade jumped out of bed and grabbed his flashlight and his .44 Magnum pistol, and out the door we went. We got to the garden, and we could hear this godawful screaming noise. We walked through the corn rows, and I shined my flashlight ahead of us, and there sat a coon caught in the trap by his nose. Man, was he squealing and thrashing around. I yelled at Wade, "SHOOT HIM IN THE HEAD!" Wade took careful aim as the coon was running back and forth as I held the flashlight. Suddenly, I heard *BANG!* The coon fell on his butt and looked around for a bit and took off running into the night. We went over and looked at the trap, and Wade had missed the coon and blown the jaw off the trap, which released the coon. As we stood in amazement, we could hear something in the shop making a horrible noise.

We quickly ran over to the shop and discovered we had caught the raccoon breaking into the shop and truck for the past week. We had not only caught him but also caught him by the nose. He was not happy and was throwing an absolute fit in the trap. I held the flashlight and told my brother, Wade, "Aim carefully and try not to blow the hell out of my trap!" All of a sudden, *BOOM, click, BOOM, click, BOOM, click, BOOM!* Wade would not let this one get away. He blew the hell out of that raccoon on the cement floor in the shop. I think that was the moment that I lost my hearing and have had ringing in my ears for the past forty years. Man, that .44 Mag pistol was sure loud when it went off in the shop.

When the coon finally came to a rest, it looked like you had killed twenty with all the blood splatter up and down the walls and all over the truck. The floor was covered in blood everywhere. But, by god, we got the coon. We went over to the trap and took the coon out of the trap. It took both of us to lift the coon off the ground. This coon probably weighed over fifty pounds and to this day was the biggest coon I have ever seen in my life.

After catching two coons in one night, I decided I was probably a professional trapper by now and that peanut butter on the pan of the trap sure did the trick for catching raccoons. I headed down to Bear Creek and set myself a trap line to see how many coons I could catch. So my best dog, Blue, and I headed down to the creek with a backpack full of traps and my mother's best jar of peanut butter. Ole Blue and I laid a trap line for about one mile long. I couldn't sleep that night wondering how many coons I would have in the morning. I got up at 5:00 a.m. to go check my trap line because I had to be on the school bus six to seven miles away by 6:30 a.m.

As I checked my first trap, I noticed something I had not planned on. I had caught a skunk by the nose. I didn't want to kill the skunk because more than likely he would pee all over the place and ruin my chances of catching a coon. So as I walked up to the trap to try to safely release the skunk, my dog Blue ran up and bit the skunk right in the ass. The skunk peed all over Blue and my favorite cowboy boots. I never smelled something so rank in all my life. I shot the skunk and left it lying right there. Blue and I checked the rest of the traps, and we caught nothing. Every set had the peanut butter licked off the pan of the trap.

I jumped on my little red motorcycle and hauled ass for the bus. When I got on the bus, the bus driver said, "WHEW, did you get sprayed by a skunk?"

I said, "Yup, he peed on my boots while I was trying to let him out of the trap!"

He said, "Please sit in the very back of the bus!"

I later arrived at school and walked into my third-grade class. My teacher's name was Ms. Bootright. She was a sweet lady and had lots of patience with me. We stood up and did the pledge of allegiance; but as soon as I sat down, all the kids around me gaged and coughed and complained that they smelled a skunk. Ms. Bootright stood up and said, "All right, who got sprayed by a skunk?"

I slowly raised my hand, and all the kids around me went eww and turned up their noses. You would think nobody ever smelled a skunk before for Christ sakes. I explained to Ms. Bootright that a little skunk had pissed on my boots while I was trying to release him from the trap, and my dog Blue bit him in the ass. She said "OH MY! Could you please go outside and take your boots off for the day?"

So away I went with all the other kids laughing at me and thinking I was some redneck or something. I never forgot that day of walking all over the school in my socks and all the other kids laughing at me all day, but man, did my boots stink.

The year was 1978, and I was ten years old. Martin came across an old pea-green Jeep Wagoneer at a local farm auction and purchased it for about $400. He brought it home and told Wade and me that he had bought us a vehicle to run around the ranch with. The Jeep was about a 1968 model. It was not pretty at all. It may have been the ugliest vehicle I had ever seen in my life, but by god, it ran, and it had four-wheel drive. When I say it ran, it only ran sometimes. My brother, Wade, and I spent more time pushing that vehicle downhill to start it than actually driving it. It was very temperamental, and some days it just didn't feel like starting.

We got stranded so often that we learned to park it on a hill if we shut it off. To put it in four-wheel drive, you had to have a very large flat-ended screwdriver to turn two rusted-out screwheads on each front-wheel hub. This engaged the four-wheel drive. We got stuck in a wash about five miles from home one evening when we learned that we needed a large screwdriver to engage the hubs and didn't have one. I busted off all my fingernails and tried every coin in my pocket to turn those damn screws that night and couldn't get them to turn. This was one of many trips that my brother and I got to jog home and leave the Jeep stranded somewhere. We called this our exercise program.

One time, my brother and I took that Jeep up to Beaver Creek fishing. We parked it on a hill so we could roll down the hill and pop the clutch in third gear to get her to fire. After fishing, we jumped in the Jeep and rolled it down the hill, and I let the clutch out. The Jeep fired, coughing and sputtering with a large plume of blue-and-black smoke coming out the exhaust from behind. My brother looked at me, smiled, and said, "IT

STARTED!" Since that moment, we always used that phrase when the Jeep would start.

We got the ole Jeep fired up, and we were headed home with a mess of fish on the rear floorboard. Life was good. I rolled down the window for some air-conditioning and fired up the AM radio to hear bits and pieces of a song I didn't like. I looked up, and there was a large mud puddle in the road. The puddle was probably about two feet deep and full of water and mud. I looked at Wade and said, "HOLD ON!" I mashed the throttle of that pea-green Jeep and gave it the onion. When we hit that puddle, water flew out on both sides of us, and water came rushing over the hood onto the front windshield. The windshield wipers didn't work, so you just guessed where the road was for a while. The water hit the hot exhaust of that Jeep, and steamrolled up through the floorboards. Suddenly, the Jeep stalled right in the mud puddle.

My brother looked at me and said, "Way to go, dumbass. Hope you got your hiking boots on." The Jeep wouldn't start, the battery was dead, and we didn't have a hill to roll it down, so away we walked the six to seven miles back to Bear Creek. Back then, we had no cell phones or ways to communicate with anybody. When you broke down, you were just broke down. What I later learned was I had hit the puddle so hard that I threw water up into the engine compartment, which drowned out the distributor cap and would allow no spark to fire. If I would have driven through the puddle more slowly, we would not have stalled and had to walk home again. We might have got stuck, and we didn't have our emergency screwdriver either.

The winter of 1978 was the worst winter I have ever seen even until this day! We got a huge snowstorm at Bear Creek Ranch that lasted for days. I remember a snowdrift that covered the entire front door of our house. The wind howled and howled for days, and large snowdrifts covered the roads. We were snowed in for at least one week. The county had a large four-wheel-drive grader with a huge V-plow on the front and was chained up on all six tires. The grader could not get through the huge drifts and became stuck for several days near Leavitt Reservoir, which was about six miles from our house. Wade and I were okay with this because we got to miss school and ride snow machines all day—that is, if you could keep them all running. It seemed we would work on them all week to get one full day of riding without something breaking down.

Because of the great snow conditions, my brother and I took the old

Puma 440 snowmobile out in the hayfields at night and chased jackrabbits. The rabbits were nearly impossible to run over because of their quick movements and fast running abilities. The headlight on the old Puma would only shine about ten to fifteen, so we had many wrecks from traveling too fast chasing rabbits and not stopping quick enough when we needed to.

One night, Wade had a jackrabbit right between his skis with me riding on the back. He was hauling ass across this open hayfield with the light shining just bright enough to see the rabbit right in front of us. I yelled at Wade and told him to stop because I thought we were about to run into a canal. We had been jumping the smaller ditch banks all night, and that was okay; but if we hit the canal, it might kill us because it was too wide to jump across. I could barely see a ditch bank coming up, and Wade was focused on the jackrabbit between his skis. I yelled, "STOP CANAL, CANAL!"

Wade yelled back, "IT'S ONLY A SMALL DITCH!"

I yelled, "NO, NO STOP!"

About that time, we hit the bank of that canal doing about fifty miles per hour and launched that Puma 440 into the earth's atmosphere. I don't know how high we flew that night, but we cleared the canal riding double. We landed hard, and the snow flew up and over the hood and windshield of the snowmobile, blocking any vision we had from the weak headlight.

This all happened fast. I couldn't believe that we had cleared the canal and even landed upright. When I looked up and right, there in front of us was a woven wire fence. We were still traveling at high speed and could not stop fast enough from hitting the fence. We hit the fence so hard that the old Puma stretched the fence out about ten feet and threw Wade and me over the handlebars for an undisturbed launch into some nearby grease wood. The old Puma was still running with a dim light when we got back to it. We pulled it back out of the fence, and Wade looked at me and yelled, "WHEN DID YOU BUILD THAT FENCE THERE?"

I said "It's always been there, DUMBASS. You just didn't know where you were at!"

My brother laughed and said, "Goddamn RABBIT—I can't believe we cleared that canal."

We quit chasing rabbits that night and drove home slowly and carefully after that little crash.

The winter of 1978 brought high fur prices for coyotes, bobcats, raccoons, foxes, beavers, and muskrats. A coyote pelt was worth $100; raccoons were worth as high as $50 for their pelts. I told my brother, Wade, we should learn how to trap coyotes, foxes, and bobcats because we could soon be millionaires by the end of the winter and not have to go to school anymore. We could just live off the land! We could even possibly earn enough money to trade that no-running old pea-green piece-of-shit Jeep Wagoneer for a better ride. I already knew how to trap coons with peanut butter; and at $50 a pelt, I might become the richest kid in the world. I asked Wade who he thought could teach us how to trap. He said, "I think our school bus driver knows how to trap. Let's ask him tomorrow."

Our school bus driver loved to hunt, fish, and trap. He was also a preacher and was once a sniper in the Vietnam War. My brother and I jumped on the bus that morning and asked him many questions. He said, "If you boys want to learn how to trap, I will take you out this afternoon after I drop you off the bus, and we can set some traps to show you how." My brother and I were excited on the bus ride home that afternoon, and the bus driver brought us everything we needed to set traps. This included traps, scent, lure, shovel, hammer, sifter, and wax paper. We got off the bus and headed down to Beaver Creek to set a trap line. The bus driver explained to us it was important to boil the traps to get rid of all human scent. "You also will need to wear rubber boots and rubber gloves to block your human scent," he explained.

We soon found a spot he thought looked good for a coyote set, and he took his small but sharp shovel out of the backpack and dug a small hole to place the trap in. He also dug a small hole above the trap to be used to place the bait in. He showed us how to set the trap and placed it in the hole so it was level with the top of the surface. He then placed a piece of wax paper over the pan of the trap to prevent the pan from freezing in the dirt during the winter months. Once the wax paper was placed over the pan, he took his sifter and dumped some premixed fine dirt with salt over the top of the trap. When he was done, you couldn't even tell there was a trap there. He then took some fine grass and sprinkled it over the fresh dirt to camouflage the new-looking dirt to make it look natural. He then took some beaver castors out and shoved a small bit of them in the small dirt hole above the trap. He then took a small wad of cheatgrass and shoved it in the hole and placed a small cotton ball on the grass and put some coyote urine on the cotton ball. He said the cotton ball will absorb the coyote urine and stay fresh for a long time. Once he was done with his set, he took a spray bottle full of fox urine and sprayed lightly around the whole area. He said this was to cover up any human scent.

He also said that the coyote was the toughest predator to catch. If you can catch a coyote, you are finally a trapper. They are smart and trap shy. That day, he left my brother and me with a bag full of boiled traps and all the supplies that we needed to set a trap line. He said, "You boys catch a coyote. Don't shoot it and leave a hole in the hide. Just knock it in the head with a hammer or something!" He also said, "If you boys catch something, just put it in a black garbage bag and spray some Raid in there to kill all the fleas and bring it with you on the bus. I will skin and sell the hides for you boys!" What a great man he was. Can you imagine your bus driver parking the bus and taking off with you to set a trap line at the end of his route in today's world? Can you imagine getting on the bus today with a dead coyote in a Glad bag? Well, that's how my brother and I grew up, and it was an awesome time in history.

Back then, if you screwed around on the bus, our bus driver would mash on the brakes and stop the bus right in the road and order you off the bus for a nice walk home. One day, a little boy named Tommy was screwing around, jumping up and down on the bus seats; and our bus driver stomped on the brakes of that bus and threw Tommy over the seat and onto the floor. The bus driver ordered Tommy to the front of the bus and wrote him up a pink slip. If you ever got a pink slip, you would have to have it signed by your parents before you could get on the bus again. Tommy signed his pink slip and knocked the bus driver's hat off with his hand as he ran for the open door to exit the bus. The bus driver quickly reached for the handle to close the bus door and slammed Tommy in the door as he was exiting the bus. Tommy was caught in the door and could go nowhere. The bus driver ordered Tommy to apologize and come back on the bus and pick up his hat. Tommy cried and apologized to the bus driver. He then got off the bus and limped home. I believe he had about a three-mile walk to get home.

The next morning, we pulled up to pick Tommy up at the bus stop, and he was standing with a cast on his foot and hanging on to two crutches. The bus driver said, "Good morning, Tommy. What did you do to your leg?"

Tommy yelled, "WHAT DO YOU MEAN WHAT DID I DO? YOU BROKE MY DAMN ANKLE WHEN YOU SLAMMED ME IN THE BUS DOOR LAST NIGHT!"

The bus driver smiled and said, "I guess you shouldn't have knocked my damn hat off!"

To this day, I can't believe that Tommy's parents made him walk to the bus stop every day with a broken ankle and a set of crutches for about three miles one way, and there was never a lawsuit against the bus driver.

We grabbed our bag of trapping supplies and loaded them into the Jeep Wagoneer, pushed the Jeep down the hill, popped the clutch, and rolled down the two-track road with black smoke spewing out the exhaust of the old Jeep. We were so excited to set our trap line we set several traps on the way home that day. The next day was Saturday, and I spent the entire day setting traps with peanut butter on them all up and down Beaver Creek and any other creek that looked like it might have coons living on it. I remember my mother later that night saying, "Scotty, where in the hell is all the peanut butter?" I couldn't even sleep that night counting all the money we would have in pelts the next morning. All we had to do was knock them in the head, place them in a trash bag, give it a shot of Raid, and give them to the bus driver. We would be rich almost immediately!

The next morning, my brother and I got up at daylight and set out in the old Jeep to check our trap line. We were so excited. We had a small ball-peen hammer and a bag full of trash bags and a can of Raid. We checked the raccoon trap line first—and nothing. Not a single coon in a trap anywhere. Every trap had the peanut butter licked off the pan of the trap, but nothing got caught in the damn traps. My dreams of being instantly rich were soon fading. We also checked the coyote sets and again nothing. We decided not to set any more traps until we had success. A couple of weeks had gone by, and we didn't catch a single thing.

One winter day, we were headed home in the old Jeep in the dark because the days were short during the winter months. I told Wade we should stop by and either pull the trap by the old schoolhouse or rescent it because it had been set for a couple of weeks with no new scent. We walked over to where we had the trap set, and we could hear the sounds of a chain jingling. We had something in our trap, but we didn't have a flashlight. As we got closer, it looked like a large coyote. I whispered to Wade, "HOLY shit, we just caught our first coyote. Let's go home and get a flashlight and a rifle!"

He whispered back, "Okay, but we're not supposed to shoot it and put a hole in its pelt."

I said, "Are you going to walk up to that damn thing and knock it in the head with a hammer?"

He said, "SCREW THAT. LET'S GO GET THE GUN!"

We hauled ass home very excited that we had just caught our first coyote. How would we spend all that money as their pelts were worth over $100 apiece?

We soon got back down to the old Bear Creek schoolhouse with our flashlight. Sure enough, we had a big beautiful and very white-colored coyote in the trap. Wade told me to shine the light on the coyote, and he would shoot it with his .22-caliber single-shot rifle. The coyote was running back and forth on the chain and would not stand still. He was even growling and snarling at us. It was hard for me to keep the flashlight on him because he was moving so fast. Finally, my brother said, "KEEP THE DAMN LIGHT ON HIM!" Shortly after that, I heard the .22 rifle fire and saw the damnedest thing I had ever seen. That coyote lunged forward and was gone in the night.

I yelled at my brother, "DID YOU HIT HIM? WHAT HAPPENED?" My brother said, "Hell, I don't know. I think I hit him!"

We walked up to the trap and found that the coyote had wrung its front foot off in the trap. All we had was his goddamn front foot. That would not bring us much money. So our first coyote got away. A sheepherder actually found a dead three-legged coyote about one week later close to the location we had caught him, but the pelt was spoiled by then. Wade hit the coyote with the .22 but hit no vitals, and the coyote ran off and later died.

Old Bear Creek schoolhouse

Our dreams of becoming successful trappers were slowly diminishing, and so was the thought of trading off the old Jeep for a newer model. I went to pull all my traps one night after school. I went to an old two-track road that headed northeast of our mailboxes. I would pull a trap that hadn't been rescented for a couple of weeks. I popped over a hill in the old Jeep, and lo and behold, I had a red fox in my trap. The fox was jolting back and forth in the trap. I had nothing to kill it with except a ball-peen hammer. I grabbed my hammer and walked toward the fox. The fox pulled back on the chain and snarled at me. I reached out over its head and whacked it a good one right between the eyes with my small hammer. The red fox immediately hit the ground and lay there motionless. I was so excited I finally had my first red fox, and the pelt was worth about $75. I threw the fox in the back of the old Jeep Wagoneer and headed home with a smile on my face. I couldn't wait to tell Wade I would be $75 richer than he was!!

I got about halfway home and heard a noise behind me. It sounded like something snarling and growling. I looked over my shoulder in the backseat, and that damn fox had come alive and was running all over the back of the Jeep. I hit the brakes, the fox jumped the backseat, and landed in the seat right next to me. It looked at me and ran into the front window and then the passenger-side window and finally over my lap and into the driver's-side window. It fell in my lap and spun out on my arms and legs to jump over my head and back into the rear seat. This scared the shit out of me. I slammed on the brakes, stopped in the middle of the road, and jumped out of the Jeep. I thought to myself, *What am I going to do? I have nothing to kill this fox with except a ball-peen hammer lying in the backseat with the angry fox.*

I didn't want to get back in the Jeep and drive home to get my gun because I didn't want to drive with the angry fox on the loose, and I didn't want to shoot the fox in the damn Jeep. I opened the door and went for the hammer in the backseat. When I opened the door, the fox saw daylight and made a run for the open door. It leaped right in my face as it exited the vehicle. That caused me to scream like a little schoolgirl and fall backward onto the road to get it out of my face. It spun out on my face and headed off into the sagebrush along the road. In a matter of seconds, it was flat gone! I said, "SHIT, SHIT SHIT!!" Not only was I now out $75, but I'm not sure I wanted to even tell anyone what had just happened because I just let a twenty-pound fox kick my ass. I angrily jumped back in the Jeep and turned the key to start it. All I heard was *click, click, click.* The damn battery was dead again. Now, I would have to walk home again.

I finally made it home and told my brother the story. He laughed and said, "You dumbass, you should have come home and got the .22 rifle!"

I said, "Yeah, how well did that work out for you on the coyote."

We eventually did catch a coyote that winter and sold the pelt for $110, which was an awesome price and a lot of money back then. But I'm sure if you added up all our expenses, we spent over $500 on fuel and supplies. But by god, we finally had a coyote, so that made us official trappers according to our bus driver!

For my twelfth birthday, my father, Bill, bought me a brand-new 12-gage shotgun. It was a Winchester model 870 with a beautiful woodstock. As I opened the present, my brother was looking over my shoulder and said, "What did you get, dumbass?"

I said, "A very beautiful 12-gage shotgun!"

My brother said, "12 GAGE! That's too big for you! The recoil will knock you on your ass!"

I said "Only if you're a PUSSY!"

I grabbed my brand-new shotgun and a couple of boxes of 12-gage shells and headed down to the barn to try it out. I got down to the barn and looked around for something to shoot. In the grass laid an old red metal coffee can. It made little sense to shoot the coffee can on the ground with a shotgun because shotguns are made to shoot birds flying.

I picked up the coffee can, loaded my gun, and threw the coffee can as high in the air as I could so I could shoot it on the fly. As soon as the can was in the air, I took quick aim, found the coffee can in my sight, and pulled the trigger. *BAM!* That gun kicked strongly that my thumb I had wrapped around the stock of the gun came back and hit me in the nose so hard. It bloodied my nose and knocked me over backward. *Holy shit,* I thought to myself, *that gun did knock me on my ass. Glad brother Wade didn't see that.*

I came to discover I even missed the damn can. I would not let that new shotgun kick my ass, so I threw that coffee can in the air probably thirty times before I finally hit it. Once I figured out how to hold on to the can with my front peep sight, I connected with the can and blew it all to hell. I was proud of myself as I ran back to the house to get more shells, and that's when my brother noticed my bloody nose I had forgotten to clean up. He laughed his ass off and said, "I told you it would knock you on your ass!"

I went back down to the big red barn to look for some birds to shoot now that I was an expert shot. I soon noticed that small groups of pigeons would keep flying by on the back side of the barn. I smiled and set up at the corner of the barn to shoot flying pigeons. I took several shots before I ever hit one; but once I figured out how far to lead them as they were flying, I connected. I would shoot two to three times, kill a few pigeons, run out and gather the dead pigeons, reload my gun, and wait for them to fly by again. I had been doing this for several hours and was getting a large pile of dead pigeons behind me. I was just having the time of my life when I heard this voice behind me say, "What are you shooting at, young man?"

I turned around, and there stood a game warden in a red shirt! Holy shit, I was scared to death of game wardens because my father said nothing good about them, and he did a fair amount of poaching animals over the years both when I was young and older. I replied, "Just shootin' pigeons, sir!"

He walked over and looked at my pile of dead pigeons and said, "Well, looks like you are doing a mighty fine job of that, young man!"

I was scared to death because I didn't know if it was illegal to shoot pigeons or not. And if it was illegal, I would probably go to jail for the rest of my life with my new shotgun because I had just killed about thirty!

The game warden held out his hand and said, "Hi there. My name is Bob Trebelcock, I'm the local game warden. I had heard some shots being fired down here while I was visiting with Martin and decided to come down and see what was going on down here"

I held out my hand and squeezed his hand tight and looked him right in the eye and said, "It's my pleasure to meet you, Bob. My name is Scott."

He said, "Nice to meet you, young man, and I'll let you get back to killing pigeons."

I said, "Hey, sir, before you go, I have something to ask you."

He said, "Sure, what's on your mind?"

I told Bob that several weeks ago my brother and I had a coyote trap set down by the old schoolhouse; and when we went to pull the trap, someone had stolen it because it was flat gone. Bob asked me several questions about the trap such as its size, kind, and how long it had been missing. I told him it was a number 4 long spring and kind of rusty in color. He asked me if I had my name on the trap anywhere, and I told him, "No, sir."

He said, "All right then, I will keep my eyes open and see if I can catch the dirty rascal who stole your trap."

I shook his hand again and said, "Thank you, sir!"

Bob drove off in his green pickup with a game-and-fish emblem of an antelope on both doors and some cool red-and-blue lights mounted to his headache rack next to his winch.

I was still standing there shaking from his presence. I had remembered when I was a young boy my dad had poached a big buck antelope out of season near Emblem and loaded it in the back of his International Scout. We were headed home, and my father said, "OH SHIT, there's the damn game warden!" I don't remember ever seeing the game warden, but my dad took off in that old Scout and drove it as fast as it would go down the highway and suddenly jerked the steering wheel of the Scout, causing us to go off the highway through the borrow pit on two wheels. We nearly rolled and ended up on two-track road that dropped down into a gulley out of sight. We came to a stop in the deep gulley, and the game warden shot past us on the highway with his red-and-blue lights on. My dad said, "WHEW THAT WAS CLOSE!" He looked at me and said, "You don't ever want to get caught poaching by one of those sons of bitches because they will hang your ass alive." I had never forgotten those words. Now, I had just shaken hands with one of those sons of bitches. I wondered if the game warden who chased my ole man was the same one I had just met minutes ago.

About two weeks later, Bob, the game warden, stopped back by the house at Bear Creek Ranch. Martin invited him into the house to talk about wildlife damage and upcoming hunting seasons for the area. Bob asked if I would join them in their conversation, and I replied, "YES, SIR." I thought this man in the red shirt was God maybe because my dad feared game wardens so much. We sat at the kitchen table, and Martin offered Bob a beer. Bob said, "Thanks for the generous offer, Mr. Mayland, but I'm going to have to decline the offer because I'm wearing this red shirt."

Martin said, "No problem. I certainly understand."

Bob looked at me and pulled a trap out of a brown grocery bag and said, "Does this look like your trap?"

I said, "Yes, sir that's it!"

I couldn't believe that Bob had found my trap so quickly. This guy is definitely God.

I asked him who stole it from me, he said, "I can't talk about that young man but wanted you to have your trap back." He then explained that I needed to have my traps tagged with my name on them to be legal and not allow for this sort of thing to happen again. At that moment, I decided that he was the coolest man in the world and that I wanted to be a game warden someday when I got older. I took over thirty years to figure out that Bob had stolen that trap from me because it wasn't tagged with my name. He didn't know who it belonged to until I told him I was missing one. Once he figured out who it belonged to, he was the hero by bringing it back and giving me a verbal warning for not tagging my traps. Slick game warden indeed, but at that age, I had decided that someday I wanted to be a game warden.

Chapter 6

Nip and Tuck with a Little Luck

My mother and stepfather always taught me responsibility. Work always came before play. We worked hard, and we played just as hard and sometimes harder. By now, Martin had given me four Suffolk bum lambs to feed and take care of. I would feed them morning and night. When they got old enough, I would take them to the annual Bighorn County Fair in Basin and show them and see if I could win a blue ribbon for first place or even a grand champion ribbon. I would then sell the lambs for top dollar at the local livestock auction. I would have to halter break the lambs, shear their wool, and teach them how to stand properly in front of the judges.

With school going on, caring for the baby lambs added to my day, morning, and night. I would also help Martin feed approximately two hundred small hay bales to sheep every morning before getting on the bus by six thirty and traveling approximately seven miles to the bus stop. Some days getting to and from school was difficult if road conditions were muddy or there was too much snow to travel through.

On the days that Mother worked at her salon in Greybull, she would drive us to school and drop us off. We didn't have to take the long bus ride every day. My mother drove like an asshole, and how we ever survived those days I'm not sure. The drive to her salon was about an hour long, so if she had a hair appointment at 8:00 a.m., she would leave the house at 7:45 a.m. and drive like an asshole. Other motorists would see my mother coming by the plume of dust that boiled out from underneath her suburban doing seventy miles per hour down the dirt road, and they would just stop and pull off the road to give my mother the right-of-way.

My mother had a large brown-and-white suburban that Martin eventually mounted a deer catcher on the front of because my mother had run over so many deer in one year they couldn't keep up with all the repair bills. Once my mother got the deer catcher mounted, she wouldn't even slow down for deer crossing the road. I would lie on the floor in the backseat of the Suburban, saying prayers we wouldn't meet someone coming to the other direction around the blind corners or over the steep hills, and hear a loud *BAM!* I would look over the seat to see what the noise was all about and see pieces of a deer flying over the right-of-way fence on both sides of the highway.

I would yell, "MOM, WHAT WAS THAT?"

She would say, "DAMN DEER, THEY NEED TO GET THE HELL OFF THE ROAD!"

Then she would romp down on the gas pedal, and that ole Suburban would downshift, and you could hear the four-barrel carburetor open up and suck about a gallon of fuel, and away we would go down the road. "MOM, aren't you even going to stop?"

She would say, "Why? I have a deer catcher on the front, and the deer is definitely dead."

The Game & Fish Department had to cut the number of deer tags available to nonresident deer hunters back then to make up for all the harvest between my mother and her Suburban during those years.

I had good friends who would lie on the rear floor of that Suburban and recite the Lord's Prayer on the way to Bear Creek Ranch. Some friends would never come to stay with me ever again. One friend was lying on the back floor praying when he finally looked up over the seat and whispered, "JESUS CHRIST, DOES ANYBODY EVER COME THE OTHER WAY?" That friend later became so carsick from flying around corners and over hilltops he asked my mother to stop because he needed to puke. My mother slammed on the brakes and said, "WELL, HURRY UP AND PUKE DAMMIT. WE NEED TO GET HOME BEFORE THE ICE CREAM MELTS!"

By now, I had traded off my little red Honda 80 motorcycle for a Yamaha YZ-80 water-cooled race bike. Martin didn't know what kind of bike I was bringing home, or he never would have allowed this to happen. This bike had six gears and a two-stroke engine and ran like a dirty bastard.

You could hear this bike coming down the road for miles. It sounded like a bumblebee; and every time I rode it anywhere near the sheep pens, you would see sheep jumping over the fences and running frantically for miles. Martin finally yelled at me and told me to keep that damn bike away from the sheep pens.

Martin would yell at me, "That damn motorcycle has two tires. I want to see both of them on the ground at all times." Back then, I learned how to ride a wheelie and actually got pretty good at it. Martin would tell me that I was going to kill myself on that damn race bike, and he just wanted to see me grow up someday. That bike and I had a love-hate relationship. I loved riding that bike, but it tried to kill me on several different occasions. I was a firm believer in God and guardian angels after riding this bike for a couple of years. I rarely ever wore a helmet but completely broke two different full-face helmets when wrecking this bike.

One bright sunny morning, I decided I was going to ride my new YZ-80 to the bus stop. I was getting ready to leave the house, and my mother packed me a lunch that consisted of a Ziploc bag full of powder doughnuts, a banana, and a peanut butter and jelly sandwich. My mother packed everything in a large brown Safeway grocery bag. She also placed three overdue encyclopedias in the bag and told me to take them back to the library as they were overdue. I'm not sure why I ever had three overdue encyclopedias because I never read books, hated school, and never brought home any homework. I must have been trying to impress someone by bringing them home. Anyhow, my mother loaded up my brown grocery sack and handed it to me as I was headed out the door. She yelled, "BE CAREFUL. I LOVE YOU. MAKE SURE YOU WEAR YOUR HELMET!" I couldn't wait to ride my brand-new dirt bike to the bus stop that morning. I loved to feel the fresh morning air on my face and blow through my blond hair while traveling down the old dirt road. But this morning, I would have to wear my helmet because my mother was supervising me.

I strapped on my helmet, fired up the two-stroke bumblebee, and placed my Safeway bag between my legs so it rested on the gas tank and seat. I took off like a bullet headed for the bus stop—just me, my lunch, and my overdue encyclopedias. I was probably traveling about sixty miles per hour and only a few short miles from the bus stop when something told me, "STOP RIGHT NOW!" It was an inner voice I can't explain, but I suddenly grabbed all my brakes and tried to stop quickly. There was a high sagebrush on each side of the road, making it difficult to see anything beyond the road. Just when I slowed down, a doe darted out of the brush on the right side of the road and tried to cross the road right in front of me.

This all happened fast, and it became very clear that I would hit the deer very solid. The deer's eyes became very large. She lowered her head as the front tire of my motorcycle made contact with her neck. I wasn't sure how this would end up, but I knew I needed to get as much distance between me, the bike, and the deer as possible! As soon as I made contact with the deer, I let go of the handlebars and pushed off the foot pegs with my feet and legs, knowing that my body would go forward over the deer and put me out in front of the wreck about to happen. I hit the deer so hard that the bike came to an abrupt stop, and I shot over the handlebars and did a complete flip in the air. I landed on my butt sliding down the gravel road backward at about fifty miles per hour.

At that moment, time slowed way down. Everything was happening in slow motion. I was sliding down the gravel road on my butt going backward, and the deer and the motorcycle were chasing me down the road, coming right toward me. The bike and the deer went end over end at least three times. The deer ended up lying on top of my motorcycle in the middle of the road. I slid on my butt so long that I actually had time to turn my neck around and see where I was headed. I finally slid off the road into a large sagebrush about forty yards from my motorcycle. I lay there for several minutes to see if I was still alive and if all my body parts were still working. Nothing hurt too bad, except I had torn my brand-new coat off me, and my left hand was missing all the skin on the back of my hand and was filled with gravel. I had worn a hole in my pants on both butt cheeks from sliding down the road for so long, and my nose was bleeding.

I slowly got up and walked back to my motorcycle. As I approached the motorcycle, I noticed the deer was still alive and the bike was still running. I bent down to hit the kill switch on the bike's handlebars; and the doe jumped forward and hit me right in the face with her face, knocking me over. The deer ran over the top of me and went out into the sagebrush, fell over, and died a few minutes later. I think she had a broken neck. The deer hitting me in the face scared me more than me hitting the deer. I got back up, shut the bike off, and took my helmet off. This is when I noticed my helmet was shattered in the front and had two cracks that ran from the front of the helmet all the way around to the back of the helmet, and both cracks met in the center of the helmet in the back. If I had not been wearing that helmet, I would have possibly died that day or had been brain dead for the rest of my life. I thanked my guardian angels and the Lord up above for keeping me alive that day and assessed the situation.

The front fender of my bike had bent over and was shoved between the front tire and forks of the bike. I pulled it out and straightened it back to somewhat normal. The next thing I observed was amazing. My banana was lying in the road peeled, my Ziploc bag of powdered doughnuts was now a bag of powder and no doughnuts, never did I find the peanut butter and jelly sandwich, and I finally rounded up all three of the overdue encyclopedias scattered everywhere. My brown paper grocery bag was shredded and of no use.

I fired up the motorcycle and headed to the bus stop with only the three encyclopedias. I'm sure I was in shock as my hands and body trembled. I was so paranoid of hitting another deer I drove about twenty miles per hour the rest of the way to the bus stop. Thank god, I didn't miss the bus. He was just pulling away when I arrived. I boarded the bus and told the driver what had happened. He got out his first-aid kit and cleaned me up the best he could, and we headed to town. This was a new bus driver who had not been driving long. The "preacher" or the previous bus driver who taught me how to trap had recently retired.

My new YZ-80 motorcycle

The bus driver arrived at the next stop, and a little girl boarded the bus. The bus driver asked her if she had her pink slip signed from last Friday by her parents. She had forgotten to have it signed. This little girl had been jumping up and down in her seat last Friday, and the bus driver hit his brakes on the highway and pitched the little girl over the top of two seats. He then turned on his flashers on the highway, called her to the front of the bus, and wrote her a pink slip.

The bus driver told her to catch a ride back to the house with the hired hand and get the pink slip signed by her parents, or she would not be able to ride the bus until she had it signed. He waited about ten to fifteen minutes for her to return. Her dad came hauling ass down the road toward the bus in an old ranch truck. The truck had a couple of rifles hanging on the gun rack in the rear window with a lariat also hanging over the guns. The truck was a flatbed with several small bales of hay and three or four blue-eyed blue healer dogs riding on the bed of the truck. Her dad came to a screeching halt right in front of the bus, and he jumped out of the ranch truck and yelled at the bus driver, "GET YOUR SORRY ASS OFF THE BUS!"

The bus driver jumped up and ran out the door to meet the girl's dad outside of the bus. They got into an argument and pushed each other back and forth. Quickly, the little girl's dad hauled off and punched the bus driver in the face, knocking him to the ground. The bus driver quickly jumped up and yelled, "I WOULD LIKE TO SEE YOU DO THAT AGAIN!" The girl's father hauled off and punched him again, and down to the ground he went. The bus driver slowly got up with blood coming from his nose and crawled back on the bus. He slowly got in the driver's seat, revved up the engine on the bus, and flipped off the girl's father and yelled "FUCK YOU, YOUR DAUGHTER WILL NEVER RIDE THIS BUS AGAIN!" He slammed the door with the hand lever and peeled out in the bus as he went back up on the main highway. Man, I would never guess you could get a bus (cheese wagon) to spin its tires out and actually make them squeal down the highway. I was having quite a morning. Both the bus driver and I had a bloody nose, and he drove like an asshole all the way to school that morning, mumbling, "What an asshole, what an asshole!"

We finally arrived at school safely that morning, and I headed down to the library to turn in my three overdue encyclopedias. The librarian lady was old school. She wore tiny reading glasses that covered half of her eyes. Her light-blue hairdo stood tall and looked like there might be a bird's cage hiding in there somewhere. I laid the books up on the counter and said, "Here ya go, madam. Sorry they are late!" She thumbed through the pages of the books to make sure I had left no bookmarks or other papers in the book. As she was thumbing through the pages in the books, she found deer hair, gravel, dirt, blood, and grass stains across entire pages and some missing pages.

She looked at me over the top of her reading glasses and whispered, "My god, where have these books been?"

I said, "I'm sorry, madam, but I had a little crash this morning and killed a deer on my dirt bike while heading to the bus stop."

She said, "Good Lord Almighty, does your mother know about this?"

I said, "No, madam, but I'm all right and reckon I can get my dirt bike back home safely tonight after school"

Back then, I couldn't notify my mother because we had no phones at Bear Creek Ranch, and cell phones had not yet been invented. Shortly thereafter, the bus driver got relieved of his full-time bus driving duties and was demoted to driving activity bus only.

I made it safely home that evening and told my mother and Martin what had happened. They were both relieved that I was still alive and not injured. Martin said, "I have some bad news for you. Your dog was chasing sheep this morning and wouldn't come to me, so I had to shoot him!" Man, that broke my heart. That dog was my best friend, and we did everything together. He was supposed to be a "sheepdog," and that was the only reason I had a dog. He was a great dog and must have just got excited and chased sheep. If I would have been there, he would have listened and wouldn't be dead right now. I felt horrible but understood that I couldn't have a dog that chased sheep and didn't mind others. It took me a long time to get over losing that dog.

Back then, we had working dogs. They weren't considered pets or another member of the family. Our dogs lived outside and got primarily table scraps, not expensive dog foods on the market today. When a dog didn't work or listen to its owner, it was shot on the spot. You never took a dog to a vet to have it put down. But I would have to say that Ole Blue was not only a pet then but also my best friend and companion. I would never forget all the days he rode between my legs on that little red Honda motorcycle just happy to be with me. And I will never forget the morning he bit that skunk in the ass and got us both sprayed, causing me to have to take my boots off in school all day in the third grade.

I had spent the day with Martin all day helping him irrigate and put up hay over at White Creek Ranch. We left the ranch late in the day and headed through a little town named Shell on the way home. Shell was a small town, population of fifty. It had only a small bar, a small post office, and an old stone building named the Shell Store. The owner of the Shell Store had a couple of red-bone coon hounds that would fetch him a beer from the cooler when ordered to do so. Once they fetched a beer, they would quietly walk back into the living room of the house and sit on an old green footstool with their front feet on the ground and their rear ends up on the footstool and go back to watching television.

The store was full of dirty old antique furniture and antique bottles with an old antique bar back in the corner. The owner of the store was a heavyset guy with a lazy eye. He always wore a dirty white T-shirt. Most days, he would be playing dice for dollars at the front counter with some old rancher or farmer and drinking beer. He was a scary-looking fella but was always nice as a young kid. The walls in the store were lined with old buffalo skulls. There must have been at least twenty old buffalo skulls in that store. The buffalo skulls always fascinated me as a kid, and I wanted to find one myself someday. I would ask the owner of the store where he found all those old buffalo heads, and he would just say, "Up in them there mountains somewhere!" I'm not sure why they fascinated me so much, but I was determined that someday I would find my buffalo skull.

So Martin and I headed through the town of Shell on our way home. Then Martin said, "I think I will stop at the Villa for a quick drink. Then we need to get you home to feed your bum lambs before it gets dark." I was good with this because I knew Martin would buy me a soda pop, and I was thirsty from working in the fields all day. We went into the small bar and saw all the familiar faces from around the community. I used to love to sit at the bar as a child and listen to all the grown-ups tell crazy stories about their lives and their jobs. They would be dirty from working hard, most wearing old dirty cowboy hats with a grease stain around the brim of their hat from working long hours in the hot sun. They would tell crazy stories, get drunk, and get loud when they laughed and talked. They would chew tobacco, spit on the floor, and smoke rolled cigarettes while telling stories. The bartender was a cute female they all flirted with, and she would flirt right back until she had all their money that was in their pocket. Some would get so broke that they would start a tab and pay their bar bill once a month. If they didn't pay their tab, they were no longer welcome in the bar until it was paid.

Martin seemed to have a great time and kept ordering more drinks for himself and others. It was almost dark, and I told Martin several times I needed to get home and feed my bum lambs before it got dark. Martin would say, "One more, and we will get headed home!" He finally tired of me bothering him and gave me money to walk over to the Shell Store and buy something to snack on. I headed over to the Shell Store hungry for something to snack on. I remember walking into the store and heading over to a rack that had all the doughnuts and Twinkies for sale. I looked down, and a tomcat lying on a bag of hamburger buns and eating a jelly-filled cinnamon roll. He had bitten into a bag of hotdog buns and ate on a bun and then decided the cinnamon rolls tasted better. I looked on the top shelf of the rack, and another cat was lying comfortably on a tray of loafed bread.

It was late, and there was nobody at the front counter to wait on me, so I had to ring a bell for service. As soon as I rang the bell, two red-bone coon hounds came running out of the living room and into the store barking loudly like they were about to tree a coon. Both cats spun out on the bread and cinnamon rolls and hauled ass across the store and jumped up on top of the old antique bar where the coon dogs couldn't reach them. The store owner came walking out rubbing his eyes with his hair standing on end and asked if he could help me with something. The dogs were barking loudly and jumping up and down on the bar, trying to kill the cats. The store owner turned on the light and yelled at the dogs, "GODDAMMIT, YOU DOGS, LEAVE LARRY AND JOHN ALONE!"

Apparently, he had named his cats Larry and John. I finally grabbed a bag of grape-flavored licorice and threw it on the counter. The store owner said, "Will that be all for you today, young man?"

I replied, "Yes, sir, and sorry to bother you at this hour of the night!"

I grabbed my grape-flavored licorice and got the hell out of there and headed back over to the bar across the street. I was feeling very let down that my bum lambs were home starving to death, and it was past dark, and I was not home to feed them.

I walked back into the bar; and it was loud with people yelling, laughing, and telling stories. Everyone in the bar was pretty shit-faced by now. Some of the old cowboys yelled at me, "WHERE THE HELL YA BEEN, OLE SON? CAN WE BUY YOU A DRINK?"

I said, "No thanks, I've been over at the Shell Store getting me something to snack on." I walked over to Martin and interrupted him as he was telling a story, and I said, "MARTIN, I need to get home and feed my bum lambs right now!"

He looked at me and slurred his words, "Well, go get in that damn truck and go home and feed your damn lambs!"

So I left the bar and jumped in the '77 Chevy truck and fired it up. I could hardly reach the foot pedals to put in the clutch, and I couldn't see over the steering wheel because I was too short. I folded up a couple of coats and sat on them so I could see over the steering wheel and headed for Bear Creek Ranch. I had driven the truck out in the hay fields before, but I had never driven a truck on a public road before. I had a short distance to drive on the pavement, and then I would be on the dirt the rest of the way home.

I never forgot that night. I was scared to death because it rained hard and lightning was flashing all around me. Every time a bolt of lightning would strike, the AM radio in the truck would make a loud squelching noise. I could barely understand the words to the songs as I drove home. The CB radio kept squelching I finally shut it off. It rained even harder, and quickly, the windshield wipers couldn't keep up with the rain hitting the front windshield. I slowed way down and had both hands gripped tightly on the steering wheel, knowing that if I slid off the road in the mud, I would be stuck and my bum lambs would not get fed that night. I was nearly home pawing my way through the mud in the four-wheel drive when I rounded the sharp schoolhouse corner and almost had a head-on with a vehicle coming to the other direction. The vehicle was driving fast. I swerved hard to the right and ran off the road to avoid having a head-on collision with this vehicle!

I mashed on the brake pedal with both feet and came to an abrupt stop, stalling the engine of the '77 Chevy. The vehicle I passed also hit the brakes and came to a quick stop in the road behind me. I looked in my mirror. This vehicle was backing up toward me. It scared me because I didn't know who this might be this late at night. The vehicle backed until they were even with me and my driver's-side window. It was raining so hard I couldn't tell who it was until a flash of lightning hit nearby and lit up the sky. When the sky illuminated, I recognized the vehicle as my mother's Suburban. I rolled my window down with rain hitting me in the face and heard my mother yell, "OH MY GOD, WHERE IS MARTIN?" My mother was just sure that something terrible had happened to Martin because I was driving his truck and it was late at night.

I yelled back, "HE IS AT THE SHELL BAR, AND I NEEDED TO GET HOME AND FEED MY LAMBS!"

My mother yelled back, "YOU GET YOUR ASS HOME AND GET IN BED. YOU CAN FEED THEM DAMN LAMBS IN THE MORNING!"

My mother mashed down on the gas pedal of that 1979 suburban, and I could hear the four-barrel carburetor sucking for air as she headed for the Shell Bar. I was relieved that Martin would now have a ride home from the bar, and I could get home and take care of the poor bum lambs.

I soon got home and mixed up some powdered milk and headed out to feed my lambs. They were happy to see me and starved to death. It made me feel good they could now go to sleep on a full stomach and not worry about where I was anymore. I went back to the house and crawled into bed and fell asleep quickly as I had had a long day. I had only been sleeping a short time when I heard a voice in the front living room. It was Martin. I heard him yell, "WHERE IS THAT LITTLE BASTARD? I'M GOING TO KILL HIM!" I'm sure I was that little bastard he was referring to, but I couldn't understand why he was so mad at me. He told me to take the damn truck home and feed my damn lambs. I then heard my mom's voice yell back at him, "HE IS IN BED. DON'T WAKE HIM. GET YOUR ASS TO BED, AND WE WILL DISCUSS THIS IN THE MORNING!" Martin was very upset with me for taking his truck home that night. He told me to do it while he had been drinking too much, but he didn't actually think I would do it. He learned a good lesson that night about me; and as for him and my mother, they nearly got a divorce over that night in the Shell Bar.

The bum lambs I raised were Suffolk rams. They had black heads, white wool, and four black legs. They all grew big and strong and filled out nicely. A guy from Shell came out one day and taught me how to shear them with a pair of handheld sheep shears. He also taught me how to make them stand pretty for the judging at the fair coming up in a few short weeks. I had a short amount of time to get the lambs halter broke, sheared, and behaved properly to show them in front of a crowd. The day finally came. I hauled them to the fairgrounds in Basin, Wyoming. I would have to leave them in small pens for about a week and feed them morning and night and show them in front of the judges during the daytime. This was a lot of work for me because it required me to travel from Bear Creek Ranch to Basin each day and take care of the lambs.

My lambs all behaved well for me on show day, and I got three first-place ribbons and one grand champion ribbon for my lambs and all my efforts. I was so proud of myself. I would show the lambs one more time in front of a crowd, and they would be auctioned to the highest bidder. Several adults told me I would do well on my lambs and make a bunch of money. I would show them the next day. I fed and watered them that evening and headed home. I could hardly sleep that night thinking about all the money I would make off my lambs the next day.

The next morning, I showed up at the fairgrounds to feed my lambs and get them ready to show. They didn't look well. They were bloated up, and they all had horrible diarrhea. None would walk around or even get up! I was heartbroken. What had happened to my lambs? I went running to find someone to help me. I was very scared that my lambs were dying. I finally found an older gentleman who knew a lot about sheep and asked him to please come to look at my sick lambs. When we arrived back at the pens, one lamb had died. The man looked at me sadly and said, "I'm sorry, son. Your lambs have bloated. Did you use the water here at the fairgrounds to water them?"

I said, "Yes, I did."

He said, "That's too bad, son. Didn't anyone tell you not to use this water at the fairgrounds because it can cause animals to become sick?"

I said, "No, nobody said a word to me about using this water!"

He said, "I'm sorry, son, but more than likely, all your lambs are going to die. They are very sick."

Sure enough, they all died right in their pens at the fairgrounds with blue ribbon hanging on each of their pens. That was one of the saddest days I can remember. It was embarrassing for me to have to drag those dead bloated lambs out of their pens in front of other spectators to throw in the back of a truck and haul them to the local landfill. So much for raising sheep and so much for making any money with all my efforts that summer. My days of raising bum lambs and going to the local fair were over. Between losing my favorite dog Blue and now my bum lambs, I was forced to grow up fast and soon understood that life was not always peaches and cream.

One of my bum lambs

Later that fall, my mother told me one day I should invite a bunch of my friends out to the ranch and spend the weekend fishing or doing something fun. My first thought was, why is my mother wanting me to invite a bunch of my friends over? We usually drive her nuts. So I did just that. I invited three of my good friends to come to stay with me for the weekend to go fishing. Mom met us in front of the schoolhouse on Friday afternoon. We were standing on the corner waiting for Mother to pick us up when I heard her Suburban's four-barrel carburetor as she rounded the corner off Main Street headed right for us. She locked her tires up, came to a sliding stop, rolled down the window, and yelled, "HURRY UP AND GET YOUR ASSES IN THE CAR. WE HAVE WORK TO DO WHEN WE GET HOME!" My friends looked at me like, "What do you mean *we* have work to do? We are going fishing!" I just shrugged my shoulders and jumped in the Suburban, not wanting my mother to make a scene in front of my friends. Again, she drove like an asshole all the way home, and all my friends lay on the back floor reciting the Lord's Prayer. We made it home safely, and all my friends slowly got out of the Suburban and staggered into the front yard. They were all carsick, and their faces were as pale as a chicken egg.

My mother said, "Before any of you disappear for the evening, grab a bag of groceries and haul them to the house. Oh, and I forgot to mention, there will be no fishing until all these leaves are raked up and hauled off in the yard!" You should have seen the look on my friends' faces. They looked at me like "REALLY?" "Come on, boys, I have a rake for each of you, and it won't take you that long!" my mother said.

Our yard was as big as a football field, and the entire yard was lined with huge cottonwood trees that caused the leaves to be about one foot deep across the entire yard. I said, "Come on, guys, let's try to get it done tonight so we can go fishing in the morning!" Everybody grabbed a rake, and we raked hard until dark but didn't get even half the yard done. I'm sure my friends would be so sore the next morning and have blisters on both their hands that they wouldn't even be able to fish if they wanted to.

The next morning we got up early and went to raking leaves. We had huge piles of leaves all over the yard. My brother, Wade, came out of the house and said, "What are you guys doing?"

I said, "We are raking all the leaves and then going fishing!"

He said, "Well, I'm going fishing with you!"

I said, "All right, we will rake the piles, and you pick them up, and we will get done sooner!"

He said, "Sounds good!"

Quickly, we had the entire yard raked, and there were huge piles of leaves everywhere. We all sat down to take a break and watch Wade pick up piles of leaves. Wade looked over and said, "Come help me pick up these piles!"

I said, "NO, we had a deal. We rake them, you pick them!!"

He yelled at me, "IF YOU DON'T HELP ME, I'M GOING TO KICK YOUR ASS!!"

I said, "Well, you better get to kickin' cuz we ain't helping you with nothing! We had a deal. Now get to picking up your piles so we can go fishing!"

My brother became very angry and ran toward me fast. I took off running and climbed a large cottonwood tree because I knew Wade couldn't climb trees. I went almost to the top of the tree and climbed into my treehouse with a wooden floor and a small railing around the front of the treehouse. I leaned over the railing approximately thirty feet in the air, looked down at my brother standing in the yard, and yelled, "TOO BAD THAT YOU CAN'T CLIMB TREES BECAUSE YOU'RE SUCH A PUSSY!!"

He yelled back, "COME OUT OF THAT TREE RIGHT NOW, OR I'M GOING TO SHOOT YOUR ASS OUT OF THE TREE!"

By now, my friends were all laughing at my brother and me for having this little spat, so I yelled at Wade, "PICK UP YOUR PILES SO WE CAN ALL GO FISHING, YOU BIG PUSSY!"

Wade turned and ran into the house. He returned about three minutes later with a compound hunting bow loaded with an arrow with a razor-sharp broadhead mounted to the tip. He yelled, "COME DOWN NOW, OR I WILL SHOOT YOUR ASS OUT OF THE TREE!"

I just laughed and said, "GO AHEAD, PUSSY!"

My brother quickly drew that compound bow back and fired that arrow up toward me. I said to myself, *OH SHIT* and quickly lay flat on the wooden floor of the treehouse. About that time, I heard a loud thump and noticed the tip of a broadhead sticking through the floor of my treehouse about three inches from my face. My brother actually tried to shoot me out of the damn tree.

I jumped up and yelled, "ALL RIGHT, YOU CRAZY BASTARD, I'M COMING DOWN. DON'T SHOOT ME!" All my friends quit laughing at this point and joined in on the picking up of the leave piles. Later that afternoon, we finally got all the piles of leaves picked up, and I said, "Good job, guys. Now, let's go fishing!" Martin said he would give us a ride to Beaver Creek as he had some irrigating to do over at that ranch. We all happily jumped in the back of his '77 Chevy with our fishing poles and couldn't wait for the seven-mile drive to end because we were about to be catching huge cutthroat trout—and plenty of them. All my friends had blisters on their hands from raking leaves all weekend. I'm not sure any of them had ever worked that hard in their entire life, but it was now all worth it because we were going fishing.

We all jumped out of the truck with our fishing poles. Then Martin said, "I'll be back to pick you guys up in about three hours!" Martin left, and all you could see was his dust cloud lingering in the air as he went over the hill and around the corner out of sight. I looked at my buddy and said, "Did you grab the worms out of the back of the truck?"

He got this terrified look on his face and said, "NO, I thought you had them!"

I said "NO, I don't have them!"

The four of us stood there holding our fishing poles with no worms to fish with. I looked over at my brother, and he said, "You big dumbass!" We had enough time on our hands we did scrounge around and found a few worms underneath wet rocks to fish with. But the worms were hardly big enough to thread on a hook, so it just wasn't the same as having a big ole fat angleworm for bait. My friends talked about that trip for a long time and never did offer to come back and spend the weekend with me again. One thing about my mother was she always knew how to get work done—and done quickly.

It took a while before my friends would ever come back and stay with me again. But they would occasionally ride their motorcycles from their home to mine. We would spend the day riding motorcycles around the ranch. On one particular day, four of my friends met me at Bear Creek Ranch with their motorcycles and wanted to go for a ride. Three had dirt bikes, and one of them had borrowed his dad's street bike. The friend on the street bike was not an experienced rider and never hung out with us as much as the other friends. He was usually the kid who got put out first in a game of dodgeball.

His name was Mason. Several times that day, Mason had missed a corner on his dad's street bike and ran off the road, wrecking the bike out in the sagebrush. I stopped several times to ask him if he was all right, and then I would help him get back on his heavy street bike and start it again. About noon, it rained, so we stopped by the house and ate lunch. After lunch, all my friends decided they better get headed home before the roads became too slick from the rain. Mason said, "Scott, I'll stay here and ride with you." I thought this gesture was very kind and showed me that Mason needed a friend and wanted to be my friend.

Once everyone left, Mason said, "Come on, Scott, let's go for a ride. I want you to ride double with me so that I can pull a wheelie more easily with you on the back!" I didn't want to ride with Mason because he had been wrecking all morning long and was not an experienced rider. There was a little voice in my head that kept saying, "DO NOT RIDE WITH HIM! DO NOT RIDE WITH HIM!" Mason kept begging me to ride with him, and I finally agreed. I jumped on the back of the street bike. He took off as fast as that bike would go. We were traveling down a rough dirt road on a street bike doing about seventy miles per hour when I looked over the top of Mason's shoulder and could see he was headed for a deep rut in the road. If he hit the rut like I thought he was going to, we would have a bad, bad wreck. I yelled at Mason and said, "WATCH OUT FOR THAT RUT!" Mason never slowed down and hit that bad rut in the road with his front tire. The rut was a deep tire track that a pickup truck tire had made in the mud when the road was wet. The rut was about one foot deep and ten inches wide and now dry hard dirt.

The rut caused the front tire of the street bike to quickly turn sideways and got wedged into the rut. All I remember was saying to myself, *OH SHIT, THIS IS GOING TO HURT!* Before I knew it, the rear end of the bike flew forward off the ground and projected me forward over the top of Mason and the street bike he was getting tangled up in. When I flew over his head, his right leg was pinned between the handlebars and the gas tank of the motorcycle. I actually landed on my feet and took three huge strides before planting my head into the hard surface of the dirt road and then slid later on my back.

When the dust cleared, I was about twenty-five yards from Mason. I was lying facedown on the road looking toward Mason. I took a few minutes to catch my breath and figure out that I was still alive and no body parts appeared to be broken. My back hurt really badly. I had split my head open just underneath my hairline on my forehead. I could feel the warmth of the blood as it poured down both of my cheeks. I slowly got to my feet and walked toward Mason and his father's mangled street bike. I had not seen Mason move or heard him say anything. I was praying that he was still alive.

Once I got over to Mason, he was breathing but unconscious. I was scared and didn't know what to do, so I slapped him on his bloody face and yelled, "MASON, MASON, ARE YOU ALL RIGHT?" Mason finally came to and moaned in pain. I was just happy that he was still alive. I asked Mason if he was all right. He moaned and said, "I think I broke my ankle!"

I said, "Well, try to get up and walk. If you can't walk, maybe your ankle is broken." It seemed a logical way to approach the situation. As Mason tried and got up, I noticed his ankle bone sticking through the side of his leather cowboy boot. I quickly said, "SIT DOWN, SIT DOWN! Your ankle is broken. I can see it sticking through your boot!"

Mason looked down and just cried. I said, "Don't move. I will walk to the house and call your mother."

He said, "Thank you, and please bring me a glass of tea and a pillow when you return."

I walked toward the house, and my back was killing me. I stopped and yelled back at Mason, "How does my back look?" I raised my tank top. Mason picked up his head and squinted one eye and said, "Just a little scratched up. You will be fine!"

I made it back to the house and got ahold of dispatch on the mobile radio and have them leave a message for Mason's mother he was in an accident up at Bear Creek Ranch and that he was lying in the dirt road approximately one mile south of the ranch house. I also told dispatch not to alarm Mason's mother, just tell her that her son *may* have broken his ankle. I quickly gathered up a glass of tea and a pillow and headed back out the door. As I was walking out of the house, my back was killing me with pain. I dropped everything and went into the bathroom to have a look at my back through the large mirror hanging on the back of the door. I lifted my tank top and almost passed out when I saw just how bad my back was.

It was far from a little scratch as Mason had stated earlier. I was missing my entire back from my left shoulder down to my right hip. The scratch was approximately twelve inches wide, and the wound was deep. I could see dirt and small pieces of gravel stuck to my flesh all the way across the wound. The entire back side of my pants was covered in blood from the wound draining down as I walked. I knew Mason needed help; so I pulled my shirt back down, took a deep breath, and headed back down the road with his glass of tea and pillow.

When I arrived back at the scene of the accident, Mason was still lying facedown in the road and moaning. I felt sorry for him to see him in all that pain. While waiting for Mason's mother to show up, Martin came riding up on his Suzuki motorcycle. Martin had been out irrigating and was heading back home. Martin asked me what had happened, and I explained the whole situation to him. I told him that dispatch would try to contact Mason's mother, but I didn't know if they actually got ahold of her or not. Martin tended to Mason and looked his injuries over. Once he saw the bone sticking out of Mason's boot, he looked at me and gave me this horrible look on his face.

I knew from that look that Martin was very concerned and upset. I could feel blood trickling down my face again. Martin looked down at me and said, "OH MY GOD, WERE YOU RIDING ON THAT BIKE AS WELL?"

I said, "Yes, I was."

He said, "My god, you have a big gash under your hairline. Are you injured anywhere else?"

I said, "Yes, my back is pretty torn up!"

Martin walked behind me and lifted my shirt and said, "Oh my god! Your back is horrible. We need to get you to a hospital as soon as possible!" I told Martin I thought I would be all right. I just needed to give it a good cleaning when we get back to the house.

Mason's mother soon arrived in an old beat-up pickup truck with her other son, Robby. She came sliding alongside Mason still lying on the road next to the mangled bike. She cried and yelled, "OH MY GOD, MASON, ARE YOU ALL RIGHT?"

Mason cried and said, "Mom, I broke my ankle. Look at the bone sticking out of my boot!"

Mason's mother almost passed out and yelled for Mason's brother, Robby, to come to help her load Mason into the truck. Once they got Mason in the truck, Robby walked over to the mangled motorcycle and said, "Man, is Dad going to be upset! I guess it doesn't matter how we load this bike!" He then picked that heavy bike up with both hands and threw it over his head and into the back of the pickup truck. Mason's brother was as strong as an ox. I had no idea he was that strong. Mason's mom jumped in the truck, revved up the engine, popped the clutch, and spun gravel as she sped out of there headed for the hospital approximately fifty miles away.

Martin loaded me up on his motorcycle, and we headed for the house. Once we got in the house, Martin lifted my shirt and said, "Oh my god, we need to get you to a hospital!"

I said, "No, I don't want to go to the hospital. Just clean it out good, and I will be fine!"

Martin grabbed a warm cloth and scrubbed the small pieces of gravel and sheep manure out of my back. The pain was horrendous! I thought I would die. The pain was so severe. Martin said, "We need to make sure that you don't get an infection, so I'm going to pour some peroxide on your wounds." This stung badly. The pain shot through my whole body. My mother returned to the house from working and about fainted when she looked at my back. She said, "Oh my god, we need to get you to the hospital!"

I said, "I think I'm okay. Let's wait and see how I feel in the morning."

The next morning, I woke up, and my back was stuck to the bedsheets since it had drained so much during the night. My mother had to peel the sheet off my back and apply new dressings to my wounds. She said, "You need to get dressed. We are headed to town for church." I got dressed and headed for the front door of the house. Suddenly, I didn't feel well and shivered. My temperature went through the roof. I told my mother I didn't feel like going to church. I just wanted to lie on the couch for a while. My mother took my temperature. It was 103 degrees. She said, "Oh my god, Martin, I think he is going into shock!"

My parents quickly made a bed for me in the back of the 1979 Suburban and carried me out and laid me in the back of the Suburban. My mother yelled, "WE NEED TO GET HIM TO THE HOSPITAL IMMEDIATELY!"

I thought to myself, *Oh, dear LORD, will I survive the trip to town knowing that my mother would drive like an asshole?*

And that she did! But by god, we made it alive. She pulled up to the emergency door, and I was greeted by two nurses and a doctor who loaded me on a bed with wheels. I remember the sheets were baby blue and the nurses were cute. They rolled me down the hall and I noticed Mason lying in a bed with his leg elevated and a cast on. I gave him a thumbs-up as they rolled me past his room with an open door. I was in the hospital for three days, and I had to take 120-degree whirlpools. Once out of the whirlpool, the nurses would scrub my back repeatedly, still trying to get all the gravel and sheep manure out of my wounds. I came to discover our sheep had been bedding in the road where Mason and I had wrecked, and that's where all the sheep manure came from. I had an infection from the sheep manure, and that caused me to go into shock and have a high fever. After three days in the hospital, I returned home with a slight scab all the way across my back. I was just happy to be home and out of that hospital.

My mother roared up to our house in the Suburban and told me to climb in bed and get some rest. As I was walking into the house, Martin was coming out of the house. I said, "Where are you going?"

He said, "I'm running up to the reservoir on my motorcycle to open the head gate."

I said, "Can I please go with you?"

He said, "No, you better stay home and get healed up!"

I said, "Please let me go. I feel fine!" I recently had a new Suzuki three-wheeler and hadn't got to ride it much yet that summer. I wanted to go with Martin so bad because this would be a nice five- to six-mile ride on my new three-wheeler. Martin finally said, "All right, but you be careful!" Martin went ahead of me on his motorcycle, and I followed on the yellow Suzuki three-wheeler. We got near the reservoir, and I noticed a herd of about thirty elk up on the hillside above the reservoir. It was unusual to see elk in that area this time of the year. I noticed a nice bull elk in the herd. It looked like he might be a six by six, meaning that the bull had six points on each antler.

I was so excited to see the elk I climbed the hill on my three-wheeler and got a better look at them. The hill was steep. It had large rocks and tall sagebrush all the way up the hill. As I was climbing the hill, I hit a large rock with my right-hand tire, causing me to veer to my left and head down a steep embankment. Before I knew it, I was out of control, heading down a steep hill toward the bottom of a deep gulley full of high sagebrush and lots of cactus. I was wearing a tank top and summer shorts with a slight scab all the way across my back. I remember thinking, *This is not good. I will crash at the bottom of the hill and will more than likely go over my handlebars. Once I go over the handlebars, I can't land on my back and tear open the newly formed scab.*

This thought process all happened quickly. The next thing I remember was flying over the handlebars and sticking my left arm straight out to catch my fall and not land on my back. I hit hard and felt a pop in my left shoulder as I hit the ground. I not only broke my collarbone but also tore the entire scab off my back. The new three-wheeler was lying upside down with fuel pouring out of the carburetor and gas tank all over the ground below.

I had done it now! Martin has no idea where I was at now lying in a deep gulley with a broken collarbone, bleeding back, and a body full of cactus. I finally got to my feet and tipped the three-wheeler back onto its wheels. This was a struggle with one arm. Now I must start the three-wheeler and drive it out of the steep ravine. The three-wheeler's engine was flooded from being upside down and didn't want to start. I had learned that when an engine gets flooded, you need to hold the throttle wide open for it to start. I had to hold the throttle wide open with my left hand and pull the starter cord with my right arm. My back was now bleeding profusely down my legs and all over the yellow three-wheeler.

After about ten pulls on the rip cord, the three-wheeler finally fired up and blew black smoke out of the exhaust. I was so excited. I didn't think it would ever start and was not looking forward to walking five to six miles home. I jumped on the three-wheeler and could feel the cactus break off in my butt as I sat down on the seat. This was the least of my worries. I needed to get this three-wheeler out of this gulley without wrecking again. I put it in first gear, leaned as far forward as I could, and gave it the onion.

The three-wheeler lunged forward as I headed up the steep hill. The front tire came off the ground, and we nearly went over backward.

I never let off the throttle and just kept leaning forward to prevent the three-wheeler from going over backward. Thank god, the throttle was on the right side because my left arm was useless. I think I had some guardian angels looking over me that day as I made it back up the hill, down the steep hill, and back on to the road again. I drove to the head gate expecting to find Martin, and he was nowhere to be found. Did he leave me up here by myself? Apparently so! I headed back down the road and couldn't wait to get back home. My shoulder was killing me, my back was in horrible pain, and I had cactus sticking out of me everywhere.

I finally arrived at the house safely and walked through the front door of the house. Martin was sitting in his favorite leather chair drinking a cold beer. As I walked through the front door, Martin said, "Where in the hell did you disappear to?"

I said, "I was chasing some elk and wrecked my three-wheeler. I need to go back to the hospital!"

My mother overheard our conversation from the kitchen. She came storming out into the living room and yelled, "WHAT IN THE HELL HAVE YOU DONE NOW?" She looked at my back now bleeding all over the living room's orange shag carpet and said, "OH MY GOD, DID YOU BREAK ANY BONES?"

I said, "I think so. I felt a bone snap in my shoulder, and I can't move my left arm."

My mother yelled at me, "GET YOUR ASS IN THE CAR AND DON'T GET ANY BLOOD ON THE SEATS! Martin, what in the hell did you leave him up there by himself for, and why in the hell did you let him ride that damn three-wheeler?" Mother was mad, and I was about to make another flying trip to the hospital in the ole Suburban. About this time, my brother, Wade, came walking into the living room eating a handful of Oreos; and he looked at me with a smirk on his face and said, "Way to go, dumbass!!"

My mother looked at Martin and yelled, "Get off your ass and put a blanket over the seat, so he doesn't bleed all over the damn car!"

I quickly arrived at the hospital, and the same cute nurse greeted me at the front door. She smiled and said, "Didn't you just leave here this morning?"

I smiled back and said, "Yes, madam, I just missed your cute smile and had to come back to see you!"

I broke my collarbone and spent a few more days in the hospital recovering and squealing every time the cute nurse pulled a piece of cactus out of my butt cheeks. I even got to go spend time with my buddy Mason in his room as he was still recovering from his broken leg. I never did get a very good look at those damn elk.

Chapter 7

SHEEPHERDERS

Sheepherders were a big part of my life as a young child and helped shape my life for many years to come. I spent many hours visiting with sheepherders over a cup of very strong black sheepherder's coffee. I learned even at a young age they were all unique people with various unique talents. Some made knives out of old metal files. Some were talented leather workers and could make beautiful saddles, bridles, or whatever you wanted them to make. It was later in life I realized many had learned these skills in prison. Many took jobs as sheepherders to hide from the law or society. The sheepherders didn't always get along with one another, and they were generally very introverted people who loved to just be left alone. Most sheepherders took a liking to me as a young kid and always enjoyed visiting with me and telling wild stories about themselves.

During the winter months, all the sheepherders would stay together down at the sheep shed during lambing season. They each had sheep wagon, and they would

Old abandoned sheep wagon

park them in a line down by the main sheep shed. We would lamb out about four thousand ewes over a few months, and everyone worked long hard hours taking care of the sheep. During this busy time, we would feed the sheepherders lunch every day at either our house or down at Wally's house.

During lunch one day, I learned from a sheepherder named Red that years ago a cook was shot in our house. Apparently, a sheepherder got in an argument with the cook and pulled a pistol on him. The fight erupted, and the cook took off running through the house with the sheepherder shooting at him. The cook was allegedly shot in every room of the house and died in the kitchen. Red got up from the table and showed us some bullet holes in the kitchen cabinets and some bloodstains still present in the corner of the wooden kitchen countertop.

That was the first time I had heard that story. It freaked me out to think somebody had died in our kitchen and somebody had also been shot in my bedroom. Red was a small man who wore a large-brimmed cowboy hat, a stained red long-sleeved shirt, and little round spectacles. The cowboy hat was stained black with dirt and had holes in the front and back of the hat. This hat had seen better days, and Red probably wore the same hat for over fifteen years. Red had a temper. He carried a pistol on his side and didn't get along with anyone.

Red had no teeth. When he would chew his food, his chin would touch his nose with every bite. As a young child, I would stare at him across the table while he ate because I couldn't believe he could actually touch his nose with his chin. Red was the man in charge of the drop lot. Whenever a ewe had a newborn lamb, Red would drag the lamb with a sheep hook into the main sheep shed with the ewe following behind the newborn lamb.

One day, Red was having a tough time getting an old ewe to follow him and the newborn lamb into the main sheep shed. The ewe had come right to the door several times and would not go through the door. The ewe would go back outside into the herd, and Red would have to take the newborn lamb back out each time and try to coax her to come back in. On the third try, he almost had her in, and I came walking around the corner and scared her back to the herd. I didn't realize what Red was trying to do, and I didn't mean to screw things up. He yelled at me, "Get the hell out of here, you little bastard!" He threw a pitchfork at me as hard as he could. I saw the pitchfork coming at me, and I quickly ducked. The pitchfork went over my head and stuck into the wooden wall of the sheep shed. I learned that day to stay the hell away from Red.

The sheepherders earned little money back then, and they were paid once a month. I think they made about $600 a month plus room and board, but they worked every day of the month. Some hoarded their money and saved every dime, placing cash in a coffee can and hiding it under their mattress. Some would find a ride to town and end up in a bar all night. They would buy everyone in the bar a drink all night long and into the early morning hours until their entire paycheck was gone. Most of the time, they would be arrested for public intoxication and thrown in jail for the night and sometimes the next day. Martin would get a call from the sheriff's office they had one of his sheepherders in jail and needed him to come to pick them up. Often, Martin didn't even know they were gone from the ranch or the mountain. The sheep would go unattended and end up all over the mountain, sometimes mixed in with other sheep producers' herds.

Martin hired a Hispanic sheepherder named Willy. Willy was always happy and always cracking jokes about anything that he could laugh at. He was a short man with a stocky build and wore a small round-brimmed town hat that was very dirty and weathered. Willy wore bib overalls and would tuck his pant legs inside his worn-out cowboy boots. He spoke broken English and had a lazy eye. His laugh was loud. You could always tell when Willy was in the sheep barn because you could hear his laugh all the way across the barn. Every morning, Willy would yell, "GOOD MORNING, SENOR MARTIN!" and then he would laugh out loud. Willy was probably the funniest, most outgoing sheepherder we ever hired. But I soon learned as a young boy that Willy could not be trusted and lied almost every time he opened his mouth.

One morning, I was driving Martin's old Chevy truck down to the sheep shed to start work. Willy walked out of the sheep shed and came toward me as I was driving down the road. I was driving slowly as Willy approached the truck. I thought Willy wanted to talk, so I slowed down almost to a stop. Willy walked up to the truck and smacked the hood of the truck really hard with his hand. He then fell to the ground in front of the truck. I got out and asked him what he was doing. He never laughed and slowly got back to his feet. He looked at me and said that I needed to learn how to drive because I had just run him over. He looked at me and said, "Wait until I tell your dad that you just ran over me and broke my ankle." I thought he was kidding, so I just laughed and told him to have a good day. Willy walked into the sheep shed dragging one of his legs.

About three hours later, Martin found me working out in the drop pen outside of the sheep shed. He came running up to me and said, "WHAT THE HELL DID YOU RUN OVER WILLY FOR?"

I laughed and just said, "What are you talking about?"

He said, "Willy—you ran over him and broke his leg. I just hauled him to town to the doctor's office."

I said, "That's a damn lie. I never ran over him!"

Martin was very upset with me and said, "If you can't learn how to drive responsibly, I will take your damn keys away from you!"

This hurt my feelings because I always wanted to please Martin and would do nothing irresponsible for operating equipment. I said, "Martin, please believe me. I did not run Willy over with your truck!"

"Well, he said you did, and now he is in town at the doctor's office, and I will be the one who gets to pay the damn bill!"

I was mad, and my feelings were hurt. I told Martin, "I'll bet he is not at the doctor's office. He lied to you so that he could get to town and go to the bar and get drunk!"

Martin turned around and stormed off mad.

Apparently, Willy's leg healed just fine because he was back to work the next day with no limp. Martin had to bail him out of jail and bring him back to the ranch. To this day, I know for a fact that I did not run over Willy. A few months later, Martin and I were up on the Bighorn tending sheep camps. We drove into Willy's sheep camp where his sheep wagon was located. His horse named Whiskey was running loose around camp with a saddle on him. We could locate no sheep, Willy, or any of his dogs. Willy was nowhere to be found, and his sheep were gone. Martin became very concerned and told me we needed to get to town and look for Willy because something bad had happened. We unsaddled Whiskey and put him on a picket chain, closed the front door to the sheep wagon, and headed for the town of Lovell, which was the nearest town from where we were located.

We drove into Lovell, and our first stop was at the sheriff's office. Martin went inside and met with the sheriff and asked him if he or his deputies had seen a Hispanic sheepherder lately. The sheriff told him he had not but would keep a lookout and let Martin know if he showed up anywhere in town. Our next stop was the local tavern. Martin told me to wait in the truck and that he would be right back. A few minutes later, Martin came walking out of the old western bar with Willy and his three dogs. Willy was intoxicated and could hardly stand up. He had a knot on his forehead and blood running down his face.

Martin asked him, "What the HELL are you doing down here at the bar, Willy?"

Willy replied, "My horse Whiskey had a runaway with me, and I hit my head on a tree branch and went off the back of my horse and knocked myself unconscious."

Martin asked Willy, "Why did your horse run away with you?"

Willy replied, "Because we had a black bear encounter us on the trail in the heavy timber below camp." Willy then claimed that the horse took off and headed for camp and that he walked off the mountain down to the highway and hitched a ride to town with some real cute tourists.

Martin asked Willy how long it had been since he was at his sheep camp. Willy said, "I'm not sure but probably three days or so!" Martin asked Willy if he had been to the doctor to take care of his wound. Willy replied, "I was headed there, and then I met this pretty senorita in the bar, and she took me home and showed me a real good time. I was going to try to hitchhike back to my camp today and take care of my horse and find my sheep."

Martin said, "Well, jump in the truck. Scott and I will give you a ride back to your camp!"

We had to load Willy in the truck because he was too drunk to step up into the cab of the truck. We loaded his three dogs in the back of the truck and headed for Bald Mountain where Willy's sheep wagon was located. About halfway up the mountain, after going around several sharp curves in the road, Willy yelled, "STOP, I HAVE TO PUKE!" Martin slammed on the brakes, and Willy puked in my lap and then passed out with his head in my lap.

We finally got Willy back to his camp and cleaned him and me up. We later found that about 1,500 of his sheep had mixed in with another sheep producer's sheep in the adjacent pasture. We had to build a temporary corral on the mountain and run all the sheep into the fenced-off area and sort them one by one until we got them all separated again. Willy finally sobered up and helped us sort sheep. When we were done sorting, Willy invited me into his sheep wagon for a cup of coffee. He built a fire in the small wood stove next to the front door and warmed up some chili and coffee on top of the stove. He asked me if I wanted a bowl of chili for lunch. I said, "Yeah, that sounds really good."

He poured the chili into a coffee cup and handed it, saying, "Be careful. A little of this goes a long way, amigo!" Then he laughed out loud. I took a small bite of the chili and thought I might die right in the sheep wagon. He had loaded that chili with red-hot peppers. I couldn't even breathe. It was so hot. Willy laughed out loud and yelled, "Hurry up, amigo. Wash it down with some coffee!" He handed me a cup of his lukewarm coffee, and I took a big gulp of it. The coffee was as thick as mud, and you could even hardly pour it out of the cup because it was so thick! It was the worst-tasting coffee I had ever tasted. It did little to kill the pain in my mouth from the red peppers. I stumbled out of the sheep wagon and picked up his dog's dish full of water and drank the entire bowl of stagnant warm water.

Willy just laughed and said, "You want another cup of chili, amigo?"

I coughed and said, "Hell NO, that will do!"

Willy never did apologize for lying to Martin about me running over him with the truck and breaking his ankle. Because of this, I never trusted Willy any further than I could throw him. I will never forget the day that Willy showed up at our house with a perfect buffalo head he had found near Bald Mountain. The head was perfect and still had the sheaths on each horn. I had never seen a buffalo head this beautiful before. Willy gave it to my mother and told her he would trade her the buffalo head for a homemade banana cream pie. My mother accepted his offer and took the buffalo head. I was ten years old when this happened, and I remembered thinking, *Maybe someday I would find a buffalo head.* Over the years, my mother painted a picture on that buffalo skull depicting a picture of Martin riding a horse and leading two pack horses. My parents later gave me that buffalo skull, and I still have it today.

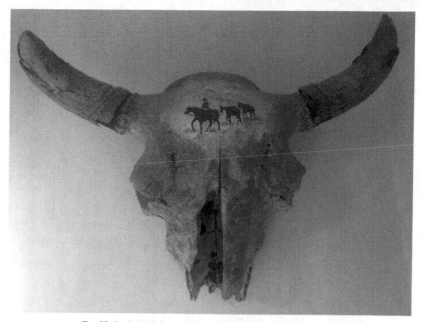

Buffalo head found by Willy the sheepherder

One of our most unique sheepherders was named Bob. Bob was an elderly man probably in his mid- to late sixties. He never said much but deeply cared for his dogs, his horse, and his sheep. Bob would spend his entire paycheck buying canned Alpo for his dogs and apples for his horse. His dogs were well trained. Bob would yell something at the dogs. They would circle out for over a mile and round up all the sheep and bring them back to him. I could never understand what he was saying to the dogs, but they understood every word he said. I'm not sure, but he may have been talking to them in German. I could never understand a word he said, but those dogs would do whatever he wanted.

One day, we're loading and sorting sheep up on Bald Mountain, and Bob brought along his three dogs to help. We were loading sheep onto a semi-truck, and the sheep would have to travel up a long loading chute to get onto the trucks. Invariably, the sheep would bunch up at the base of the loading chute and wouldn't go up the ramp into the large truck. We would have sometimes over one thousand sheep in the pen, and you couldn't walk through all the sheep to get to the base of the loading chute to start the ewes back up the loading chute.

Bob would yell at his dogs, and they would jump on the backs of the sheep and run all the way across the herd of sheep to the front and bite the

109

ewes on the butt standing at the base of the loading chute. The dogs would then run all the way back to Bob on top of the sheep's backs. This got the sheep moving; and they quickly learned that if they didn't keep moving, they would soon have a sheepdog on their back nipping at them. It was always an amazing sight to watch those dogs run back and forth on top of all those ewes and lambs. These dogs saved us a great deal of work, and I'm sure that's why they always got fed so well.

In the winter months, Bob would come down to the main sheep shed. He always carried a hammer with him. He would sit next to a wooden feed bin full of alfalfa cubes and crush up every cube in the feed bin. Sometimes the cubes were too big the ewes would choke on a hay cube and die. Bob hated to ever see a sheep choke on a hay cube and die, so he would take his hammer and break up every cube in the large feed bins. He would spend hours and days breaking hay cubes and never saying a word to anyone as they walked by.

Bob chewed tobacco and had no teeth. When he would spit, the tobacco juice would just run down the front of his chin and all over his shirt. He rarely changed his clothes, so the front of his shirt became a caked-up mess of chewing tobacco. His T-shirt was probably so caked full of dried-out tobacco spit it would probably fall apart if he ever removed it. Bob would buy a new pair of blue jeans at the beginning of the summer and wear that pair of jeans the entire year without washing them. Most sheepherders would generally buy the jeans too long in the leg and just fold up the cuffs. Once the cuffs were folded up, they could store fencing nails, cigarettes, tobacco, or whatever else they didn't have room for in their pockets.

When Bob took his sheep to the mountains in the summer, he would build sheepherder monuments with neatly stacked rocks. These monuments were a landmark so sheepherders wouldn't get lost in a storm. Some stood over six feet tall. He would also take an ax and chop sagebrush all day long and build huge sagebrush wind blinds. He felt that the more sagebrush he removed, the more grass that would grow for the sheep to eat!

When Martin and I would tend his sheep camp, all he ever wanted to eat was jelly-filled cinnamon rolls and canned milk with an occasional dozen eggs and a bag of ginger snaps. Whenever we moved his sheep wagon from one location to another, it would take us several hours to clean up all the canned dog foods lying on the ground around the wagon. I think he fed his dogs at least six cans of dog food per day. I can't imagine how much money Bob spent on dog food over thirty years of herding sheep.

Bob was not ever married or had any kids, but I don't know because he never said much. I do know that his pride and joy was his old sixties Cadillac he kept parked in our barn with a tarp over it. He had stored it there for years. I only saw him drive it one time to go to church one bright Sunday morning. The demise of the Cadillac came one winter morning when my mother was running late for work. She couldn't get her Suburban to start, so she ran down to the barn and uncovered Bob's Cadillac. In all its glory, there it sat without even a spectacle of dust on it. DJ jumped into the Caddy and pumped the accelerator about twenty-five times and turned the key over. The car eventually fired up and blew some black smoke out of the tailpipes.

Mom yelled at us kids to shut the barn door and get in the damn car as she was running late for work. Wade and I jumped in the front seat of Bob's beautiful Caddy, and away we went down the dirt road. We made it about five miles, and the car's engine made a horrible grinding noise and quickly came to a stop. My mother said, "Now, what in the hell is wrong with this car?" She turned the key and went to turn over the engine, and it wouldn't turn over. We ended leaving the car to sit along the roadside and caught a ride to town with someone else. Later that night, I heard my parents arguing and learned that the Caddy had no oil in it and my mother had blown the engine. Martin was not happy with my mother, and I'm sure Bob was less than impressed. Martin bought him a new car when it was all said and done.

Sheepherder Bob with his Cadillac car headed for church

One cold winter night, Martin asked me if I would go down to the sheep shed and check on Bob as he hadn't been feeling well. I took my motorcycle down the hill and found Bob's sheep wagon. The inside of Bob's sheep wagon was lit up with a kerosene lantern hanging from the ceiling over his bed. I looked through the small window on the front door of the sheep wagon and could see Bob lying in bed through the light of the lantern. I knocked on the door, and Bob didn't move or say anything. I banged harder on the door and still nothing. I thought to myself, *Oh my god, is Bob dead?*

I looked closer through the window, and Bob was wrapped up in orange plastic irrigation dam with just his head sticking out. The dam had mud all over it. Bob had been spitting and chewing tobacco down the side of the orange plastic dam. After no response, I was sure that Bob was dead, so I kicked open the door and walked into the wagon. I yelled Bob's name several times and still no response. I walked over to the edge of his bed to see if he was breathing. I was feeling scared, and all I could see was his frail little face sticking out of the orange plastic dam glowing from the light of the lantern.

He must have been lying there for several days because he had been spitting his chewing tobacco down the side of the plastic dam. His spit had pooled up on the floor at the base of his bed. I needed to check his pulse but did not want to peel his tobacco-soaked shirt away from his neck. I finally grabbed the edge of the orange plastic dam and gently pulled it away from his neck to check his pulse. When I slowly moved the crinkly plastic dam, Bob's eyes quickly opened; and he yelled "AH, AH, WHAT DO YOU WANT?" Suddenly, one of Bob's arms came out from underneath the orange dam, and a pistol was pointing right at my head.

I yelled, "I'm sorry, Bob. I just wanted to check on you. I didn't mean to scare you!"

Bob had cocked the hammer on the pistol. He slowly released the hammer on the pistol and put his arm and pistol back under the orange plastic dam. He mumbled something that I didn't understand, and he went back to sleep.

I got the hell out of there and was scared to death I could have been shot. I went back up to the house and told Martin what had happened. He said, "Thanks for checking on him. I probably need to get him out of there in the morning and get him to a hospital." That was the last I remembered of Bob, and I think he ended up passing away sometime later at a veteran's hospital.

Inside a sheepherder's wagon

A couple of mornings later, I went down to the sheep shed to have a cup of coffee with some of the other herders. This morning, it was very cold. The sheepherders had the woodstove fired up in the bunk room of the sheep shed. Grady and Ed were sitting in a pile of straw on the floor drinking coffee and telling stories about years and years of herding sheep together. They were both in their early to midseventies and had herded sheep together most of their lives.

Both wore bib overalls, and Grady had white hair and a white beard. He reminded me of Santa Claus. Grady was always happy and probably drank whiskey in his coffee early each morning. Ed always had bloodshot eyes from drinking heavily. He smoked rolled cigarettes one after another and had the shakes. His two fingers that held the rolled cigarette were stained dark brown from smoking so long. Neither of them had any teeth left; and when they would laugh, you could see both top and bottom gum lines with no teeth.

On that morning, another sheepherder sat in the straw pile with them, telling stories. I had not met this herder yet, but he was rough looking with long greasy hair and a shaggy beard. He also smoked rolled cigarettes and coughed loudly while laughing at Grady and Ed telling stories. He had a tattoo across his knuckles on one hand that read *ace*. The other hand read *lucky*. While telling stories, I watched him take off his scotch cap and quickly catch a mouse in the straw stack by slamming his hat over the mouse. He grabbed the mouse around the body with the hand that read *lucky* and slowly squeezed the head off the mouse. The herders just kept telling stories, and nobody even said anything about the headless mouse now quivering on the floor next to his cup of coffee. I never forgot that moment or that tattoo. All I remember is that guy didn't work for Martin long.

Grady told the story of how he had just received a case of government cheese and that he hadn't been able to shit for over a week. He looked at me and said, "You want some plug 'em, Scott? Eat a brick of this, and you won't shit for a week!" Then they cussed the local government trapper. They hated the government trapper because they didn't think that he ever caught enough coyotes, and coyotes were always killing their sheep. Grady laughed and said, "That worthless son of a bitch couldn't track an elephant in a snowstorm even if it had a bloody nose." I sat there and listened to them tell stories all morning long. I thought to myself, *Man, I wish I could have recorded them conversations because I could write a book about them stories someday.* Well, here I am, over forty years later, trying to remember all those damn stories!

Ed told a story of how he and Grady got drunk one night and left the ranch on a trail ninety motorcycle headed for a bar in Lovell. The ranch was about forty-five miles from the bar, and they had run out of beer. They rode the bike double and headed for the bar. Their three sheepdogs went with them. Grady laughed and said, "Remember when you kept running over them damn dogs!"

Ed replied, "That's because you were drunk and kept falling off the back of the damn motor sickle."

Grady said, "Yeah, shit, we finally made it to Lovell. You got so drunk they threw your ass in the slammer, and I didn't know how to drive that damn motor sickle home!"

Ed laughed and said, "Yeah, you ended up wrecking the motorcycle in town and left it lying on the sidewalk in front of the bar. You then gathered up all the damn dogs and hitchhiked home at two in the morning."

Grady said, "Oh, that was a bad, bad night. Nobody would pick me up, so I finally stepped out on the highway in front of a truck to get them to stop. They never even tapped on their brakes and hit me so hard that it pitched me out in the borrow pit."

Grady looked at me and said, "Man, that hurt, Scott. I lay in that borrow pit for several days before someone finally stopped to try to catch my dogs and found me lying facedown in the grass."

Ed laughed and said, "Yeah, you were pretty busted up on that deal and ended lying in the hospital for several weeks."

Ed and Grady just went on and on one story after another. I laughed so hard I almost peed my pants several times. I thought it was neat to listen to a couple of old guys telling stories of their lives and laughing about hard times and still maintaining a positive attitude. They had little, but they were damn sure happy and enjoying life working together.

One of my favorite sheepherders was named Curley. Curley was an older guy, maybe seventy years old, and he never said much. But when he talked, you listened because he was always trying to tell you great words of wisdom. Curley was a small skinny man who wore thin wire-rimmed glasses and a top hat. Curley had a gimp and used a wooden cane when he walked. Curley dressed nice and was always cleaned up. He smoked a pipe and chewed WB Cut tobacco. He always said that WB Cut tobacco looked like pussy hair, and that's why he liked it so much. He would always ask me if I wanted a small pinch of pussy hair and would offer his WB Cut.

I told Curley I didn't know what that might look like, and it sounded gross, but I would try it. It actually did taste good, but I liked my Copenhagen better. Curley was getting up there in years, and his health was failing him. One evening, Martin asked me if I would help Curley in the morning get his band of sheep up the face of the Bighorn Mountains from Crystal Creek to Bald Mountain. He was worried about Curley not making the trip alone anymore.

I was about ten to twelve years old, and I told Martin I would help Curley in the morning get his sheep to the top of the mountain. Martin said, "You better pack a lunch tonight because we will need to leave before sunup." I made a tuna fish sandwich and grabbed a can of soda pop out of the refrigerator. I grabbed my bright-orange backpack and loaded it up with my lunch and a light coat. We got up early in the morning and headed for the trailhead at the base of the Bighorn Mountains near Crystal Creek. We arrived at the trailhead right at daylight. Martin got his binoculars out and glassed the steep face of the huge mountain range. The mountain was covered with mahogany and bitterbrush with scattered patches of timber near the top. Martin told me we were supposed to meet Curley at the trailhead at daylight, but it looked like Curley had left.

Martin continued glassing the steep mountain slope with his binoculars. I looked over at Martin, and he had a concerned look on his face. He said, "I don't see Curley anywhere. He must have gotten an early start. Do you think you can hike up that mountain by yourself and catch up with him?"

I looked up the mountain, and I couldn't see any band of sheep anywhere. Curley might have made it to the top. I said, "Yeah, I think so."

Martin said, "Whatever you do, don't ever go downhill, or you will be going the wrong way and may end up getting lost. Just head up that trail, and you should catch up with Curley shortly." He also told me that if a bear attacks me, just shove a rock in its mouth so it can't bite down and hurt me. I grabbed my bright-orange backpack and started up the mountain. Martin said, "I'll see you later this evening at Bald Mountain."

I vigorously headed up the steep mountain trail hoping to soon catch up with the band of sheep and Curley on his horse. The trail that I was hiking on didn't have any sheep tracks on it at all. As I headed up the steep mountain trail, I became worried that I might not ever catch up with Curley. I had not ever thought about a bear encounter before; but now, as I was hiking alone with no firearm to protect myself, it crossed my mind. What if I do run into a bear?

I was young and in great shape, but my legs began to tire as I climbed up the steep mountain slope. The higher I climbed, the more tired I became. Soon I had completely lost the trail that I had been hiking on. The trail just flat disappeared. I just kept climbing uphill remembering Martin's words: "Never go downhill, or you will be lost." I finally reached the timber about two-thirds the way up the mountain. The shade of the timber felt cool on my body because I had been sweating from the steep climb. I still had seen no sheep tracks or any sign of Curley. I kept traveling upward, but the trees became thick, and the terrain became rough. The next thing I knew, I had traveled down and up several steep ravines in the heavy timber. I finally stopped and looked around, and everything looked the same. I was not even sure which direction was up anymore. I panicked and ran through the trees, hoping to find a trail or hear sounds of a sheep bleating somewhere. The next thing I knew, I had been running in circles and had returned to the same area I started from! It was at this moment a little voice told me, "You are lost."

I was scared and out of breath, and I cried. I thought to myself, *What if I never see my family again?* I felt like I had let Martin and Curley down because I could not find him and help him with moving the sheep up the mountain. I needed to sit down, breathe, and compose myself as I was hyperventilating. I looked over and saw a large white rock sitting at the base of a large pine tree. I thought to myself that rock would be a good place to sit on top of while I rest for a minute. While sitting on the rock and looking down between my legs, I observed something weird in the rock. The texture of the rock was rough, and it had several large cracks on the surface. The closer I looked, the more I could see something protruding from the front and top side of the rock.

It looked like tiny feet protruding from the rock. The closer I looked, the more the rock looked fossilized and different from any other rock I had ever seen before. I stood up off the rock and looked down at it. Oh my god! This was not a rock. It was a fossilized turtle shell. I could actually see the two small turtle feet protruding out of its shell. I could even see a small fossilized turtle head protruding outside of the fossilized rock shell. I was not sure how much this fossilized turtle shell weighed, but I was sure there was no way I could pick it up. I remembered gazing at it for a few minutes, wishing I had a camera to take a picture, when I realized I was still lost and this fossilized turtle shell was the least of my worries at that moment in my life.

I sat back down on top of the turtle shell and closed my eyes. I got quiet with myself and meditated and tried to figure out what I needed to do to get myself out of this predicament. While sitting there quietly, I thought I could hear the sound of sheep bleating in the distance. It was a very faint sound. I couldn't tell what direction the sound was coming from. All at once, I felt a sign of hope and climbed upward through the thick trees toward what I thought was the sound of sheep bleating in the distance. I climbed clear to the top of the mountain and stood silently listening. All I could hear was the sound of my heavy breathing and the pounding of my heart against my chest.

I would need to sit down, catch my breath, and let my heart rate decrease if I would ever want to hear that faint sound again. I sat down and listened closely for about ten minutes. There was the sound again! I could hear sheep bleating down below me. I looked off the cliff to my right, and the sound was coming from the bottom of the canyon below me. The canyon was steep and deep with black timber that no one had probably ever tried to pass through. Way down in the bottom, I could see a small creek and meadow. It looked like it was miles away. I asked myself, *Did Curley go a different way with the sheep? Was Curley lost? Should I hike down there and not follow Martin's directions in fear of becoming lost?*

I knew better than to hike down that steep canyon. But I must do something, and I was sure I could hear sheep bleating at the bottom of that canyon. I later learned that I was heading down to the bottom of a canyon called Bear Creek Canyon. This was a canyon that few people had ever traveled because of its extreme rough and steep terrain. After several hours of hiking down through thick downed timber and sliding on my butt down steep rocky ravines, I reached the bottom of the canyon.

I had found a game trail along the creek and was glad to finally have a trail to follow. I listened quietly and could no longer hear sheep bleating. I was sure I was losing my mind. I kept walking down the trail and listening. Quickly, I observed some bear tracks in the trail and heard a loud *wuff* noise, and I looked up to see a large black bear facing me in the trail! I thought, *OH MY GOD!* I never grabbed a rock to shove in its mouth if it bites me like Martin had told me to do. I yelled at the bear, "GET OUT OF HERE!!" The bear ran off into the thick trees to my right. It was at that moment I told myself, *You need to get the hell out of this canyon before you die down here!*

I quickly headed back up the steep canyon through the thick downfall. I wanted out of that canyon and out of it quick. After several hours of hard climbing, I finally reached the top of the canyon and was back to the spot I had earlier dropped off. I was now very tired, hungry, and thirsty. I sat down, cried some more, and ate half my tuna sandwich. I saved the other half of my sandwich in case no one rescued me for several days, and I needed something else to eat to survive. I also saved my soda pop as I might need it later to survive. After eating my half tuna sandwich, I hiked farther up the mountain and got as high in elevation as possible so that maybe I would recognize something or be able to spot the sheep.

I topped out of the trees and spotted a small grassy knoll ahead of me. I climbed to the top of the grassy knoll and peaked over the edge to the north. HALLELUJAH! A lone ewe stood on the back side of that grassy knoll. I only saw one sheep, but I knew in my heart that Curley would know he was missing a sheep and come back looking for her in time. I took my backpack off and laid it on the ground. I rested my tired head against the backpack and fell asleep in the warm afternoon sunshine.

I don't know how long I had been sleeping but was eventually awakened by the sound of a voice yelling, "SCOTTY, SCOTTY, WHERE ARE YOU?" I woke up and could see Curley, Martin, and my mother coming down a steep slope headed in my direction.

I jumped up and yelled, "I'M OVER HERE! I'M OVER HERE!" Thank god, they had found me! I had been rescued!

My mother came running off the hill in the lead. She was screaming, "OH MY GOD, SCOTTY, ARE YOU ALL RIGHT? WE WERE WORRIED SICK ABOUT YOU!"

They all hugged me, and I even saw a tear in Curley's eye as he gave me a hug. This old sheepherder was worried about me.

I soon ate the rest of my tuna sandwich and guzzled down my warm soda pop. Apparently, Curley had left at three that morning and took a different route up the mountain than he usually had done in the past. Martin had picked up Curley's sheep wagon that morning and picked up my mother at the house before heading all the way around through Shell canyon and up to Bald Mountain. It had taken them all day to drive around to the top of the Bighorns with Curley's sheep wagon. When they arrived, Curley was with the sheep; and they asked Curley where I was. Curley told them he hadn't seen me all day! They thought he was kidding at first, but they soon discovered that he was telling the truth. This was when they all went into a panic and set out looking for me.

I didn't know it, but the rest of the band of sheep was right over the hill from the single ewe I had seen. I told them the story about the bear and not having a rock to stick in its mouth if it tried to bite me. I also told them about the beautiful fossilized turtle shell I had found in the trees while being lost. I never went back looking for that turtle shell again, but I'm sure I could never find it again. And if I ever found it again, I knew it was too heavy to lift and pack out of there. I also told Martin I would never do that trip again without a horse and a rifle. Martin smiled and said, "I will get you your horse someday." I never forgot those words because I had always wanted a horse.

We loaded up in Martin's old Chevy truck and headed down the rough two-track road with my mother sitting between us on the bench seat. The road was rough as we drove by the Bald Mountain cabin. My mother held her stomach tightly as if she was in pain or uncomfortable. She looked over

at Martin and whispered, "Please slow down. Remember, I'm pregnant!"
I was not supposed to hear this! But I did, and I remember thinking,
Holy cow! I will have a baby brother or sister someday! She didn't look
pregnant, and I had never heard them talk about it before.

Bald Mountain cabin in the Bighorn Mountains

A few weeks later, I came home from school one day; and Martin said,
"Take a look down in the corral by the barn. I found you a horse!" I couldn't
wait to see my new horse. I jumped on my yellow three-wheeler and headed
down to the barn. The horse was about a two-year-old sorrel mare. She was
racing around the corral and whinnying at the top of her lungs. She tried
to jump the fence in several places but kept hitting the top rail of the eight-
foot-high post and pole fence. This was not what I expected for my first
horse. This mare was wild and had never been handled before. She would
try to jump the fence and fall over backward onto her back. She would then
get up and paw the ground, snort and buck, and try to jump the fence again.

I soon crawled between the high fence rails and entered the corral with
her. She quickly ran toward me and stood on her hind legs and struck out
at me with her front legs. This horse was very upset and did not want to be
touched or handled at all. Martin later showed up on his motorcycle and
said, "What do you think of her?"

I said, "She seems wild as hell."

Martin said, "Yeah, she will need a little work. She has never been handled before. A buddy of mine roped her off the range yesterday and wanted you to have her."

I'm not sure how this worked, but apparentlly, this horse had been roped off the open range and never been handled before. Martin told the ole boy I had been looking for a horse, so he damn sure found me one.

I didn't know anything about training a damn wild horse. I wanted something gentle and ready to ride the mountains and foothills. Over the next few days, I took this as a challenge. I told myself, *I will catch that damn horse, halter-break her, and soon ride her!* I could not get near that horse or even touch her. I finally found myself an old lariat in Martin's truck and decided it was time to rope this mare if I would ever get my hands on her. I chased her around that damn corral for hours and never could throw the right loop to catch her. I swung that lariat until I thought my arm would fall off. Finally, I decided I needed to outsmart her and run her into the barn and get her in a corner and rope her. I finally got her in the barn and a corner. She was facing me and snorting as she pawed the ground. She stood on her hind legs and lashed out at me with her untrimmed hooves. I finally had a clear shot at her head, and I swung a perfect loop right around her neck. At that very moment, I questioned myself, *What in the* hell *have I just done?*

That young mare took off headed right for me, and I stepped aside to avoid being run over or kicked. She was headed toward the back door of the barn with the lariat around her neck, and I would not let go of that rope She and I would have a little understanding, by god. Well, by god we did. She jerked me off my feet and was headed for the back door of that barn at a high rate of speed. I was dragging on the floor of the barn shortly behind her and would not let go of that rope. The next thing I knew, my body had torn all the trim pieces off the frame of the barn door as she pulled me through the doorway and back out into the open corral.

The corral was large and had a creek flowing through it at the far end. The weeds in the corral were over three feet tall because we rarely had used that corral that summer. She pulled me on my belly all the way across the corral, through the creek, and down through all the tall tumbleweeds. I couldn't see, I couldn't breathe, my face was full of cheatgrass and dirt— but damn if I would let go of that rope. We soon made about three circles around that entire corral when she finally slowed down and eventually stopped running. The lariat had choked off her airway, and she lay down in the dirt, gasping for air.

I was gasping for air. My chest, arms, and face were bleeding from being dragged through the dirt and weeds. I quickly jumped to my feet and hog-tied her legs with the other end of the lariat while she was lying down gasping for air. She snorted and kicked but couldn't get up. My knot was good and tight and was not coming undone. I quickly ran into the barn and grabbed a halter and lead rope off the wall and headed back out to the corral.

It was difficult to get the halter on her head because she was flailing her head back and forth, beating it off the hard ground. I

Me practicing with my lariat, getting ready to go rope my wild mare

finally got the halter on her and untied her legs. She pulled back on the lead rope hard and dragged me around the corral some more. She finally got tired and stood still. She no longer had the strength to drag me around the corral. I reached over and tried to pet her neck. She just snorted and pawed at me. I even offered her a sugar cube I had put away especially for her in my bib overalls before I left the house earlier that day. She did not see this offer of kindness and continued to strike at me with her untrimmed front hooves.

I tried to get her to lead for about an hour. I just simply was not strong enough to overpower her. Finally, I had a brilliant idea. I would tie her to the back of my three-wheeler and break her to lead. There would be no way she could outpower my three-wheeler. I quickly tied her lead rope to a solid post and excitedly headed to get my trusty three-wheeler. When I returned, she was still tied to the solid post and snorting at me through both nostrils. I tied the lariat onto the end of the lead rope and quickly tied the other end of the lariat to the metal rack mounted on the back of my three-wheeler. I fired up the three-wheeler and pulled the rope until it was taut. She pulled back, and I gave it the onion. We lunged forward, and she was soon running behind me in the corral. She would squeal, lock up all four legs, and jump straight in the air and squeal more. But she couldn't outpower the ole yellow Suzuki. After about three laps in the corral, it was time to hit the open road and get her used to being outside of the corral.

Martin had gone back to the house earlier and was probably resting in his leather recliner by now. We headed out of the corral and up the hill. She was still resisting but couldn't outpower the three-wheeler. By the time we went by the house, I was in third gear and she was at a high trot. Martin looked out the front window and couldn't believe what he had just seen. He yelled at Mother and said, "Look at Scott. He's about got that damn mare broke to lead already!" We went on down the road to the spot where Mason and I had our motorcycle wreck, and I turned around to head home. The ole mare was lathered up, breathing hard and damn near halter broke at this point. I headed back home and saw if I could get her in a full gallop and maybe hit fourth gear.

We were soon galloping down the road, and the fresh air was blowing through my air. I had a smile on my face because I had just halter-broke my first horse. About that time, the mare spooked at something along the road and locked all four of her feet up. The three-wheeler came to an abrupt stop, and this change in acceleration threw me over the handlebars. I skipped down the road on my head a few bounces and looked up to see this mare dragging my three-wheeler backward. All I could hear was the sound of the horse bucking and farting as she veered off the road and out into the high sagebrush. The three-wheeler was now upside down and being dragged through the sagebrush. She later made it back onto the road and was now dragging my three-wheeler upside down back down the road and right past the front living room window of our house. Martin got back out of his leather recliner and looked out the window and said to Mother, "OH, MAYBE NOT!"

The mare finally tired of dragging my three-wheeler upside down, and she stopped just short of the barn. I walked about one mile back home and got the horse untied from the three-wheeler. I looked at the horse, pulled on the lead rope, and said, "Come on, girl." All be damned if that mare didn't take off leading and follow me back to the barn. I had no problems leading her after that. Breaking her was another story for later. I named her Daisy, and she did eat that damn sugar cube by end of the day. I later led Daisy up to the house and told Martin as the blood dripped off my forehead down the front of my bib, "There's more than one damn way to halter break a colt."

**Suzuki three-wheeler with trail 90 motorcycle
that a sheepherder gave me one day**

Growing up on the ranch was not always easy, and I'm sure it made me grow up much faster than most. I got to see and do things as a child that most people today wouldn't even understand. Martin turned me into a young man at a very young age because of the level of responsibility he entrusted in me daily. I was often forced to learn things through the school of hard knocks or just go without.

One bright summer day, I rode with Martin to tend sheep camp. We were going to a sheepherder's camp located at a lower elevation in the bentonite hills. We arrived at the sheep camp about noon in Martin's old white Chevy pickup. The sheepherder named Big John came walking out of his wagon to greet us. Big John didn't look good. His face was pale white as he approached Martin and me. Big John's first words to Martin were "Martin, I'm not feeling so well. Could you please take me to town to see a doctor?"

Martin said, "You don't look so good, Big John. Go sit in the truck, and we will get you to town as soon as possible."

Big John went and sat in the truck. Martin and I packed in his groceries, fed his dogs, and made sure his horse was fed and watered.

Big John was a big man and weighed well over three hundred pounds.

He soared up every horse he ever rode because of his excessive weight. I remembered on this day John was riding a bay horse named Lucky. I had ridden Lucky before in the Bighorn Mountains near Snowshoe Pass. He was a very nice, gentle horse to ride. Lucky's front foot was picketed to a chain next to the sheep wagon. Lucky had a huge sore on his withers where Big John had worn all of his hair off him from riding too long with too much weight on him.

Big John had smeared some purple goopy-looking cream on Lucky's withers to help heal the wound. We soon got camp tended and headed over to the truck. Big John was sitting in the center of the bench, seat ready to go to town. Martin and I jumped in the truck, and Big John said, "Martin, I sure am sorry, but I just haven't been feeling well for a while."

Martin said, "No problem, John. We will get you to town and get you checked out."

You never knew when to believe some herders because oftentimes they just wanted an excuse to get to town and drink away another paycheck. But Big John didn't look good. I felt he was being very sincere.

We fired up the truck and headed down the road. Martin seemed like he was driving faster than normal and talked little. We went around a sharp corner, I felt the weight of Big John's heavy body slump against me. I tried to shove him back over to my left, but he didn't move! Quickly, his entire upper body fell into my lap face up. I slapped Big John on the face and said, "Big John, Big John, wake up!" There was no response from Big John. I looked at Martin and said, "Martin, I think Big John is dead!"

Martin hit the brakes and pulled off the shoulder of the road. Martin reached over and checked for a pulse on the side of Big John's neck. Martin couldn't find a pulse and looked at me and said, "I think you are right. He is dead. Can you take care of his sheep for a few days while I take him to town?"

I said, "Sure, I think I can do that!" Back then, nobody knew how to perform CPR. When you were dead, you were just dead. Martin turned his truck around and took me back to Big John's sheep wagon. I pulled myself out from underneath Big John's dead body and slipped out the passenger side of the truck. Martin said, "Doctor that poor damn horse before you ride him, and I will see you as soon as I can."

Martin sped off and left me standing there in front of the sheep wagon. It was a beautiful blue-sky day. I walked around to the back of the sheep wagon and noticed a dead buck deer hanging in the shade off the back of the wagon. It was a small two-point buck, and it looked like Big John had eaten about half of the deer. It was pretty common back in those days for sheepherders to get themselves some "camp meat." This was July, and there was no season open for hunting deer. I noticed the back window of the sheep wagon was open and the front half door was also propped open. I could see sheep off in the distance to the north, but I'm sure I was only seeing a portion of what was in the herd.

I decided that I better saddle Lucky and go check on the sheep while the weather was still nice. I could see big black clouds forming off to the north several miles away. I doctored Lucky with the purple ointment and gently put a blanket and saddle on him. Lucky was fun to ride and would do whatever you asked of him. I soon found the sheep, and Big John's dogs went about their business and quickly rounded up all the sheep. I felt much better once I had all the sheep accounted for because I didn't know the lay of the land well and didn't want to lose a bunch of sheep on my watch.

Once comfortable with the situation, I pulled a set of hobbles out of my saddlebags and hobbled Lucky. Lucky seemed to enjoy himself as he would feed in one spot for a while and then hop with both front feet in the air and move to a new spot with better grass. I enjoyed myself and relaxed once I had everything under control. I even spent some time searching for an arrowhead on a bare hillside a short distance away from the band of sheep. Between me looking for arrowheads and Lucky slowly hopping off the other direction, we became separated for about one mile in distance. I looked up to see where Lucky was headed. He was quickly hopping back toward camp! About that time, the wind blew. I looked up to see a huge very nasty-looking black cloud coming straight toward me from the west. I had found two arrowheads and didn't want to leave the area because I had also just found some teepee rigs where Indians have camped before. I was very eager to search for more artifacts.

I could hear the sounds of thunder in the distance and could see flashes of lightning headed in my direction. The sheep bleated loudly and quickly gathered in a tight bunch. Lucky was headed for the wagon on his hobbles. I needed to catch him quickly, or I would be walking home. I finally got a foot in the stirrup and boarded Lucky and headed for home. The storm approached quickly with little warning. The clouds were black above and swirling in a large circular motion that moved slowly. Suddenly, it became very calm and eerie out. I heard a huge *crack*, and a bolt of lightning struck right next to Lucky and me. The lightning was so close that the sound deafened me, and the flash of light was so bright that all I could see were little black circles flashing around in my eyeballs. I could feel my hair standing on end, and I could hear lightning snapping on the ground below between Lucky's metal horseshoes. I quickly jumped off Lucky knowing I was probably just seconds from being bucked off even though he was a gentle horse. This was too much for any horse to put up with, and we were both scared to death. It hailed. The hail stung my face and arms as it hit me. Then it rained harder than I had ever seen it rain before. It was a good ole Wyoming cloudburst out on the prairie, the type of rainstorm that produced gully washers within minutes.

I grabbed ahold of Lucky's lead rope and led him back to the sheep wagon. It was raining and lightning so hard that I could hardly keep my eyes open or see anything if I could keep them open. I lowered my chin into the collar of my light coat, and rain poured off the brim of my green cap that read *skoal* across the front of the cap. We soon came to a gulley roaring with rainwater. It looked too wide to jump across. The water was moving so fast it could wash me down the ravine if I slipped and fall in. A bolt of lightning cracked right next to me, and Lucky reared up on his hind legs and whinnied.

I could not lead Lucky across the ravine because it was too wide to jump and the water was raging down the ravine. I finally led Lucky about twenty-five yards away from the ravine so we could both get a run at the ravine and jump over the raging water together over to the far bank. I took off running with Lucky's lead rope in my hand and him running behind me. Once I jumped to clear the ravine, Lucky spooked and reared backward and jerked me into the raging water below. I hit the cold water with only a lead rope and bridle in my hand. (I had pulled Lucky's bridle off his head.) As I was washing down the ravine, I could see Lucky running in the opposite direction. I could see him bucking and hear him fart loudly with every jump as he ran off.

I rode the ravine downstream in the raging water for about fifty yards and finally pulled myself out of the strong current and onto the bank on the opposite side of the river from Lucky. Thankfully, we had hit an oxbow in the ravine; and that caused me to hit the bank on the opposite side of the ravine, washing me up onto the shore. I quickly walked up and down the stream of heavy-flowing water looking for a place to cross to get Lucky and the dogs. It wasn't happening. I needed to get back to the sheep wagon and warm up and get dry before hypothermia set in. I figured the dogs and horse would be fine and make it back on their own once the water level in the ravine went down. At least, I hoped so. I headed for the sheep wagon in the heavy rain located about two miles away. I was so scared I think I might have run the entire way back to the wagon.

Once I got back to the wagon, I realized the rear window and front door had been left open in the sheep wagon. The floor had about two inches of water on it, and the bed was soaked from the rain blowing through the back window. I quickly jumped in the wagon and shut the doors and windows tight. I quickly fired up the kerosene lantern hanging from the ceiling. This produced both heat and light. I then grabbed a small hand ax and split some kindling to build a fire. I placed the kindling in the woodstove and poured some diesel fuel over the wood and lit a match. Voila! We had a fire on the stove. I soon got the chills and shivered. I couldn't get warm with all the wet clothes still on me. I quickly stripped off all my wet clothes and searched for anything dry to put on. The only thing I could find was one pair of Big John's dirty pants underneath the bed. I jumped into his big ole pair of trousers and stood with both arms tucked down the pant legs. The waistband came clear up to my neck, so I ran some baling twine through the belt loops and cinched the waistband tight around my neck. The wagon soon warmed up, and I was able to partially dry out my wet clothes.

Scotty riding Lucky near Snowshoe Pass, wearing my favorite cap

Nightfall soon came. Neither the dogs nor Lucky had shown up. I was worried about them, but it was still raining, and there was nothing I could do at that moment. I waddled out the front door of the sheep wagon in Big John's trousers and carved a chunk of poached deer meat hanging on the back of the wagon. I put a small metal pan on the hot stove and filled it full of Crisco oil, cracked a couple of store-bought eggs in the pan with some deer venison, and fried it up. It might have been one of the best meals I had ever had. Or maybe it was just because I had cooked it myself. I later crawled into Big John's dirty sleeping bag that night and lay there trying to go to sleep. I could hear coyotes howling in the night. I could also hear dogs barking, Lucky whinnying, and sheep bawling over the sound of the kerosene lantern hissing in my ear. I was worried that everything would be a huge mess in the morning, but there was nothing I could do about it tonight. I finally shut the lantern off and fell asleep to the sound of a battery-operated alarm clock ticking next to my head. *Tick, tick, tick.*

The next morning was beautiful. The sky was shining bright blue. I woke up to find Lucky and the dogs outside the wagon wanting to be fed. I fed them and let the dogs in the wagon get warmed up and dried off. They were soaking wet and smelled like wet dogs. I made a pot of sheepherder's coffee and cooked more store-bought eggs in a frying pan. I came to later discover it had rained so hard that Martin could not get back and pick me up because of the muddy road conditions. Martin finally showed up on the third day in the afternoon to pick me up. I was excited to see him.

I became a man over those short three days herding sheep alone, and I felt good about it. I survived eating poached deer, black coffee, and store-bought eggs. Big John had a massive heart attack and died right in my lap. I kept the sheep gathered up safe and cared for the dogs and

Artifacts found near sheep camp
after a heavy rainstorm

Lucky. I was always close to that horse after that experience together in the rain and lightning. This had been an adventure I had never forgotten about. I even found a couple more artifacts over the next few days because of the heavy rains washing out the deep ravine and causing additional erosion that uncovered several more artifacts.

Chapter 8

SCHOOL/SPORTS

I did enjoy my childhood just as long as I wasn't in school. The school was boring. I could never pay attention to what the teachers were trying to teach me. My mind would soon drift off to hunting, fishing, and trapping. I went to kindergarten in a small town named Otto. Our class size was small, and so was our one-room schoolhouse. The only thing I remember was we kids had dug a dirt hole in the backyard of the school. It became our underground fort during recess. How that dirt hole never caved in on us and killed us all I will never know. The hole had a small round entrance and went about five feet deep underground. The hole was deep enough that we kids could stand up once in the hole and not hit our heads on the ceiling. We would gather up a handful of salt sage and eat it for lunch while in our fort.

My parents went through a divorce about this time. Wade and I moved to Greybull and attended Greybull Elementary School. My first-grade teacher was a sweet lady named Mrs. Dentley. She always had a smile on her face. she spoiled me every chance she could. By second grade, I had joined the USA wrestling team in Greybull. I had two dedicated wrestling coaches, and they taught me a handful of moves I became very proficient at. I was a strong boy, stronger than most probably because of all my hard work on the farm and ranch as a child. I won wrestling matches and could pin most of my opponents quickly. I qualified for the state tournament in Cheyenne, Wyoming, that year. I was seven years old. I remember Cheyenne being a big city, and I had never seen so many wrestlers in my life. I would quickly take my opponent down and pin them and move on to the next match. My coaches would hug me and say, "Good job, Scotty. Just keep winning!" There were thirty-two wrestlers in my bracket that year, and I ended up with a second-place finish at the state tournament.

Second-place finish, state wrestling tournament, Cheyenne, Wyoming

I never liked wrestling, but all my friends wrestled, and I was apparently good at it, so I continued to go out for USA wrestling each year. My coaches would load up about five to six of us kids in the back of a 1977 Ford pickup with a camper. We would travel many miles to attend wrestling tournaments all over the state including Utah. These were fun times for us kids. We raised a lot of hell in the back of that truck in the camper traveling to various wrestling tournaments. On one particular trip home, we ended up in a blizzard in Wind River Canyon. The wind blew so hard it felt like it might blow the truck and camper over. I remember our wrestling coach stopping along the highway and telling us kids to lie on the floor for weight so the truck wouldn't blow over in the wind.

My third-grade teacher was sweet and pretty. She always gave me special attention and called me Grumpy Gus. She always told me I needed to smile more. I never knew what was wrong with me, but I was an angry child. I did not get along with others often, and I was a bully to other kids in school. Maybe my behavior stemmed from my parents getting a divorce when I was a young child?

One day, another kid who was also a bully kicked me hard in the shin of my left leg. He was wearing a brand-new pair of hiking boots with those red laces. Back then, if you didn't have a pair of those new hiking boots with the red laces, you weren't considered to belong in the popular-kid circles. This hurt bad, and it put an egg-sized lump on my shin bone. The blow to my shin hurt so bad I didn't fight back. I came limping into our classroom after recess, and my teacher noticed me limping. She said, "Scotty, what is wrong with your leg?"

I said, "Nothing, ma'am, just got kicked while playing during recess!"

She said, "Who kicked you, and did they do it on purpose?"

I said, "Yeah, Charlie kicked me for no reason with his new hiking boots!"

She became very mad and asked me to step out into the hallway. She poked her head back in the classroom and yelled, "CHARLIE, get your butt out here right now!"

Charlie came out into the hallway and looked at me and smiled. The teacher looked at Charlie and said, "Did you kick Scott in the shin during recess?"

Charlie smiled and said, "Yes, I did!"

The teacher asked him why he kicked me, and Charlie replied "I just wanted to try my new hiking boots out." The teacher showed Charlie my egg-sized lump on my shin bone and asked Charlie to raise his pant leg on his left leg. Charlie raised his pant leg, and the teacher looked at me and said, "Well, go ahead and kick him back, Scott!" Man, did that bring a smile to my face. I hauled back and kicked Charlie in the shin bone just as hard as I could with my worn-out cowboy boots on. I got him good too. You should have seen the look of pain on his face just before he cried like a little schoolgirl. The teacher told him to get his butt back in class and get seated. Charlie and I got along after that day and never fought with each other again.

I remember all the kids in my class would stand up each morning and place their hands over their hearts and recite the pledge of allegiance. We got a small carton of white milk every morning and chocolate milk on Fridays. I would save my empty milk carton container and place it inside of my desk, so I had something to spit my chewing tobacco in during class!

When I tired of class, I would fake being sick and ask the teacher if I could go to the nurse's office. I would walk into the nurse's office looking like I might die at any moment and tell her I wasn't feeling well. The school nurse was a sweet lady who always took good care of me even when I wasn't sick. She would take my temperature, give me an aspirin with a small cup of water, and tell me to lie down on the couch for a while. After about 20 minutes, she would ask me if I felt any better; and I would moan and reply, "No, not really." She would then give me a saltine cracker and a carton of milk and say, "Try this, honey, and see if that helps!" She would then say, "Try to get some sleep. You will soon feel better!" I would lay there for another thirty minutes and moan again. I knew if I kept moaning, she would eventually call my mother and send me home sick.

Once I was sent home sick, I would go skipping down the street to my mother's beauty salon and hang out there for a while. My mother would yell at me, "ARE YOU REALLY SICK?"

I would moan and say, "Yes, Mom, very sick!"

She would say, "Well, fold these two baskets of towels and empty all the garbage in the salon. Then you can lie on the couch for a while!" Once I did all the chores, Mom didn't care if I lay down or not. I would sneak off and play with my friends who just got out of school. I guess I didn't care for school and would avoid going if I could figure out a reason not to be there.

Wade and I spreading manure

Wade and I would actually like to stay with my father, Bill, in Emblem for a few days here and there. It seemed my dad always had a girlfriend, and they were always nice to Wade and me. Either we would ride the school bus to Greybull from Emblem, or my dad's girlfriend would give us a ride to school each morning. Wade and I would help our dad do chores while he was busy working.

I was never a morning person. I hated getting out of bed early each morning, especially to go to school. My dad would tire of yelling at me to get out of bed each morning. He invented interesting ways to get me out of bed in the mornings. He would throw a pot of ice-cold water in my face or use an electric cattle prod. (This worked well!) He even threw a live bullsnake in bed with me one morning and lit a pack of firecrackers in a coffee can and placed it next to my head to wake me up, only to find the damn snake slithering across my chest. This method also worked well. My dad would always try to do something with us kids if he had time away from his work. Doing "something" with my dad was not always legal and sometimes very dangerous.

I went with my dad to check his traps one winter day. He had caught a bobcat in one of his sets and had used a "drag" fastened to the trap so the bobcat wouldn't chew its foot off from being securely anchored to the ground. This way, the cat could travel slowly and would usually get hung up in something along the way. This drag was an old cedar fence post. Once you found the trap missing, you could follow the drag marks on the ground until you could catch up with the bobcat. On this day, the drag marks in the snow led us to a large deep hole in the ground. My father shined his flashlight down the hole but could not see the bobcat because the hole was deep and dropped straight down about ten feet before it went around a sharp corner.

My father told me to go down in the hole and get the bobcat out. He told me to hang on to the end of his rifle as he lowered me down the hole. The hole was so deep that once I was hanging from the end of his rifle, my feet were still several feet from touching the ground. I hung in the air for a short time and finally let go of the barrel of the rifle and dropped down into the deep and *very* dark hole! As soon as I hit the ground, the bobcat let out a loud growling noise and hissed at me. The sound was loud it sounded like a woman screaming. The lighting was very poor; but as I looked to my left, I could see the bobcat backed into a corner about two feet from me. The bobcat hissed and growled at me and lunged forward, trying to attack me. I quickly kicked the bobcat in the face and yelled at my dad to throw me the flashlight and the rifle. My dad quickly dropped the flashlight down to me and lowered the rifle down as far as he could. He said, "Are you ready? I'm going to drop the rifle down to you."

I said, "Yes, hurry up!" I caught the scoped .223-caliber rifle and quickly chambered a round. I then turned on the small flashlight and placed it in my mouth. Once I had it shining on the bobcat, I raised the rifle and aimed. The bobcat was so close. All I could see was hair in my scope with no detail of where I was actually aiming. The bobcat continued to growl at me. Finally, I could see the glow of the bobcat's red eyes in my scope from the light of the flashlight. I aimed and fired. I hit and killed the bobcat with one shot. I was so relieved that the bobcat was dead and not me.

I grabbed the cedar post with the trap and bobcat wired to it. I wired the rifle to the cedar post and handed the cedar post up to my dad. He reached down in the hole as far as he could reach and pulled out the bobcat, trap, cedar post, and rifle all at once. He then took the trap and bobcat off of the cedar post and lowered the post down to me. I grabbed the post with both hands, and my father pulled me out of the deep dark hole. I was still shaking but thankful to be alive and out of that damn hole. My dad smiled, looked at me, and said, "Good shot, son. Let's get back to the truck and warm up."

Once back at the truck, my father said, "Let's head over to Dry Creek and see if we can find a beaver to shoot." We eventually made our way over to Dry Creek and parked up on a hill where we could look down in the creek for any beaver activity. After sitting for about twenty minutes, my dad whispered and said, "Look down there in the creek!" I looked down and saw a large beaver swimming upstream. My dad slowly and quietly got out of the truck with his rifle and lay down next to his truck. He quietly chambered a round with his scoped .223 rifle and took careful aim. All was quiet, and the beaver was slowly swimming upstream—*BOOM!* My father had hit the beaver. The beaver turned and headed downstream and eventually went underwater. My dad jumped up and yelled at me, "COME ON, WE HAVE TO GO!" My dad took off running down the hill toward the creek with me following close behind. My dad said, "We must hurry and get downstream and wait for the beaver to come floating by us." The creek was not that wide, and the water was moving slowly.

After running several hundred yards through the tall brush, my father stopped on a bank next to the creek. The bank was about three feet high above the creek. My dad said, "Get ready to grab that beaver when he comes by!" I looked upstream and saw the beaver coming toward us floating down the middle of the creek. My dad said, "Come here, and I will hold you out over the creek so you can grab the beaver when it comes by." My father then quickly grabbed me by my ankles and held me out over the creek. He said, "GET READY. HERE HE COMES!" The closer the beaver got, the more I realized it was still alive. I didn't want to grab a beaver, let alone a wounded live beaver. But I knew their pelts were worth a lot of money, and I knew my father needed the money, so I would not let my father down. The beaver was coming quickly, and my father lowered me down by my ankles until my head was almost touching the water. He yelled, "GRAB HIM!" I grabbed the wounded beaver with both hands and held on for dear life.

My father lifted me and pulled me toward the bank. Once the beaver came out of the water, he bit me! It hurt like hell, but I would not let go of him and have him escape down the creek. I screamed when he bit me, and my father yelled, "DON'T LET GO OF HIM!" My father pulled me and the beaver to shore and dropped my feet and legs to the ground. He told me to grab the beaver by the tail and hold it in the air so it couldn't bite me anymore. I grabbed the beaver by the tail and tried to lift it off the ground. The beaver was too heavy for me to lift off the ground. My dad yelled, "HANG ON TO HIM!" My father then grabbed his rifle and smashed the beaver's skull with the butt end of his rifle. The beaver kicked a few more times and was dead.

My dad didn't want to shoot the beaver again because he didn't want another bullet hole in the pelt of the beaver. This would just be another hole he would have to stitch up before selling. My hand was bleeding in several spots where the beaver had bitten me, and it hurt badly. My dad looked at me and said, "Good job, son. Not everybody can say they have been bitten by a beaver!" Between the bobcat and the beaver, that was a day I never forgot. When I returned home to Bear Creek, I told Wade the stories, but I never would tell Mom or Martin the stories that happened between me and my dad because I was worried they might not let me see my father anymore.

My dad continued to drink heavily. I'm sure my dad was drinking nearly a case of Budweiser beer and a fifth of Peppermint Schnapps a day. I can honestly say I never observed my dad act like he was drunk; he held his liquor well. He was content to drive around in the remote hills, drink his beer, and shoot about anything that moved. He was a good shot. I observed him several times kill large buck antelope while they were running at speeds over fifty miles per hour! He told me, "If the antelope are running single file, aim behind the shoulder of the antelope running in front of the antelope that you want to kill. Gently squeeze the trigger, and you will hit the antelope behind this antelope right behind the shoulder." I learned at a young age that if my dad intended to shoot something, he never missed. My dad would shoot cottontail rabbits, jackrabbits, prairie dogs, antelope, deer, and an occasional wild horse if it screwed up and scared away an antelope he might have been stalking. I never understood why my dad liked to kill animals and drink so much beer.

The fourth grade was a tough year for me. I was almost held back a year because of my poor grades and lack of ability to pay attention. Back then, the teachers would mail a handwritten report card to my parents four times per year. My brother, Wade, and I soon figured out when the report cards were mailed out, and we would run about two miles to our mailbox at Bear Creek Ranch and intercept the report cards before our mother could read them. We would carefully open the envelope and review our grades. We soon learned that we could change an F into a B; and if you were careful, you could also change a D into a B. We would use our best penmanship and carefully change the grades and gently place the report card back in the envelope and reseal and place it back into the mailbox. Changing our grades, undoubtedly, saved us many unnecessary groundings and beatings over our childhood years.

Again, my brother and I would stay with our father as much as our mother would allow it and my father would have us. We liked to stay with our father because he would let us shoot his guns and we could go hunting with him. This weekend, Wade and I wanted to go duck hunting. My grandpa Lester loaned me his single-shot .410 shotgun. Wade and I dug through Dad's shotgun shells and headed out to Dry Creek to hunt a pheasant or duck. I flushed a mallard duck out of some cattails, and it flew out over a pond away from me. I put my little metal peep sight on the mallard as it was flying away from me and squeezed the trigger. Down went the mallard duck right in the pond.

I had not anticipated actually hitting and killing a duck let alone how I would get it out of the pond without a dog. I was so proud of myself for hitting and killing that duck with my grandpa's 410 shotgun I was not going home without the duck. I stripped off my clothes on that very cold winter day and swam out and retrieved the damn duck. I nearly froze to death before I returned home. I killed my first pheasant on that day. I was proud of that single-shot 410. When you have only one shot, you have to make it count. I returned home with the duck. My dad said, "Well, I guess I know what's for dinner tonight." My dad cooked that damn duck up. It was the worst-tasting thing I had ever eaten in my life. That was the first and last duck I have ever killed.

My dad had goats that he kept around to eat all the weeds around the house. They did a great job eating the weeds and the vinyl off the roof of his Lincoln Continental car. My dad didn't like them eating the roof of his car, so he loaded up some salt shot in some of his 12-gauge shells and shot them in the butt to get them off the roof of his car. One day my dad looked out of the kitchen window and observed a goat on top of the car chewing on the vinyl roof. My dad said, "Goddamn goats!" He then grabbed his 12-gauge shotgun, loaded it with what he thought was his "special" salt-shot shells, and pulled the trigger. *BOOM!* The goat dropped dead on the roof of the Lincoln car. I heard my dad yell, "SCOTTY, YOU BEEN MESSING WITH MY SHOTGUN SHELLS AGAIN!"

Me with my dad's goats in the background, not sure which one ended up dead on the roof of my dad's car

My dad would often have friends come over in the evenings. They would drink beer and play cards for money. My brother and I would sometimes play cards with them, but we never had much money to lose. But it sure was fun when you could win and take all their money. One particular night, my brother and I were in the living room watching *The Dukes of Hazzard* while my dad was playing cards and drinking beer with several of his friends. They were getting loud, and it was hard to hear the television.

Wade reached over and hit me over the head with a pillow he picked up off the couch. He got me good because I wasn't paying attention, so I reached over and grabbed another pillow and smacked Wade hard over the head while he was trying to watch Daisy Duke in her short cutoff jeans. Wade jumped, and the fight was on, except this time he threw a punch instead of a pillow and caught me square in the jaw. This pissed me off because it hurt so bad. I threw a punch back at him. The fight was on! The next thing I knew, we were in a full-blown fistfight and knocking the hell out of each other and destroying the living room.

My dad heard the commotion going on in the living room. He and his friends jumped and came running into the living room to watch the fight between my brother and me. My dad's drunk friends cheered for us, yelling, "KNOCK HIM OUT! KNOCK HIM OUT!" They then started a Calcutta, and they bade on my brother and me to see who would be the winner. Once the bidding was completed, they all made side bets on who would win the fight. The fight went on until my brother and I nearly destroyed the living room. We had knocked the television set off the table, tipped over a large plant, and broke my dad's oak table in half by me throwing my brother on top of it.

Apparently, my father finally tired of us destroying the house. He came into the living room, grabbed a pillow, and hit me over the head so hard that he knocked me out. He then turned and hit Wade with the same pillow and knocked him out as well. When I came to, I could hear his buddies laughing. There were white chicken feathers all over the living room floor and walls. My dad had broken the pillow open over our heads, and all the chicken feathers went everywhere. My brother finally came to, and my dad yelled from the other room, "PICK ALL THEM DAMN FEATHERS UP AND GET YOUR LITTLE ASSES TO BED!" Yet another story I failed to mention to my mother and stepfather.

During the fifth grade, I became more disrespectful in class and found I was in trouble most of the time. My teacher became less patient with me and would send me to the coatroom for a time-out whenever I misbehaved in class. On one particular day, I was sent into the coatroom for being disrespectful in class. The room was dark, cold, and quiet. I did not want to be there while all the other students were having fun in the classroom. I was sitting in a small yellow plastic chair facing the wall. I became bored and found a box that contained about twenty-five pairs of scissors. I bent the metal scissors back and forth until they broke in half. I sat there and broke every pair of scissors in that box. I then found a box full of small plastic bottles of blue paint. Each small bottle had a screw on it with a paintbrush mounted to the underside of the plastic lid. I painted all the soccer and footballs blue so that when the kids would run into the coatroom for recess and grab a ball, they would get blue paint on their hands. I also painted a cute-girls coat blue because I thought it looked better than pink.

Whatever caused me to do those things, I didn't know. But it sure was funny when the kids ran into the coatroom to be the first to grab a ball for recess, and their hands would stick to the wet blue paint on the ball. They would yell, "EWWW! What happened to the balls?" The little girl grabbed her freshly painted blue coat and screeched, "Oh my god, what happened to my coat?" I just sat back and giggled.

The next thing I knew, I was taken down to the principal's office and interrogated. I quickly denied any wrongdoing, and the principal checked under my fingernails for any signs of blue paint. I had no blue paint on my hands. He then showed me the box of broken scissors and asked me if I had broken them. I responded, "No, I'm not strong enough to break a pair of scissors. Let me show you" I took a pair of scissors out of the box and tried my best to bend them, but I just wasn't strong enough to break them in half. The principal knew that I was lying, but he couldn't prove it otherwise. He told me to get back to the classroom and behave myself. The funny thing was, after that, they never sent me back to the coatroom ever again.

We had an intercom system set up in each room of the school. If the principal needed you or a teacher for anything, he would simply get on the intercom and make an announcement. It seemed like every other morning I would hear the principal's voice come over the intercom system and say, "Scott Werbelow, please come to the principal's office!" It seemed I was always in trouble. Most of the time, I would be headed to the principal's office walking down the long hallway trying to think of what I had recently done wrong to be in trouble. Once in the principal's office, I would usually see some young boy or girl sitting there crying because I had called them a bad name or beat them up during recess.

Back then, we had real fights in the alley after school. If you had a beef with someone, you just told them to meet you in the alley after school. The word would quickly spread; and by the end of the day, every student in school knew who would be fighting who in the alley after school. Kids would show up and cheer you on, and you would fight until one or the other could no longer carry on or until a teacher would break up the fight, whichever came first. Back then, the principal and the teachers still gave students swats with a wooden paddleboard. The board was about two feet long and eight inches wide and had holes drilled through the wood to make it sting when it came in contact with your behind. I received many swats as a child, and to be honest, that was probably the best discipline tool the teachers had to keep me in line back in those days.

That fall, my brother and I again would go stay with my father in

Emblem and do some hunting. One particular night, my father took us out spotlighting someone's private property. He started shooting jackrabbits with a .22-caliber rifle. I'm not sure if we had permission to be hunting on that private property that night or not. We came around a corner. My dad was driving slowly and panning the spotlight mounted to the roof of his Jeep pickup across an alfalfa field. Quickly, I could see a deer illuminated by the bright light about one hundred yards away, feeding in the field. My dad quickly stopped the truck and locked the spotlight on the deer. He said, "This is the one we been looking for, boys!"

I looked up and observed a very large mule deer buck in the spotlight. The deer had a huge set of horns on it. My dad slowly opened his driver's-side door and slid off his seat and exited the Jeep. He then leaned over the hood of the Jeep and aimed his rifle at the deer. My brother and I sat nervously inside the truck and watched. We couldn't believe my dad was about to shoot this deer. *BOOM!* Down went the large buck deer. The deer went down but did not die. We could see it lying down with its head still up in the air. My dad quickly put the gun away and told my brother and me to run out in the field and cut the head off the deer. He said, "I will stay in the truck and hold the spotlight while you boys cut the head off!" As he took a sip of his beer, he handed my brother a sharp knife.

We both ran out into the field with the spotlight on our backs. It was tough to see because the light cast shadows of our bodies in front of us as we were running through the alfalfa field. We both tripped and fell into an irrigation ditch as we couldn't see where we were running. We got back up and ran again. I was scared because I knew we were doing something wrong. I just didn't know how wrong it was, and the damn deer was still alive!

We finally reached the large buck deer, and his back was broken from the shock of the bullet that had just traveled through its spine. It couldn't stand up, but it was very much alive. My brother said, "Quick, put him in a headlock, and I will slit his throat." I put the deer in a headlock and lay on the ground next to the deer. It was all I could do to hold the strong deer down while my brother slit its throat and cut its head off.

My brother struggled to try to cut the deer's head off. The deer was blowing fresh warm blood out of its nostrils all over my coat and arms. The deer would make a gurgling, coughing noise as my brother continued to cut its head off. Finally, the deer went limp, and I could smell fresh blood and deer-in-the-rut smell. We both grabbed the large deer's head and headed back to the truck. It was hard to see anything with the spotlight shining in our eyes. We both fell in the same irrigation ditch again, and my father finally shut the spotlight off. It took a few seconds for our eyes to refocus, and we got up and headed for the truck. We finally reached the truck, and both of us were covered in blood. My dad said, "Throw the head in the back of the truck and let's get the hell out of here."

It was a quiet trip home and my brother and I smelled like a dead buck deer in the rut. If you have never smelled it, you won't know what I'm talking about. You just have to experience it yourself! We were both covered in blood and deer hair.

We got home and washed our hands and clothes and went to bed. Nobody had said a word to one another the whole trip home. As I was lying in bed, I felt like we had done something wrong, but I was with my dad, so it must be all right. I was too young to understand just what had happened, and I felt confused. The questions that ran through my mind were, was it deer season? Did my father have a license? Is it okay to use a spotlight and hunt at night? Did we have permission to be hunting on private property? Why did we not take the whole deer and only the antlers? I became very upset thinking that some needy person could have eaten that deer, and now it's going to waste!

I loved my dad, but why did he do this? I then thought of the game warden named Bob I had met on Bear Creek Ranch several years ago. How could I ever become a game warden someday if my father was a poacher? What if my father got caught poaching? I would never become a game warden someday. I cried myself to sleep and swore I would never allow myself to get in that situation again. What kind of a father would have his kids cut the head off a live deer in an alfalfa field under the bright light of a spotlight? How am I going to get rid of this smell on my new coat? Will my mother discover what happened when she smells my coat when I get home?

Once I got into the sixth grade, I had a whole new set of teachers, and they seemed more mature and less likely to put up with any of my crap. I never did apply myself and actually do any studying or homework. I never remember bringing any homework home ever. When I got home from school, I was busy hunting, fishing, trapping, riding my motorcycle, or working on the ranch. My teachers labeled me as a C student and passed me through their classes. I didn't disrupt their class, and I was good at sports, so I passed. This was a new start for me because we just got a new middle school and a new principal. The school building was brand-new and nice. We also had a state-of-the-art new gymnasium. I continued to wrestle and did well.

That fall, Martin and I headed out to check sheep camps one day, and Mother wanted to ride along with us. We ended up on a rough road on top of the Bighorn Mountains. My mother was about seven months pregnant. The road was rough, and my mother would scream at every bump in the road. She screamed at Martin, "MARTIN, I CAN'T TAKE THIS ANYMORE. I THINK I'M GOING TO HAVE THIS BABY RIGHT HERE!"

Martin said, "Diana, I don't know what to tell you. I have several more sheep camps to check on, and the road is going to be very rough!"

My mother yelled, "WELL, LET ME OUT OF THE DAMN TRUCK. I CAN'T TAKE THIS ANYMORE!"

Martin hit the brakes and let Mom out of the truck. He pulled an old cream can full of water out of the back of the truck and placed it alongside the road. He told Mother, "You sit right here on this cream can until I return later today!" We went about our business and tended sheep camps for the rest of the day and returned several hours later to pick my mother up. She was much more pleasant and had even found a perfect arrowhead that day. I think she was tired of sitting on the cream can and riding in the rough truck.

My mother later went into labor on December 14 and gave birth to my first and only baby brother. He was named Daniel Martin Mayland. I was so excited! I would finally have a younger brother to play with someday, even though I was eleven years older than Dan and would have to wait several years before he could tag along with me.

Before I knew it, I was entering the seventh grade. I went out for football for the first time. Our coach was very hard-core and worked us to death during every practice. During our first practice, we had to run from the high school to the cemetery and run the cemetery hill twenty-one times in a row. Up and back counted as one. Everybody had to run the hill up and back in a certain amount of time. If someone failed to make the set time, that run didn't count, and the whole team would have to run it over again. Once we completed that hill, we moved over to a smaller but much steeper hill. Each player would have to sprint up that hill and back down in a certain amount of time, or it didn't count. We had to sprint up and back eleven times on this hill, and you didn't want to be the one who didn't make it on time and because the whole team would have to run it over again.

Once the team completed the running exercise, about half the players were left lying on the ground puking their guts out. We still had to run back to the high school about two more miles away. I thought I would die that day and stopped at someone's house along the way back to the football field and drank about five gallons of water from their garden hose. Our coach was hard-core, and losing was not an option. I played fullback and linebacker and special teams, and we went 7–1 for the year.

These were interesting times. My parents just had a brand-new microwave oven, a small DustBuster vacuum cleaner, and a brand-new VCR. We could now rent movies from the grocery store and bring them home and watch them. You just had to remember to rewind them and have them back by the next day, or you would be charged a late fee. The microwave oven weighed about fifty pounds, but, man could it warm your food up quick. Wade and I loved to cook microwave popcorn in it because it would be ready to eat in about two minutes. If you were smart enough to program your VCR, you could actually tape movies off your television up to two weeks in advance. None of us ever figured that option out, but it sure was nice to watch movies since we got only two television channels while living at Bear Creek Ranch, and that was only if you had the antenna on the roof pointed in the right direction and tin foil on the television's antenna's inside.

That year was also a very special Christmas for me. Santa brought me a brand-new pair of Moon Boots, a pair of parachute pants, a Stretch Armstrong Man, and a Rubik's cube. I was jealous because Santa brought Wade a Bionic Man, a Sony Walkman, and a brand-new LED watch with a built-in calculator. Wade and I stretched out ole Stretch Armstrong until he broke in half. The fluid inside of him looked like thick red pancake syrup and was very sticky. (very difficult to clean off Mom's new carpet). I never did figure out how to solve the Rubik's cube, but I was smart enough to take it apart and put it back together in the correct way with all sides matching the same color. I was so proud of myself that I took it to school the next day and showed all my friends how I had figured out how to solve it. They were all impressed with me, and I inspired them all to figure it out on their own. They all thought, if Scott can solve it, anybody can solve it!

The Moon Boots were warm and probably the warmest boots I had ever owned to this day. The parachute pants—well, chicks just dig them. That's all about that! I stole Wade's fancy calculator watch and got kicked out of math class for getting caught cheating on a final exam with that damn watch. Back then, you weren't allowed to use calculators in math class. You were just expected to know how to do math without one. My seventh-grade history teacher confiscated my Rubik's cube for playing with it in class and added it to his collection of over thirty Rubik's cubes in his lower desk drawer. He also confiscated my whoopee cushion for disrupting class on several occasions that same day!

Once Wade and I were both in sports together and having to practice after school, Mom felt it necessary to buy us a new car so we could transport ourselves to the bus stop and back each day. We came home from school one day, and Mom said, "Kids, I bought you a new car today for $400. I took $200 out of each of your savings accounts and paid for the car!" We were excited and couldn't wait to see what our new car looked like. We went outside, and here sat the ugliest game-warden green car we had ever seen in our lives. The car was a 1974 Datsun B210 Hatchback. The entire driver's side of the car had been T-boned by a drunk driver. The car had low miles. The previous owner decided to total the car and take his insurance money and not fix the car. The little car got excellent gas mileage and had a four-speed manual transmission with a small four-cylinder engine. I quickly jumped in the car and took it for a test drive. The speedometer didn't work; the needle on the gauge just spun in full circles. The faster you went, the quicker the needle spun around in circles. Wade and I were not initially impressed with this contraption of a car, but, what the hell, it ran better than the Jeep Wagoneer!

As soon as we got done test driving our new car, Wade stepped out and said, "Well, dummy, I guess if we are going to pick up any chicks in this car, we better do it from the passenger side because the driver's side is flat ugly."

I told Wade, "It will buff out with about five gallons of Bondo. I'll take care of it. I'm a trained professional." I drilled a hole in the center of the large dent on the left-rear quarter panel. I hooked a heavy-duty chain through the hole and hooked the other end up to my three-wheeler. I pulled slowly thinking the dent would slowly come out; but after several attempts, nothing would happen! Finally, I got slack in the chain and hit it hard. I dragged the little car sideways in the dirt for about eight inches, and the dent still didn't pop out at all. That's when I filled the entire dent with Bondo and sand it down. I didn't have a clue what I was doing, and the Bondo was so thick it took days to dry. A couple of years later, the Bondo in the center of the dent where it was the thickest never did dry, and it stank. All my buddies named our car Cancer because that's the only way you could describe that little green car.

I quickly decided that I wanted the car to sound and look better. I cut off a good exhaust system and welded some two-inch irrigation tubes to the exhaust pipe just under the passenger- and driver's-side seat. I bent the pipes to come out the side of the car instead of the rear. This made the car cackle when you revved it up. Wade was not impressed. I then ordered some brand-new mag wheels and a lift kit for the rear end. I lifted the rear end about four inches and put a brand-new pinstripe down the passenger side. I couldn't stripe the driver's side because of the large dent and damp Bondo!

I then installed a brand-new stereo system in the car. The stereo system consisted of me hard-wiring an eight-track player with a T handle. The eight-track player sat in the backseat, and you could change songs by clicking up and down on the T handle. When you started the car, the eight-tracker player would automatically turn on. Chicks would really dig this new state-of-the-art sound system. Wade again was not impressed. He hurt my feelings when he said, "What in the hell is that?"

Wade and I later learned this little car would go about anywhere even in the mud. It became our primary hunting and fishing buggy. We actually took it antelope hunting one year and placed a "dressed out" antelope carcass in the hatchback. You couldn't fit a large buck deer in the hatchback because the large horns sticking out wouldn't allow the hatchback to close, so we would just strap buck deer to the roof of the car with a rubber bungee cord or two.

One day I caught a limit of trout and threw them in the backseat to take them home. I forgot to take them out that night, and they slid underneath my driver's seat. Several days later, I could smell something horrible but remembered that I had filled a five-gallon bucket with water to water my horse Daisy, and it spilled in the backseat. I wrote this smell off as mildew in the carpet because of the spilled water. The smell persisted for week's maybe even months. Finally, I moved the front seat forward one day only to discover six fish skeletons lying on the floor under the driver's seat. They had lain there so long baking in the hot sun that the only thing left was bones and a metal fish stringer. I had driven that car with the windows rolled down for weeks because of that horrible smell.

We didn't know it at the time but my brother and I would drive that car all the way through high school. You couldn't kill that car. It just kept going. I later learned how to quickly check the oil in the car. I would just drive fast and mash on the brakes. If the red oil light came on, you were two quarts low on oil. I would rev it up and drive like an asshole and then mash on the brakes and look at the dash. Wade would look over at me and yell, "WHAT THE HELL ARE YOU DOING, DUMBASS?"

"Just checking the oil!"

Our hunting buggy pictured with infamous yellow Suzuki three-wheeler

In the eighth grade, I again went out for football and played in the linebacker and running-back position. I loved to hit and play hard. I was never fast at running the ball, but I could take a hit and always get a first down when short yardage was needed. Our team played well that year, and we finished with a 6–2 record for the year. I also continued to wrestle and did many push-ups and sit-ups each night before I went to bed. I built noticeable muscles and became much stronger. I still didn't care for school. I received poor grades and was in trouble at the principal's office more times than not.

It was also in the eighth grade when I took my buddy Biff fishing with me on Beaver Creek one day after school. We both sat together on the bank and tossed a hook with a worm on it down below us into a deep hole filled with large cutthroat trout. We had just fished when my buddy looked up and said, "IT'S MINE!"

I said, "WHAT?"

He said, "That buffalo head sticking out of the bank over there on the other side of the creek!"

I looked over and saw the most beautiful buffalo head I had ever seen in my life sticking halfway out of the dirt bank. I couldn't believe that I had fished that hole a hundred or more times and never seen that buffalo head before. We quickly jumped and raced to the other side of the creek and dug with our hands and a sharp stick.

Once the head became more exposed, we noticed a tree root about two inches in diameter had run through both eye sockets of the buffalo skull. This would make it even more difficult to dig out. We dug and dug and dug, and finally, we lifted the head out of the bank. The buffalo head was perfect. It had both nose pieces, both lower jawbones, and all its teeth. The head was full of compacted dirt and was very heavy to lift. It took both of us to lift the head off the ground and carry it back across the creek. We were both so excited because neither of us had ever found a buffalo skull before.

We high-fived each other and jumped up and down in joy for several minutes. I said, "You know, if we just found one head, maybe there are more to be found." We reeled up our fishing poles, threw them on the ground, and headed

My friend's first buffalo head sticking out of the bank

upstream to look for more buffalo heads. We only went a short distance, and I jumped across the creek to get to the other side. I tried to place my foot on a rock just under the surface of the water as I jumped the creek. I didn't want to get my feet wet, so I used the rock in the creek as a stepping stone to get across. As I went over the rock and looked down to place my foot on it, it looked like a buffalo skull.

Once on the other side of the creek, I looked closely in the water at the rock that I had just used as a stepping stone, and all be darned if it wasn't another buffalo skull lying face up in the middle of the creek. I quickly pulled it out of the water and couldn't believe how much it weighed. This one wasn't perfect like Biff's, but it was petrified from lying in the water so long, and the nose pieces were broken off it. I screamed at Biff, who was just downstream from me, "HOLY SHIT, LOOK AT WHAT I JUST FOUND!" Biff was just as excited for me as I was for him. We both just had found our first buffalo skull. We had to make two trips back to the Datsun B210 with our buffalo heads, and it took both of us to carry Biff's buffalo head because it was so heavy.

Biff and I both became addicted to hunting for buffalo heads after that successful day. Every free moment we had after school or on weekends, we would comb that creek looking for old buffalo heads. Over a couple of years of searching about fifteen miles of that creek, I later ended up finding eight buffalo skulls.

My first buffalo skull

Another buffalo head found in this area

Chapter 9

GOOD AND TOUGH TIMES

It was October 1981. My brother, Wade, had drawn his first bull elk tag in elk area 41. We were so excited to meet my grandpa Lyle and grandma Peggy at the Anthony Timber cabin for a weekend of hunting. Martin and my mother, Diana, were also staying at the cabin. All of us would be hunting together. The cabin was in a remote area surrounded by a beautiful grove of aspen trees. The aspen leaves were always so beautiful in the fall with their bright colors of red, orange, and yellow. The cabin was made of logs and very rustic and simple with a small deck built off the front of the cabin. Martin would hook an extension cord with battery clamps onto the battery in his truck. This would provide lighting for the cabin. Our single lightbulb hung over the small dining table. When the lightbulb went dim, it was time to go outside and start the truck and charge the battery. If you waited too long, the battery would go dead and the truck wouldn't start.

The cabin had two bunkbeds against the back wall and an old antique cookstove that Martin loved to cook over. Each morning Martin would get up early and cook bacon, eggs, and pancakes over the old cookstove. I will never forget the smell of bacon and pancakes cooking in that small little cabin. The aroma would fill up the cabin and wake me up while sleeping on the top bunk of the bed. Martin would proudly say, "Breakfast is ready. Come and get it!" We would all jump out of bed, run to the table, and eat as much as we could. For dinner, Martin loved to cook elk liver and onions if one of us was lucky enough to harvest an elk. It sounded gross, but it actually tasted good. After dinner, Martin and Grandpa loved to have a drink, and we would all play a card game for quarters each night. The games we played were called 99 and 31. I would usually win everyone's money, and they would volunteer me to go outside in the cold and start the truck to charge the battery backup.

The next morning Wade and I jumped in Grandpa Lyle's old International Scout to go look for an elk for Wade to shoot. Grandpa Lyle could roll his cigarettes, drink his morning coffee, and drive simultaneously. His favorite hunting hat was faded orange and had hat ear flaps that hung down over his ears. He would bend the bill of the hat, so it went straight up in the air instead of straight out over his face. That way, the bill of his hat didn't interfere with his binoculars when searching for game. Grandpa could build about anything with sheet metal. He built a custom thermos holder he screwed to the dash and mounted right next to his custom binocular's holder. He also made a gun rack and screwed it to the dash of that old Scout for quick access to his rifle if an elk runs in front of us while driving later. Grandpa would light up his rolled cigarette with a small metal lighter he always kept in his front shirt pocket. He would then fire up the Scout, let it warm up for a few minutes, and then turn on the CB radio mounted under his dash. Wade and I loved to listen to the CB radio and would even talk to truckers when Grandpa wasn't around.

We drove out on a long ridge that morning and drove until the road ended. The road was rough and finally ended just before going off into a steep canyon below. We all got out of the Scout and walked over to the edge of the hill to look down into the canyon below for an elk. There was a barbed-wire fence that ran along the top of the ridge. We all three leaned over the wire fence and looked through our binoculars into the canyon below. We did some glassing for a while but saw no elk. The fence we were leaning on went down off the steep ridge and into the canyon below.

Wade and Grandpa had given up glassing for elk and walked back toward the Scout. I kept looking down in the canyon, just hoping to see an elk for Wade to shoot. As I walked back to the Scout, I heard the fence make a screeching noise in the canyon below. It sounded like something had run into the fence or hit the top wire while trying to jump the fence. The noise made a screeching sound down below me where I couldn't see because the hill was so steep. The noise reminded me of the sound that the fence made when Wade hit it that night on the Puma 440 snow machine chasing after that damn jackrabbit.

Wade and Grandpa were almost to the Scout when I yelled at Wade,

"Come over here! I think there is something below us!" Wade came running over with the brand-new .270-caliber rifle that my dad had given him for his birthday. I told wade, "Keep a look out below. I just heard the fence screech like something may have run into it or tripped over the top wire." My brother was leaning over a large cedar fence post with his rifle looking down below. Pretty quickly, we could see a spike elk below us running down an old cattle trail away from us. The spike had its tongue hanging out of its mouth, indicating that he was tired and had been running for many miles. That's probably why he tripped over the fence while jumping. He was just flat tired from running.

The elk was running about four hundred yards away from us and covering ground pretty quickly. I yelled at my brother, "HURRY UP AND SHOOT!" *BOOM* went the .270 rifle. I was watching the spike elk in my binoculars when he ran a few steps after the shot and lay down on the trail. My grandpa was so excited. He yelled, "Great shot, Wade. You got him!" My grandpa yelled, "Let's get down closer to him and put him down!" We walked within about twenty feet of the spike elk lying on the cattle trail. The elk looked sick and didn't get up. Wade aimed at the elk and shot it in the head to put it down.

We were all excited. Wade had just shot his first bull elk and made one heck of a shot on the elk running about four hundred yards away from us. We high-fived one another and congratulated Wade. We then rolled the elk onto its back and dressed it out on the cattle trail. Once we were done dressing out the elk, Grandpa said, "I never did see or find a bullet hole in this elk. I wonder where you hit him." We all looked closer for a bullet hole because we felt that Wade had made a great shot as quickly as that elk went down. We looked and looked, and finally, Grandpa laughed and said, "The reason we can't find a bullet hole is because you blew his balls off!"

Sure enough, the elk was missing both of his testicles! I thought to myself, *Well, they must have gone somewhere.* I got up and walked down the trail about twenty feet and noticed both of the elk's testicles were lying in the cattle trail. We all got a good chuckle about that. We even saved them so Wade could fry them up and eat them later that night for his celebration dinner. I looked up, and it dawned on me how in the world we're going to get this elk dragged back up to the Scout. The hill was steep, and the Scout was a long ways.

Grandpa pulled a rope out of his backpack and put one end around the elk's neck. He said, "It's not going to be easy, boys, but we must get it out of here." We all got on the end of the rope and heaved one pull at a time together. We would move the elk about two feet with each pull as we headed straight up the hill. We finally got about halfway up the hill when my grandpa said, "Hold up, boys. I'm not feeling so well. I need to rest." My grandpa sat down next to the elk and coughed heavily. He would cough hard and then gag. He would gag until he puked. This was horrible for me to watch my grandpa feeling so sick. His puke was a nasty dark-green color with bright-red blood mixed in it.

I told Grandpa to sit and rest and that I would run up to the Scout and try to reach Martin on the CB radio. I ran up to the Scout and fired up the Scout. I was so glad that the Scout started. I reached down and turned on the CB radio, put it on channel 14, and squeezed the squelch button on the mic. "WHITE FANG, DO YOU HAVE A COPY, OVER?" I stopped and listened for a few seconds and squeezed the mic button again. "WHITE FANG, DO YOU HAVE YOUR EARS ON OVER?"

The radio squelched, and I heard, "GO AHEAD, LITTLE ONE. I HAVE MY EARS ON!" Thank god, Martin answered the radio. I explained to him we had an elk down and needed his help. He said, "10-4, Little One, I'll be there shortly!"

I raced back down the hill, and Grandpa had recovered and was ready to drag more. We all got on the elk again and dragged again. My grandpa would say, "One, two, three—PULL!" and up the hill we went again. Grandpa went into another coughing-puking frenzy again and had to quit and rest. Martin finally showed up, and we got the elk to Martin's truck and loaded it. Martin was excited and congratulated Wade on his first elk. We got the elk back to the cabin and hung it on a meat pole behind the cabin in the shade. This was the largest bodied spike elk I had ever seen. To this day, I don't know how we ever dragged that elk whole up that hill. This was the first sign I had ever seen my grandpa sick. We later found out that my grandpa was suffering from lung cancer, and he would not be with us much longer. I was so excited that he got to be with his grandson that beautiful day when he killed his first elk.

The next morning, Wade and I woke up right at daybreak and went outside to split some firewood. I heard a noise in the aspen trees directly behind the cabin. I looked closely through the brightly colored aspen leaves, and I could see a handful of elk moving through the trees. If the elk kept traveling the way that they were headed, they would be coming out of the trees right next to the cabin and out in the open. I quickly ran into the cabin and yelled, "ELK, ELK, get out of bed!" Martin jumped out of bed and was wearing a white underwear with red hearts on them. Mother must have given him them this pair of sexy underwear for Valentine's Day or something.

Martin quickly grabbed his 7mm Weatherby rifle hanging on a nail by the front door. He stepped out on the deck of the cabin and was trying to focus his eyes on the bright sun as it was peeking over a distant mountain peak. The elk ran out of the trees about seventy-five yards from the cabin. Martin leaned over the railing of the cabin deck and fired his 7mm rifle. *BOOM* and down went a cow elk right in the two-track road that ran right by the cabin. He quickly handed the rifle to my mother and shouted, "Hurry up. Shoot that cow next to the road." My mother grabbed the 7mm Weatherby and also leaned over the railing of the deck. *BOOM!* Down went the second elk. They had two elk down within one hundred yards of the cabin.

My grandpa stepped out of the cabin wearing only his underwear, squinting in the bright morning sun, and said, "What the hell is going on out here?"

Mom turned around and looked at Grandpa Lyle and excitedly said, "I just got my elk, Dad!"

Grandpa said, "Congratulations, but you also scoped yourself, and your forehead is bleeding badly." My mother was so excited she didn't even know that the scope from the rifle had hit her forehead when the rifle kicked as it fired the bullet.

The 7mm Weatherby kicked hard when fired and was too much for my mother to handle the recoil. Everyone got dressed. My mother cleaned up her wound on her forehead and placed a Band-Aid over the small gash above her right eye. We all went out, even Grandma Peggy who had been babysitting my little brother Danny. We dressed out both cow elk and dragged them to the meat pole behind the cabin with the pickup. We now had three elk on the meat pole, and Wade's spike elk was considerably bigger than both adult cows.

Martin cooked us elk liver and onions for breakfast that morning. Wade ate one fried elk testicle that morning from his elk but couldn't get the second one down. Our dog got the other elk testicle for breakfast that morning. Mother left the cabin a short time later and said she was going for a walk to look for arrowheads. She left wearing her fluorescent-orange sweatshirt and headed down the two-track road south of the cabin. Later that afternoon, Grandpa loaded Wade and me up in his International Scout, and we headed down the two-track road south of the cabin to go look for my mother and to find a deer. My mother had a deer license for this area, and we were eager to find a big buck for her to shoot.

We traveled about one mile south of the cabin. I looked over to my right, and I could see my mother sitting on the ground next to a sandstone bluff. She was waving her arms back and forth, trying to get our attention as we were driving by her. She was easy to see because she had her fluorescent-orange sweatshirt on. I told Grandpa to stop because Mother wanted us for something. I heard my grandpa say, "OH MY GOD, LOOK AT THOSE BIG BUCKS!" I looked forward out of the front window of the Scout, and there stood seven of the largest buck deer I had ever seen in my entire young life. Each deer was standing broadside about one hundred yards from us. Every buck had a huge rack, and some had drop tines and freak points sticking out on each side of their antlers. Most were supporting racks nearly thirty inches wide or even wider on a couple of them.

I said, "HOLY COW, LOOK AT THOSE HUGE BUCKS!"

Wade said, "Quick, get Mother her gun. That's why she is waving us over because she has a deer license and wants to shoot one of those bucks."

My mother was about seventy-five yards from us, and the big bucks were standing just south of her location about one hundred yards away. I quickly jumped out of the Scout and grabbed Grandpa's .300 Savage scoped rifle and ran to my mother's location as quickly as I could run. When I got to my mother, I said, "HERE, TAKE THIS RIFLE AND SHOOT ONE OF THOSE BUCKS OVER THERE!"

She said, "What bucks? I wanted you guys to help me load this pretty rock that I have found."

I said, "Screw the rock, MOM! Hurry up and shoot one of those large bucks before they run off."

She stood up and aimed the rifle toward the seven buck deer still standing broadside watching us.

She was shaking as she aimed the rifle and said, "Which one should I shoot?"

I said, "It doesn't matter, Mom. They are all trophy bucks. Just pick one and shoot."

She quickly pulled the trigger, and I heard a loud boom. She hit low in front of the deer. I saw the dirt fly up right in front of the largest buck in the bunch. I said, "Mom, calm down. You hit low. You need to aim higher." The deer were still standing broadside at about one hundred yards. Suddenly, *BOOM* went the .300 Savage rifle. The deer took off on a run and ran away from us. Their huge racks became sky lined as they ran over the hill away from us. We all stood in awe and couldn't believe the size of those seven buck deer and that my mother had missed them twice.

My mother handed my grandpa's rifle back and said, "Go get your grandpa and brother and help me load this fossilized rock for my flower garden at home." She wasn't nearly as disappointed about missing that trophy buck as I was. The deer were long gone and had run off into a deep canyon. We would probably never see those deer ever again. To this day, those were the largest magnificent buck deer I have ever laid eyes on. I named them the Magnificent Seven. I guess I wasn't surprised that she missed them twice with Grandpa's .300 Savage rifle. I had never seen my grandpa actually hit anything before with that rifle—ever. It may have needed sighted in.

We continued to hunt for a few more days, trying to get my grandpa an elk and my mother a deer. We finally packed up and headed out of the cabin, driving through the grove of aspen trees. I was riding in the back of the truck, and I spotted a nice four-point mule deer buck standing in the trees to our left. I banged on the roof of the old Chevy truck, and Martin quickly stopped. He rolled his window down, and I said, "Look over there in the trees. It's a nice four-point buck!" Mother jumped out of the truck and leaned her rifle over the hood for support, and *BOOM* went the 7mm Weatherby Mag rifle that Martin had loaned her. The buck deer dropped dead, and I heard my mother scream, "GODDAMMIT!"

I said, "What's wrong, Mom?"

She said, "THIS DAMN RIFLE BIT ME AGAIN!" Sure enough, the scope from the rifle smacked my mother hard in the forehead, and she was bleeding again. We quickly dressed the deer out and loaded it in the back of the truck and headed home. It was a successful hunt with three elk and a nice four-point buck deer.

Mom's deer at Anthony Timber cabin

My grandpa Lyle would become very sick soon after this hunting trip. Over the next year, he lost a bunch of weight and went through terrible chemotherapy treatments, causing him to lose most of his hair. He became so sick and lost so much weight I could hardly recognize him anymore. This broke my heart. I didn't want to lose my grandpa. He meant so much and was such a nice and kind man. He was my best friend and took Wade and me on so many camping, hunting, and fishing trips over the years. My grandpa had taught me so much in life. He taught me how to clean my first fish and cook it over an open campfire. He taught me how to shoot his rifle and how to dress a deer out. He taught me how to build things with my hands while using his tools in his metal fabrication shop in Greybull.

Now, my grandpa lay helpless and desperate on his deathbed in a nearby hospital with all my close family gathered around his bed. We all said prayers and our last goodbyes to Grandpa Lyle that day. His eyes were closed, and his breathing was shallow. The nurses had him hooked up to so many machines. He had various tubes going up to his nose and stuck in his arms. After everyone had said something special to Grandpa Lyle, he slowly opened his eyes and smiled. He said, "I had a wonderful dream last night. I was in a large gymnasium shooting baskets. I was having the time of my life and couldn't miss a basket from anywhere in the gym, and, hell, I've never even played basketball before!"

He explained that the gym was huge and the lights were bright. He told us that the entire gym was painted bright white with bright lights, and there was only one small door, and it was in the corner of the gym at the far end of the room. He told us he was having the time of his life shooting baskets from half court, full court it didn't matter he could not miss a shot. Finally, he said, "The small door opened at the far end of the gym, and a very beautiful woman wearing a white dress with long black hair came through the door and entered the gym. The beautiful women slowly walked across the gym floor toward me."

She smiled and said, "Be prepared, Lyle. We are coming to take you tomorrow!"

Grandpa then said, "She turned and walked away with her long beautiful black hair dragging on the floor of the gymnasium. I think she might be an angel!"

My grandpa closed his eyes with a smile on his face and peacefully passed away later that day.

This was a beautiful angel, and she put my grandpa at ease in his final hours! I would never forget that dream that my Grandpa told us about that day just before his passing. This dream would come back to haunt me nearly twenty years later with possibly the same angel that spoke to my grandpa.

Losing my grandfather was huge for all of us but more devastating for his wife, Peggy. They had been together their whole life and done so much together. My grandma Peggy seemed very lost after Lyle's death, and my mother wasn't dealing with it very well. After Grandpa's passing, Grandma took more prescription drugs to cope with life. It was that I overheard my parents, Martin and Diana, arguing one night in the bedroom. I heard Martin tell my mother he was concerned about losing Bear Creek Ranch to the bank because he could no longer make his annual interest payment.

I was too young to understand everything about Bear Creek Ranch and the bank at that time in my life. The way I understood the situation was that the International Implement Dealership and snow machine business were purchased using the ranch as collateral. Employees who ran the implement business were stealing money under the table and selling equipment sometimes for less than what was paid for it. All the money that Martin made the entire year went toward an interest payment at the end of the year. Interest rates with banks back then were high, sometimes as high as 14 percent. When you couldn't make your interest payment, you would just get further and further behind each year to where the bank would force you into foreclosure.

Martin was devastated. He had worked seven days a week for many years trying to make the ranch successful and pay for itself. Now his world was falling apart all around him, and he would have to figure out a way to save the ranch. I remember there was always this big oil man from Texas to purchase both Beaver Creek and Bear Creek ranches because he believed it was rich in oil. They even drilled some test wells on Beaver Creek and found that the oil in the ground was possibly the second heaviest oil find in the world. The only problem: they couldn't figure out how to get the heavy oil out of the ground.

I remember for almost two years Martin would get his hopes up every day he could either sell the ranches to the rich oil man or at least get the oil out of the ground and make money off the mineral rights. This rich oilman from Texas would tell one lie after another. He would say he would wire Martin money to save the ranch. Days would pass and no money. He would say he was flying his jet to Wyoming and settle on the purchase of the ranches this weekend. Days and days went by, and he would never show up.

Nearly two years went by, and nothing ever improved with the financial situation of the ranches. That dreaded day finally came when Martin would have to line up all his pieces of farm equipment and auction them to the general public. Martin worked for weeks and weeks cleaning up farm equipment and parking heavy equipment in rows and long lines to prepare for the big auction. At the last minute, the rich oil man from Texas finally wired Martin enough money to buy back his "good" equipment at the auction and sell all the older equipment and equipment that was worn out or broken to the public. You should have seen the look on the banker's face come auction day when Martin raised his hand during the auction and bought back all the equipment he wanted to keep. I'm not sure how this all worked out with the bank; but at the end of the day, Martin would file for bankruptcy and lose the ranches and farm implement business to the bank.

This was a very devastating time for all of us. I couldn't imagine losing the ranch and having to move to town and give up all the good hunting and fishing I had been so blessed with most of my life. There was no way I could live in town. I loved the country too much. Martin was a mess. Everything that he had worked so hard for was gone just like that. He would now have to start over and rely on my mother's income as a hairdresser. Things were about to get tight for the entire family. I was going to miss living at Bear Creek Ranch, but I was blessed that I could live there for eleven years of my life. I got to hunt and fish and work with the adults and sheepherders as a young boy. This ranch shaped my life over the years and made me the person I later became.

It was the spring of 1984. I was a sophomore in high school. Martin asked me if I would be interested in living at the house on White Creek Ranch by myself for the spring and summer months. I was excited about this opportunity in life. The ranch was beautiful and sat at the base of the Bighorn Mountains at the mouth of White Creek Canyon about four miles northeast of the tiny town named Shell. Martin said he would pay me $600 a month plus room and board but that I would be responsible for all the irrigating of the hay meadows and putting up all the hay that the fields produced. This would be a huge responsibility for me as the ranch had several hundred acres of farm ground to take care of. The ranch house was small but nice, and I was looking forward to living by myself and having more freedom from my family. I packed up my personal belongings, my horse Daisy, my yellow three-wheeler, and the trusty Datsun B210 named Cancer.

I worked hard that summer irrigating all the fields and changing water sometimes three times a day. Many fields had been reseeded, and I would need to shovel out water rows/marks to ensure that the water could run the full length of the fields and irrigate the newly seeded alfalfa. If the seeds didn't get water, the alfalfa didn't, grow and that would be a poor reflection on me and the job I was doing. Again, Martin trusted me with this ranch, and I wouldn't let him down ever. Irrigation water was scarce and only lasted a few months. The water I would irrigate with was spring water run-off from the snow melting on top of the Bighorn Mountains. Once the snow melted, the water would run down White Creek Canyon and out a ditch that led to the fields on the ranch.

That summer was hot, and the alfalfa grew very tall and beautiful. It gave me great pleasure to look out over the fields each morning and during sunset at all my accomplishments shown by the beautiful and tall alfalfa across the fields. I later cut, rake, and bale the alfalfa into small bales. Once the hay was baled, I would use a self-propelled hay wagon to pick up all the bales. I would drive the tractor, and Wade would stack the hay on the wagon. The wagon would handle about two hundred bales. Once full, we would haul the wagon with the tractor to the stackyard about one mile away and stack the hay in neat straight rows. Wade would get pissed at me and say, "Nice you can drive the damn tractor all day, and I get to stack all these damn hay bales." Wade helped me only at White Creek Ranch when his help was needed.

After a long day of working in the hot sun, I would jump in the Datsun B210 and head for the Shell store for something cold to drink. I would go back to the cooler in the store and grab a six-pack of Coors Light, bring it to the front counter, and pay for it. The sweet gal running the cash register would take the six-pack of beer and put it in a brown paper bag and say, "Better put this in a bag so that it stays cool for you." I would drink a cold beer on the way home and fire up the grill and barbecue a burger once I got home. I enjoyed drinking a cold beer on the deck of the house after work and watching the sunset most evenings after work. It took me a while to figure it out. I was only sixteen years old, and it was illegal for me to buy alcohol at the Shell store, so the sweet gal would conceal my beer in a brown paper bag so nobody would see me leave the store with it. Once my friends learned that I could purchase beer as an underage child, I seemed to end up with more friends.

I worked hard, running a shovel digging marks and changing water on most days. In the evenings I would do push-ups and sit-ups and lift weights. I wanted to get in excellent physical condition for football and wrestling seasons coming up later in the fall and winter months. My muscles developed. The more they developed, the more I got stronger and build bigger muscles. I was in the best shape I had ever been in. I never worried about getting in a fight with anyone at that age because I knew I was stronger and worked harder than most kids. If you were going to pick a fight with me, you better have your ducks in a row. I never spent much time in the weight room. I became strong from hard work on the ranch. My brother spent hours in the weight room and became very strong and fast, but he could never beat me in arm wrestling, and it drove him nuts.

It was at this age I drove my Datsun B210 to Greybull occasionally to pick up chicks. I actually had never picked one up, but I would give it a try. One evening, I met this very cute girl named Cindy in town for a couple of weeks visiting her grandparents. She was the cutest girl I had ever seen, and I finally mustered up enough courage to ask her on a date. My friends had told me they would have a "kegger" down on Shell Creek below my house on Friday night. I thought it would be fun to invite Cindy to the kegger. I asked her, and she said, "That sounds fun. I will ask my grandma if I can go with you to a kegger."

I thought to myself, *Yeah right, her grandma is really going to let her leave town to go to a kegger with some guy she doesn't even know.*

She went into her grandma's house to ask her the big question of the day as we didn't have cell phones back then. I patiently waited in the car with sweaty palms. She soon came out the front door and said, "Well, my grandma said I can go on a date with you, but I'm not allowed to go to any kegger with you, and I must be home by midnight." This seemed an easy solution to me. Grandma didn't need to know that we were going to the kegger, and I would have Cindy home by midnight.

I said, "Sounds good. Can I pick you up Friday night at six?"

She said, "Awesome, I'm looking forward to our date!"

I couldn't believe it. I actually got my first date, and she was hot. I picked her up in the Datsun B210 on Friday night at her grandma's house. She came out the front door of the house. She looked beautiful and smelled of sweet perfume. I was nervous as a fox in a henhouse. I walked her to the passenger side of the Datsun B210 and opened the door for her. I didn't want her to see the driver's side of the car because she might cancel our date once she saw how ugly that side of the car was. I opened the door for her, and she said, "Thanks, you are such a gentleman!"

We traveled the twenty-five miles to where my friends were having the kegger down by Shell Creek just below my house. She smiled and said, "What are we doing at this kegger? You know my grandma told me that I'm not going to this party with you."

I smiled and said, "I will have you home by midnight. She doesn't need to know that we went to this party." I winked at her and said, "Trust me, pumpkin', everything is going to be just fine."

We walked down a narrow path through the beautiful cottonwood trees and found my friends having a party with a large bonfire. I introduced Cindy to all my friends and grabbed a red solo cup and drank keg beer. Nightfall came quick, and the fire was beautiful. I looked overhead, and the sky was full of beautiful bright stars. I was the luckiest man in the world. I had a beautiful girl by my side and a red solo cup full of ice-cold keg beer. I must not have eaten much food that day.

The next thing I knew, I was drunk, and my head was spinning in all directions. I went to take a step and nearly fell into the fire. I was feeling sick and felt like I needed to puke. I was embarrassed and left the fire. I walked back into the trees and lay down in a thick bush and tried to puke. I never did puke, but I did pass out. Several times I could hear my friends yelling my name in the dark. They would shout, "SCOTT, SCOTT, can you hear me? Where are you at?" I could hear them, but I didn't answer because I wanted no one bothering me. I felt sick and needed to puke. I don't know how long I had been passed out. I finally heard Cindy's voice yelling, "SCOTT, SCOTT, WHERE ARE YOU? I NEED TO GET HOME RIGHT NOW!"

I was still feeling drunk and sick, but I finally answered, "I'm over here!"

She said, "Oh, thank god, I need to be home in twenty-five minutes or I'm LATE!"

I said, "I'm not feeling so well and I'm drunk. Is there anyone else at the party that could give you a ride home?"

She said, "Nope, you are it. Everyone else went home already!"

I jumped in a panic and said, "All right, hurry up let's get out of here!" We quickly ran through the trees back to the car and jumped in the car. I started the Datsun B210 up and turned on the headlights. As soon as I turned on the headlights, the car died. I restarted the car, turned on the headlights, and it died again. I said "Shit! The alternator is going out of the car, and we have no headlights."

Cindy was panicking, and she said, "I knew this wasn't a good idea to come to this party."

I said, "Don't panic, pumpkin'. I will run up to the house and get us something to drive to town. Sit tight. I will be right back." I ran up to the house in a panic. All I could think about was I would get Cindy home late, and she could never date me again.

I soon got to the house and looked around for a vehicle I could get Cindy home safely in and on time. We had a 1971 International manure spreader truck that ran great—most of the time. It had four bald tires, no taillights, no insurance, and no dash lights and was missing its exhaust system. The springs stuck up through the bench seat, and it had no power steering; but other than that, she was cherry. This only got used a couple of times of the year and was only used on the ranch. I used the truck before and knew the ole girl was plumb dependable.

I jumped in the truck and fired her up. It sounded like a demolition derby car, but man, did the motor run strong. I drove it down the hill and met Cindy sitting on the hood of the Datsun B210 crying. I yelled, "Hop in,

BABY! Let's GO!" I will never forget the look on her face at that moment, but she jumped in the truck and closed the door, except the door would not shut. I said, "Just a minute!" I jumped out, went around the truck, and slammed the door *hard*. I Hooked a bungee strap through the door handle across the door and down to the frame on the bottom of the door. The damn door wouldn't latch, but she would be fine if she didn't lean too hard on the door.

I revved up the engine and popped the clutch, and away we went down the road headed for Greybull. I yelled over the sound of the loud exhaust, "HANG ON, PUMPKIN'. THIS IS GOING TO BE A REAL TANK SLAPPER!" The truck was loud. I held the pedal to the metal all the way to town, except the truck was also low geared and top speed was about fifty-five miles per hour. About this time, only one headlight was working, but I could see well enough to keep her on the highway. Cindy never said a word all the way back to town. I couldn't have heard her even if she did say something because of the loud sound of the lack of exhaust pipe and muffler.

I parked the old truck on the outskirts of Greybull and quickly walked Cindy home. We got to the front porch of her grandma's house, and I looked at my watch. It read 12:15 a.m. *Not bad, only fifteen minutes late,* I thought to myself. I didn't feel like we had had a very romantic date, and I'm guessing a good night kiss would be poor timing on my part. I thanked her for the date and told her I was sorry that I got so drunk and sick. She gave me a small hug and ran into the house. Speaking of being drunk and sick, I was over being sick but was still drunk and needed to get myself and the old International manure spreader home.

As I was walking across the bridge on the Bighorn River to get back to my transportation home, a car went by me and stopped on the highway. My brother poked his head out of the passenger window of the car and said, "DUMMY, what in the hell are you doing?"

I said, "I'm headed home!"

My brother said, "Where in the hell is your car? I need a ride home."

I said, "It's right around the corner!"

"What's it doing right around the corner?" my brother asked.

I said, "It's been a long night. If you need a ride, come with me!"

My brother and I took off walking across the bridge. Once we rounded the corner, my brother said, "WHAT IN THE CORNBREAD HELL IS THAT?"

I said, "The Datsun broke down, and I needed to get Cindy home by midnight. Get in the truck and shut up for a while." He opened the passenger-side door on the old manure spreader. I said "It doesn't open. You will have to get in on the driver's side!" I didn't want my brother to know that I was drunk. If he would have discovered, he would have beaten my ass because he didn't believe in drinking alcohol ever. If you were an athlete, you didn't drink; and besides, look at what it was doing to my ole man.

We headed home, and I said a short prayer, thanking God for a safe trip. We were about halfway home when suddenly I heard this loud noise and could see sparks flying behind the truck in my mirror. I looked at Wade and shouted, "WHAT THE HELL WAS THAT?"

Wade tried to open the door, but it wouldn't open. He quickly rolled down the window and stuck his head out and looked behind the truck as we were slowly moving down the highway. He poked his head back in the cab and yelled, "I DON'T KNOW, BUT I THINK YOUR DRIVELINE IS BOUNCING DOWN THE HIGHWAY!"

I revved up the truck, and it would go nowhere. I yelled at Wade, "I THINK YOU ARE RIGHT!" I pulled the truck off the highway. It was very dark outside. I walked down the highway back toward town and found my driveline lying on the highway. I carried it back to the truck and burned both of my hands because the driveline was very hot from being next to the broken exhaust pipe underneath the truck. I crawled underneath the truck and got one end of the driveline hooked back up. The yolk was beaten up on the other end of the driveline from bouncing down the highway.

I found some loose wire hanging on the barbed-wire fence that ran along the highway. I crawled back under the truck and wired up the other end of the driveline so it wouldn't drag on the highway. I jumped in the truck and put the transmission in low gear. I gave her some gas and popped the clutch, and away went in granny gear. The top speed was about twenty miles per hour, but we were still moving and heading toward home.

On the way home, I explained the whole situation and the details of my date to my brother. He just looked over at me and said, "You big dumbass!" We made it home slow but safe. I ended telling Martin a few days later that the driveline fell off the old International truck while I was irrigating during a rainstorm and asked him if he could pick me up a new U-joint next time he was in town. As for Cindy, she later chose to date a more responsible man who owned a much nicer car than me. I can't blame her I guess.

At the end of that summer, Martin paid me $1,800. I found a 1969 Ford Mustang fastback for sale in Cody. I called the guy, and he was asking $2,400 for the car, but I told him all I had was $1,800. He said, "You give me $1,800 for that car, and I will hand you the keys to the car!" I got a ride over to Cody with a buddy and looked at the car. The car was beautiful. It was red with a black wraparound stripe that went off the hood of the car and down each side of the vehicle. The car had beautiful shiny chrome wheels with ten-inch slicks on the rear for racing. The Mustang came with a 302 engine and straight pipes. The car ran and sounded awesome. I bought the car and headed back to Shell with a smile on my face. The car even came with a stereo that even sounded good. I would no longer need my eight-track player with the T handle in the backseat of my Datsun, and chicks would dig me. I borrowed a cassette tape from my friend and listened to Quiet Riot on the way home. Life was good.

I soon learned that the car was not perfect. The driver's-side window was too short and would not roll all the way up. I also learned that the heater didn't work. This made wintertime driving a little chilly. The car only got about eight miles to the gallon, and I had spent every dime I earned that summer on that damn car. I couldn't afford to put gas in the car or make any necessary repairs, let alone pay for my license plates, sales tax, and insurance. I was flat broke and would have to park the car until I made money. I thought of ways I could make some quick good money. Hell, I had a horse named Daisy that was unbroke and stood around the yard at the White Creek house eating grass all day. Maybe I could break this horse and sell her for some good and quick money!

My new chick getter

I soon saddled up Daisy for the first time. She was snorty and didn't want me on her back. I led her down to the neighbor's round corral and lunged her in circles for a few minutes until she was paying attention. She seemed a gentle horse. She just had never been ridden before. Heck, any horse that will jog behind a three-wheeler can't be all that bad. I put one foot in the stirrup and swung my other leg over the saddle. This was the moment my day was about to change for the worse.

Ole Daisy reared up in the air as I mounted the saddle, and it was time for me to hold on tight. She dropped her head and went to bucking like she was in the National Finals Rodeo in the final round. The cinch on my saddle slipped, and the saddle rolled off to one side of her, and off I went. She bucked me off in a mudhole and ran across the round pen and jumped the top rail of the fence. All I remember seeing was her hind feet straight in the air as she broke the top rail on the fence and landed on her head on the other side of the round pen. She quickly got up and continued bucking across a fenced-in pasture. The saddle was now underneath her belly and her hind legs were kicking the saddle with every jump. She finally kicked the saddle off and ran through a fence consisting of five strands of barbed wire.

I was still lying in the mudhole covered with black mud. I was bleeding in several areas of my body but wasn't sure where the blood was coming from because of the heavy black mud coated all over my body. About that time, the neighborhood girl always riding horses by my house showed up riding a horse wearing only a bikini. How embarrassing. This girl was cute, and I kind of had a crush on her. She smiled and said, "Are you all right?"

I was embarrassed and said, "I'm fine, but I guess my mare didn't want to take me for a ride today."

She got off her horse and walked over to me and helped me up Out of the mud hole. She said, "You better go home and shower up and see where you are bleeding from. I will go catch your mare and clean her up. She probably has some pretty deep cuts that will need doctored!"

I said, "Thank you very much. I will run home and shower, and I will return shortly."

I returned about thirty minutes later, and this nice, pretty girl had the horse standing in the neighbor's yard hosing off her deep wounds with a garden hose. She doctored all the cuts on my mare. As I walked up to my mare, she snorted at me and reared up in the air on her hind legs and tried to strike at me. The pretty girl looked at me and said, "OH MY, I don't think she likes you. Sometimes mares just don't like men."

I said, "Yeah, I know. I just dated one."

She laughed and said, "Your saddle is lying over there, and it's in pretty tough condition!"

I thanked her for all her help and led my mare back to the house with a lead rope in one hand and a torn-up saddle in the other. What a humbling and embarrassing moment for me. I put Daisy—I mean Crazy—back on her picket rope in the front yard and decided that I would sell her at the next horse sale in Greybull.

Daisy healed up fine over the next few weeks. I ran her through the horse sale in Greybull unridden. She ran around the arena with her tail straight in the air, snorting, pawing the ground, and letting out a loud whinny. The auctioneer told the crowd of bidders that Daisy was a great-looking mare with spirit and that she was "green broke" and would make someone a fine horse. I knew he was lying through his tooth. Daisy would make no one a good horse. She was still suffering from the trauma of being halter broke at twenty-five miles an hour with a three-wheeler, and she hated men. The auctioneer started the bidding at $500, and nobody raised their number. The auctioneer finally went down to $50, and this ole boy in the back sitting on the top row raised his number and nodded. The auctioneer said, "Seventy-five, seventy-five, seventy-five, SOLD $50 to bidder number

54!" I thought this was interesting because I owed $54.50 to pay for license plates on my Mustang car. I had just sold a Mustang to buy plates for a Mustang. I marched down to the courthouse and happily bought new license plates for my 69 Mustang from the sale of that crazy damn horse.

My parents left Bear Creek Ranch and bought a nice house on top of a hill just outside of Shell. They seemed happy in the house, and Martin was relieved that he wasn't having to work as hard with the responsibility of both Beaver Creek and Bear Creek ranches. Martin later purchased some mountain ground in the Bighorn Mountains and some farm ground in Emblem from his uncle and father. He continued to run sheep and cattle, just not as many. I soon moved from the White Creek house back into my parents' new house on the hill. It was a very nice house, and I had my bedroom downstairs with a pool table. I loved to shoot pool and practiced nearly every night.

I soon learned that I couldn't climb the hill up to my parents' house in the winter when the road was slick because of the ten-inch slicks I had for rear tires. I eventually saved up enough money to buy fuel for the car and take it to town on Friday nights and drag main with my buddies. I even got a date one night with a pretty girl. I took her out to the Greybull Cemetery one night, and we parked up on the hill with our lights out and made out for a couple of hours. A snowstorm had settled in, and we didn't know it was snowing outside because the windows were all steamed up. I finally looked up because I was getting cold and noticed a snowdrift had settled across my dash because my driver's-side window wouldn't roll all the way up. It was also this night I realized the heater core had gone out of my car. When I turned on the defroster, it blew steam through the vents and fogged up the car, and made it smell like antifreeze. Not only could I not see anything, but the snow was also blowing around the cab of the car because of the defroster blowing cold air through the snowdrift on my dash. I went to pull forward, and shit, I was stuck in a snowdrift. I finally got the car dug out and my date safely home. That was my last date with that gal. I just needed a damn heater and some better tires, and hell, she might have married me someday!

That Mustang car would be the death of me. I took one buddy for a ride one afternoon, and we headed west out of Greybull toward Cody. My buddy said, "Well, let's see what this ole Mustang can do." The highway was straight for a long ways, so I romped on the throttle and held it to the floor. I was doing over one hundred miles per hour when I looked up to see red-and-blue lights flashing just ahead of me. The patrolman went by me and whipped his car around to pursue me. He took a while to catch me, but he did catch me.

He came walking up to my door and said, "What seems to be your hurry today, Mr. Werbelow?"

My buddy and I were both dressed in camouflage clothing, so I responded to the officer, "We were just trying to catch up with a herd of elephants on the horizon."

He said, "Well, they must be running pretty fast because I clocked you at 104 miles per hour." He then said, "Do I need to have a talk with your parents about this?"

I said, "NO, SIR, I will keep it at fifty-five miles per hour from hereon out." He gave me a verbal warning for 104 miles per hour. Holy shit! My parents would have killed me if they would have found this out, and there was no way I could have paid that hefty fine.

This officer knew me well and had pulled me over several times before for exhibition of acceleration. My buddies and I were always drinking alcohol while dragging main on Friday nights. We didn't want to ever get caught with alcohol in the vehicle and get a minor in possession charge against us, so we designed a system to hide our alcohol. I unhooked the hose that went to the windshield washers and ran the hose through a small hole I drilled in the dash. We would then drain the windshield wiper fluid out of the small plastic container in the engine compartment and replace the windshield cleaner with Crown Royal whiskey. When you pushed the handle to wash your windows, Crown Royal would shoot out of the hose in the dash, and you could fill your cup full of ice and Coke with Crown Royal. We were absolute geniuses!

It soon became clear that I couldn't afford to drive this car, and it was worthless to drive during the winter months. I had no money to fix the few small things wrong with the car, so I put it up for sale. The car sold quickly. I pocketed $2,400 and made $600 on this car. I was so excited that I marched down to the Honda dealership that same day and purchased a brand-new 1984 Honda XR-500 motorcycle for $1,800. I'm sure this was a *wise* decision for me. This bike was badass. I later learned how to climb steep hills with this bike, and I could ride a wheelie on this bike for over three miles at speeds over eighty miles per hour. Plus, I still had the trusty ole Datsun B210, and chicks would dig it.

Me riding a wheelie down Trapper Road

My brand new 1984 XR-500 motorcycle

At the end of that summer, I went into the doctor's office in Greybull to get a physical to participate in football practice that fall. I was sitting in the waiting room, and some guy walked through the front door of the doctor's office. The whole left side of his face was badly swollen. Both of his eyes were black and swollen. He looked like hell as he sat down across from me in the waiting room. I kept staring at the man because his wounds looked horrible. The closer I looked, the more I thought to myself, *HOLY SHIT, that's my dad!* I went over and asked my father what had happened to him, and he replied, "I slipped on some ice and hit my head on the brick wall on the front porch of the house." Was Dad telling me the truth? Did someone whip his ass in a barfight? Was he in a car accident? Or was he telling me the truth? That scarred me to see my dad's face that beaten up. I would never forget that sight on that day for the rest of my life.

Chapter 10

HIGH SCHOOL/SPORTS

In my freshman year, I played football but didn't make the varsity team. I also wrestled but did not make the varsity team that year. I continued to get stronger and stronger and worked on developing my skills in both football and wrestling. In my sophomore year, we got a new football coach. The coach knew the game well and made us kids work hard in practice. We nicknamed him Coach. We focused on the fundamentals of football and ran a very simple offense.

Greybull had not won a football game in four years when this coach came along. We won games and continued to win games. The kids all respected this coach and played hard for him. The next thing we knew, we were playing in the state championship against a team in Burns, Wyoming. It was a hard-fought game, and we came out the underdogs with a score of 19–15. At the end of the game, the players cried. The coach cried! But we developed a team of kids who learned to play together and respect one another. I again played the fullback position and linebacker position but only started varsity on special teams that year. My brother, Wade, also played running back and linebacker and started that year and played in the state championship. I thought it was interesting that my dad played for Greybull in the state championship back in the sixties, and Greybull had never won another state championship since then, but both of us boys got to play in a state championship game together for years later.

My brother, Wade, and I playing high school football my sophomore year

In my freshman year, our wrestling team traveled over to the Star Valley in Western Wyoming and wrestled very good teams from Jackson, Kemmerer, Star Valley, and Evanston. The Greybull Buffs won this tournament even though we went up against all bigger schools. This was the start of a very great wrestling team. I wrestled my first varsity match during this tournament as a freshman. I matched up with a senior who was a defending state champ the previous year. I shot in for a takedown, and he did some fancy move on me and pinned me in nine seconds. This was my first varsity match and damn embarrassing. My coach just laughed as I walked off the mat, and he said, "Congratulations, you just got pinned quicker than any other kid in the entire state." I was embarrassed but knew I would get better in time. In my sophomore year, I made the varsity team and improved dramatically.

I had a good relationship with all my teachers in high school and even went hunting and fishing with some after school and on weekends. My grades were never good, but they were passing. I learned that I only excelled in shop class, sports and PE (physical education). I was very good at building with my hands and welding. The only As that I ever earned in high school were in woods class, welding class, and PE. I hated all other classes and was bored to death with the school. I swore if I ever made it through high school, I was not going to college. I would start a business or work for someone else, but I was not going to college.

In my junior year, I excelled at sports and started on the varsity football team in the running-back and linebacker positions. I loved to hit the opponent hard and became known as a hard hitter from other players on my team. I scored touchdowns in the running-back position and loved that feeling when I would make a touchdown. I would always see my father's blue Lincoln Continental parked at the end of the football field behind the goalposts on the north end of the field. He never missed a home game. He would never leave his car and come talk before or after the game, but I knew he was at the game, and he watched me play. I didn't understand this as other kid's fathers would come out on the playing field after a game and congratulate their kids. Maybe Dad was shy around other people, or maybe he was drinking and didn't want others to know about it. I always knew he was very proud of me, and I was just happy that he took time out of his busy schedule to come and watch me play football.

Our wrestling team was awesome, and our team the Greybull Buffs won state all four years I was in high school. Other teams feared us. Other kids would stand in the hallways and look at the bracket for their weight class to see who they had to wrestle with. I would often overhear a wrestler as they were looking at the bracket say, "SHIT, I have a Greybull kid to wrestle!" Our whole team was tough, from the ninety-eight-pound weight class clear through heavyweight. If you had to wrestle a Greybull kid, you would have a tough match. It didn't matter what weight class you were in. Our coaches started us kids wrestling at a very young age in AAU and USA wrestling programs, and they continued to coach us from a young age all the way through high school. This dedication from our coaches and all the hard work in the wrestling room made us champions.

Wrestling practice was hard, and I hated it. We would do the same moves repeatedly. We would be dead tired and still practicing moves repeatedly. This built muscle memory, so you knew the moves inside and out when you were dead tired. My head coach was very dedicated. He wanted me to spend the night at his house during wrestling season so I could be in the weight room at five each morning and stay late after practice to run extra and lift weights with the team. I told him I couldn't afford the gas for my car to come in early each morning and that I wouldn't make it because I needed to ride the activity bus. He would not take no for an answer and told me he would pay for my fuel to travel back and forth to town for wrestling practice. If I didn't want to do that, I could just live at his house during wrestling practice.

In my junior year, I chased a lot of girls around and dated a few here and there. I would date a gal who was a freshman and very cute. She handed me a love note in the school hallway one day. The note read she thought I was cute and wanted to go on a date with me if I was interested. Hell yeah, I was interested. We both fell in love, and both lost our virginity that year. It's hard to focus on sports, school, or anything when you fall in love with a cute girl and lose your virginity.

My wrestling coach would get furious with me if I lost a match in wrestling. He would go through each weight class every Monday before wresting practice and critique each wrestler when they did well or when they didn't do so well. That Monday, he got to my weight class, and he said, "And now, Scott, let's talk about your overtime match that you lost on Saturday. You weren't focused on that match. All you can focus on is your damn new girlfriend. Let me ask you a question, Scott: is wrestling more important to you, or is your damn girlfriend?"

He asked me that question in front of the whole damn team, and it pissed me off. First, I wrestled my ass off and lost by one point in an overtime match to a very good wrestler I had never beaten before. I also pulled three ribs from my sternum trying to get off my back with only seconds remaining in the match to prevent myself from not getting pinned.

I looked at my coach and said, "Coach, my girlfriend is more important to me than wrestling. Wrestling is just a sport and no more. Besides that, I love her very much!"

My best buddy looked at me like "I can't believe you just fucking said that to the coach." The coach then looked at my best buddy, who was also madly in love with his girlfriend, and said, "How about you, Pat? Is wrestling more important to you or your girlfriend?"

My buddy quickly said, "WRESTLING, SIR!"

I looked at my buddy Pat like, "REALLY? YOU ARE A BIG PUSS!"

I saw my coach years later in the grocery store, and he walked up to me and shook my hand. He said, "You are looking good, Scott. Do you remember that day in wrestling practice when I asked you that question: what was more important, wrestling or your girlfriend?"

I said, "Yes, Coach, how could I ever forget that question?"

He said, "Did you really mean that when you said your girlfriend was more important?"

I said, "Yes, I did!"

He looked at me and said, "REALLY!" His next question was "Scott, I know you have been graduated for a number of years now, but was there really alcohol on the school bus on the trip back from the state wrestling your senior year?"

I drove out to my dad's house in Emblem one day after school to check on him. Last time I had seen my father, he was in the doctor's office and wasn't looking very good healthwise, plus his head was all swollen from hitting the brick wall on the front porch. The first thing I did was walk over to the front door of the house and check out the cinderblock wall that my dad had told me he fell into while slipping on some ice. Sure enough, two rows of cinderblocks had been broken. There were still bloodstains on the cinderblocks and the cement patio from my father breaking his head open. I thought to myself, *OH MY GOD, how did my father survive this fall? Did it knock him out? He could have bled to death or even frozen to death if he was passed out lying out in the cold! Did he drive himself to the doctor, or did someone give him a ride to town?*

I knocked on the front door of the house, and my father's Great Dane named Blue stood on his hind legs and looked through the top window of the front door at me. The dog was barking and growling viciously as his teeth bit at the glass in the window. My dad came to the front door and yelled at the dogs, "SHUT UP GODDAMMIT! Come on in!" My dad had two pit bulls and one Great Dane. No one would ever break into his house while he was gone without first killing those dogs. If you didn't kill them, they would kill you. My dad would poach antelope and deer and feed them to the dogs. The entire backyard was full of bones and rib cages of animals that my dad had poached and fed to the dogs. Back then, you could even find an old eagle carcass or two lying on the roof of the old outhouse located next to the apple orchard.

I came into the front living room of the house and sat down on the couch next to my father's brown leather chair. My father came from the kitchen and sat down next to me. His head looked much better, and most of the swelling had gone down. The circles around his eyes were no longer black, and his eyes were no longer bloodshot. He still didn't look very well. His skin was pale, and he had lost a bunch of weight. I noticed something strange that I had never seen before. My father wasn't drinking a beer. He was drinking a grape-flavored soda pop. I had never seen my father drink soda pop before. I asked my father how he was feeling after his accident falling into the brick wall. He said, "My head feels fine, but the doctor told me that I need to quit drinking, or I'm not going to make it much longer." He said, "You didn't know this, but I got really sick a couple of weeks ago and went into a coma while I was in the hospital up in Billings. I almost died. I could see a very bright light while in a coma, and the good Lord told me to quit drinking, or I was going to die."

He then said, "I saw the bright light, and I quit drinking two weeks ago and have been drinking nothing but this DAMN soda pop since then. It tastes like shit, but I will try to quit drinking."

I was so proud of my father. I never had told him I loved him. I never remember him telling me he loved me. Neither of us knew how to show affection, but we understood each other. I looked at my dad and said, "Good for you!" I didn't know what else to say. My dad asked me how football was and told me he sure enjoyed watching me play. I said, "Thank you, Dad!" I then got up off the couch and headed for the kitchen because I thought that soda pop looked good. I opened the refrigerator door, and it was full of only grape-flavored soda pop, not a beer in the refrigerator. I was proud of my father. We visited for more while I drank down a grape soda pop.

I was getting ready to leave when my dad pulled a hunting license out of his wallet and said, "Look here. I got a special bull elk license for the Sunlight Basin area this fall."

I said, "WOW! Congratulations!"

He said, "I didn't actually draw the license in the limited-quota draw this year, but the neighborhood girl is really good with white-out and a typewriter. Check out the job she did on this license. You can't even tell she just typed where I wanted to hunt a bull elk!" HOLY SHIT! My dad was making his hunting licenses so he could hunt anywhere in the state he wanted to. He would simply put in for an easy-to-draw limited-quota area license. Once he got the hunting license, he would have the neighborhood girl use white-out on the license to block out the valid hunt area.

Then she would put the license in her typewriter and kindly type in the new hunt area that my dad wanted to hunt. I suppose if a game warden was ever to check my father's license while hunting in the field and looked at it closely, they may have become suspicious. But if he did harvest an animal and the animal wasn't checked in the field by a warden, he would return home with no problems. I soon left my father's house shaking my head in disbelief. I headed over to Grandma Helen's house to see if she had some no-bake cookies for me and a jar of homemade dill pickles. My grandma Helen made the best dill pickles I have ever tasted.

My new girlfriend lived just across the draw and over the hill from my parents' new home near Shell. It was easy for us to spend time together because we lived so close to each other. I was forbidden to go over and see her if her parents were gone. One Saturday night we got about four inches of fresh snow. I called my girlfriend on Sunday morning and asked her if it was all right to come over and see her. She said, "NO, that's not a good idea because my parents are gone for the day!" I told her they would never discover because I would ride my snow machine over and visit for a while, and the sun would melt the snow later in the afternoon and destroy all evidence of my snow machine tracks in their driveway. She giggled at the idea and said, "Okay, see you in a few minutes!"

I rode my 1969 Puma 440 snow machine cross-country over to her house. I parked the machine in their driveway and banged on the front door. She opened the door with a big smile and said, "Glad you made it safe. Come on in!" It turned out to be a very beautiful and warm day. We sat down on the sofa, watched a movie, and cooked a bag of microwave popcorn. After watching several movies and kissing a little, I looked at the clock, and it was 4:00 p.m.! We had closed the drapes on the windows to block the sunlight, and I had lost track of time! I quickly jumped and said, "OH MY GOD, it's four o'clock, and your parents are going to be home soon."

I gave her a quick kiss goodbye and headed out the door. The sun was shining brightly, and I soon noticed all the snow had melted during the day. My snow machine was now sitting in a very muddy driveway with no snow left to get home. I fired up the trusty ole snow machine and headed home in the mud. It was very tough going because of all the thick mud I had to travel through. I nearly burned up a belt getting home, and I left deep tracks in the mud from my skis and track digging. When my girlfriend's parents returned home, it was obvious that the neighborhood boy had been over for a visit while they were gone to town. The tracks in the mud all the way to my house gave it away. My girlfriend called me later that evening and said, "I'm grounded because that was not a very good idea."

I continued to date this girl for several months, and we both continued to fall in love with each other. One night I asked Martin if I could borrow his '77 Chevy to take my girlfriend on a date. He said, "Sure, just be careful out there!" I was excited and jumped in his truck and headed the short distance to pick my girlfriend up for our date. As I was heading out of the town of Shell, a coyote ran across the road in front of me. It was a very large coyote, and its pelt looked prime. I quickly turned the truck around in the dark and shined my lights on the coyote as it was running up a private driveway that led to a mansion up on the hill. I slammed on the brakes and grabbed Martin's 22-250 rifle that always hung in the gun rack behind the seat.

I had the coyote in my headlights as it was running up the private driveway. I leaned over the hood of the old Chevy truck, got the coyote in my crosshairs of the scope, and fired the gun. *BOOM!* The coyote dropped dead in the driveway. I was so excited. I had just killed a beautiful coyote worth a great deal of money, and I could damn sure use the money right now. I loaded up the coyote in the back of Martin's truck and headed to my girlfriend's house. When her family greeted me at the front door, I excitedly told them I had just killed a coyote right outside the city limits by Shell. I said, "Yeah, I killed it right next to the thirty-five-mile-per-hour flashing speed limit sign as you come into Shell." My girlfriend had three younger sisters, and they were all excited about the story and wanted to come out and see the dead coyote in the back of the truck. I took the young girls out and showed them the dead coyote. They wanted to touch it and look at his big teeth.

I returned home late that night after my date and laid the coyote on the ground next to the front garage door. The next morning, as I was getting ready to go to school, Martin said, "Where did that dead dog come from?"

I said, "It's not a dog. It's a damn big coyote, and I shot him last night when I was headed over to pick up my girlfriend!"

He said, "There is something wrong with it. I don't think it's a coyote. I think you killed someone's dog! Look here at the dark spot on its nose!" It certainly did have a dark spot on its nose, but in my mind, it was damn sure a coyote. Martin then said, "I think you better take that one to the town dump and get rid of it" So that's what I did, but I still wasn't convinced that it wasn't a coyote.

The neighbors had recently been babysitting my girlfriend's sisters and told them they were missing their dog and that it looked just like a coyote. The girls quickly chimed in and said, "My sister's boyfriend just killed a coyote in your driveway last night. His name is Scott." The neighbors were related to the deputy sheriff, so they called him and told him that a kid named Scott from Shell might have killed their dog.

I got done throwing the coyote/dog in the dump and headed for the school that morning. When I walked into class, the neighbor's daughter, who was a very cute girl, yelled at me while she was sitting at her desk crying, "DOG KILLER!"

I thought to myself, *Oh my god! Did I just kill their dog, their family pet?* I felt horrible and didn't say anything back to the girl still sitting at her desk crying. I later went to the school cafeteria to eat lunch. As I was looking for a place to sit and eat my lunch, a whole table full of girls yelled at me, "DOG KILLER, DOG KILLER, DOG KILLER!" Now, I felt horrible, and every kid in school would know about this by the end of the day.

I got done eating lunch and headed out of the cafeteria to walk back to the high school building when I looked up and a huge deputy sheriff was approaching me. This man stood about six feet seven inches and weighed nearly three hundred pounds. We all kids were scared to death of this deputy because he had a large beard and dark voice and tolerated no one who was breaking the law. Not only that, but this deputy was related to the dog's owner. The deputy confronted me on the sidewalk in front of the high school. He said, "Are you Scott Werbelow?"

I said, "Yes, sir."

He said, "I need to talk to you about the dog that you shot the other day!"

I explained to him I thought I was shooting at a coyote and that I would have killed no one's dog intentionally.

The deputy explained that their dog was missing and it looked just like a coyote. He asked me where the dog was located, and I explained that I had taken it to the Shell dump. He then said, "If you thought you had killed a coyote, why did you take it to the dump?" I explained to him that after further investigation the next morning I had noticed a small spot on the coyote's nose and then decided that I might have screwed up, so I took it to the dump. The deputy said in a very gruff voice, "The dog did have a spot on his nose, and his name was Spot!"

I said, "I'm very sorry. I did not know who owned the dog, or I would have apologized to them!"

He said, "MY NIECE IS THE OWNER OF THE DOG!!"

I soon knew this would not go well for Scotty. The deputy said, "I think you're a good kid and made an honest mistake. I will talk to the dog owner and see if they want to press charges!" He then said, "I think it would mean a great deal to the dog owner if you meet with him in person and apologize for shooting their dog!"

I said, "Yes, sir, I will do that tonight when I get home."

I met with the owner of the dog that evening. I explained to him what had happened. I told him every detail about where I had shot from, where the dog died, and that I had shot him in my headlights.

He said, "This whole thing is an unfortunate situation, but our dog Spot did look just like a coyote, and I knew this was going to happen someday!" His voice then cracked up, and he said, "We should have had a fluorescent-orange color or something on the dog!" A tear ran down the dog owner's cheek. This was a very unfortunate situation, and the only thing wrong with this picture is that I was in it! I apologized to the man and shook his hand. I told him that if he wanted his dog back, I would retrieve it for him so that could have a proper burial. He looked at the ground, shook his head back and forth, and walked back to his house with his head hung down low. I felt horrible!

The next day I went to school, and all the girls were still calling me a dog killer as I walked down the hallway of the school. I had heard nothing from the deputy yet, and I was very worried that I would be charged with something. I went to wrestling practice that afternoon, and the deputy showed up in the wrestling room and asked the head coach if he could visit with me. Of course, every wrestler on the team now observed me leave the room with the deputy. This was truly an embarrassing moment for me.

The deputy took me out in the hallway and said, "Scott, we have some more things that we need to discuss."

I said, "Yes, sir!"

The deputy said, "You never told me that you shot this dog using artificial light."

I said, "Sir, I didn't use artificial light. I used my headlights."

He said, "Headlights are considered artificial lights."

I said, "Oh, I did not know that!"

He then stated, "Taking any wildlife with the use of artificial light is a $210 fine." He then said, "We also have a couple of other problems. You didn't tell me that you shot the dog on private property. That's another $210 fine. And finally, you never told me that you shot from a public highway. That's another $210 fine." I looked at the ground and shook my head. I thought to myself, *Man, that's $630 I don't have, and I'm in a huge amount* *of trouble right now. I hope Bob, the Greybull game warden, doesn't discover this. Will this affect my becoming a game warden someday?*

The deputy then said, "Scott, I know you are a good kid, and this was all a mistake. You did not intentionally shoot someone's dog, but you used poor judgment and broke several laws while doing so. You're a good kid, and I respect the fact that you owned up to your mistake and apologized to the owner of the dog in person. That means a great deal to me!" He then said, "I have talked to the dog owner, and they don't wish to press any charges against you." I was very excited to hear this news, but it still didn't bring back the owner's dog, and I was very embarrassed about what I had done! This one was going to take some time to heal, and it would be a long time before the girls quit calling me dog killer.

My brother, Wade, ended up getting a football scholarship and decided to go to Chadron, Nebraska, to play football and attend college. He called me one night and asked me how I was doing. I explained the whole dog story to him, and he just laughed and said, "YOU BIG DUMBASS!" He then said, "You should come down to Chadron and play football once you graduate. IT'S REALLY FUN!"

I thought to myself, *BULLSHIT! There is no way I'm going to college. I hate school.*

I got home from wrestling practice one evening, and my girlfriend asked me if I would come over to her house and talk. She sounded very sad. I finished dinner and drove over to her house; and no, I didn't shoot any more coyotes near the town of Shell. I arrived at her house, and she was crying. She said," I'm sorry, I love you much, but my father is moving the whole family to California!" She cried and said, "I told them that I want to stay here and finish school, but they told me NO, I must go with the family!"

We both cried and I told her, "Don't worry, we will figure out a way to make it work. You can come back with your dad in October when he comes back to hunt, and I can come to see you in California over Christmas break."

We knew this would be very difficult, but we would make it work no matter what. I never knew why their father moved them to California. But within a week, they were packed up and gone. We didn't have cell phones back then, so I could not talk to my girlfriend for three days as they traveled to California. I was heartbroken. I had finally found a girl who loved me, and I loved her, and now she was gone just like that. I considered going to college in California, but I knew I would never go to college. This would be very tough to get through. My heart felt like someone had put a dagger in it.

The summer of my junior year in high school was very busy for me. I landed a job mixing cement for an old fellow who laid moss rock, brick, and block. He was working on the rock wall at Shell Falls and asked me if I would come work for him for a few days as he needed to replace broken rocks in the decorative rock wall at the falls. I agreed to take the job, and he taught me how to mix the cement and mortar to repair the rock wall. I only worked for him for a couple of days, and he asked me to replace two broken rocks in the wall. I chipped out the broken rocks and mortar and carefully fit two new rocks back in place. He thought I did a great job and congratulated me on my work.

I returned home from work one day, and my mother asked me if I could lay moss rock around the entire cinderblock foundation of their new home. I said, "Mother, Christ, I have only laid two rocks in my entire life. What makes you think I can lay moss rock around the entire foundation of your house?"

She said, "Because you're good, and I know you can do it!"

I grumbled and walked off. This would be a huge job, and I wasn't sure I could do it.

I soon found places out in the hills with tons of beautiful moss rocks. I took Martin's truck out, and I have no idea how many loads of rock I hauled back to the house to complete that job. It took me several years to complete the entire house. I would generally do one wall per summer. But I did learn how to lay moss rock, and I did a very good job at it. Soon, I would start my business laying moss rock for other people. My first job would be for a rich doctor on a brand-new trophy home; my next job was for a wealthy dentist, also on new trophy home I would bid the jobs to make $100 per day. This worked out to about $8 per square foot. Once I figured out how much square footage I could cover in a day's work, I then figured out what to charge per square foot to allow myself to make at least $100 a day. I did good work, and I was reasonably priced. The word traveled fast, and quickly, I had more work than I could keep up with.

I also landed a job building a new fence along the highway right-of-way between Emblem and Greybull that summer. Wade and I both worked on this project for a couple of months. This was one of the hardest jobs I had ever had. It was very hot that summer, and digging post holes all day in the hot sun was difficult. We would drink several gallons of water a day.

Our pay was $8 per hour. Back then, this was considered a high-paying job. Wade and I felt like we had more money at this time than at any other time in our lives.

Between laying moss rock and building fences all summer, I was becoming a very strong young man. I didn't need to work out in the weight room like all my other friends did. I was becoming very strong from performing good old-fashioned physical hard work daily. I would pick up large moss rocks and carry one in each hand, often walking several hundred yards to get back to the truck. I would load heavy rocks until the truck was full and then drive home and unload hundreds of heavy rocks. Once at a job, I would have to load all the rocks up in a pickup and on a trailer and haul them to the job site, only to unload them, and eventually load all the unused rocks back up and take home only to unload them all again. It seemed all I ever did was lug heavy rocks around. This work built up my hand, wrist, and finger strength. At that age, I had never lost an arm-wrestling match.

I came home from football practice one evening when I was a junior in high school. My mother said, "I think you better go visit your father. He is in the Basin hospital, and he is not doing very well at all." This news played hard on my heart. The last time I had seen my dad, he had quit drinking. It was a Friday morning. I jumped in my car and headed for the hospital in Basin. I walked through the front door of the hospital and walked up to the front desk. A lady wearing blue scrubs and a white mask said, "Can I help you with something?"

I said, "My name is Scott Werbelow. I'm here to see my father, William Werbelow."

She looked at her chart and said, "Okay, your father is in room 111. He is not doing well. He has been in a coma for a couple of days now."

I said, "Okay, ma'am, thank you!" I walked down the long cold hallway, and it hit me like a ton of rocks. Room 111 was the same room that my Grandpa Lyle died in two years ago. I slowly opened the door into room 111, not sure what I was about to see.

Once I was in the room, it was quiet. All I could hear was the sound of a machine going *beep, beep, beep.* It was a heart monitor hooked up to my father. There were two beds in the room, but my father was the only person in the room. My father was lying in the same damn bed that my grandpa Lyle had died in. I walked over to his bedside and looked at his face. His skin was yellow, and his face was sunken in around his cheekbones. His eyes had black rings around them, and my father lay there motionless with his eyes closed. His breathing was slow and laborious.

I grabbed my father's hand and said, "Dad, can you hear me. This is your son Scott, and I'm here to see you." My father lay there motionless. His face never moved, and his eyes never opened. I thought to myself, *Can my father hear my voice right now?* I grabbed his hand tighter and raised my voice and said, "Father, can you hear me?" Nothing—my father did not react to my voice at all. I had never told my father I loved him before. I cried and said, "Dad it's me Scott, your son. I love you very much. Please don't die!"

I cried as I squeezed my father's hand. I said a prayer to God and asked God to comfort my dad and let him go in peace comfortably. I prayed to God, "Please take my father to heaven with you so that I can be with him someday" I was losing words and said my final goodbyes to my father. I turned and was walking to the door to leave the hospital room when I heard a faint voice. The voice was very weak, but it was coming from my father. He said, "Son, make five touchdowns for me in your game tonight!"

I quickly turned and walked back over to my dad's bedside and said, "Dad, can you hear me?" No response. "DAD, DAD, can you hear me?" Again, no response! Just shallow deep breaths from my father. I kept talking to my father but no response. I turned and walked out of the hospital room, asking myself, how did Dad know that I had a football game tonight? He told me to make five touchdowns for him in my game tonight. We would be playing Wind River in football later that night. We would be traveling to Wind River for an away game.

I drove from Basin to Greybull to get back to school and cried the whole way there. My life seemed empty. *WHY ME, GOD?* I lost my grandpa Lyle, whom I dearly loved; my girlfriend just moved to California; and my dad was lying in a hospital bed dying. The same damn bed that my grandpa died in. I finished the day at school and jumped on the bus early that afternoon to travel to Wind River High School to prepare for a night football game. We had a great team, and Wind River was not doing well that year. This game should not be a tough one for us. Just before the game, my coach said, "Werbelow, I want you to start in the fullback position tonight!"

I said, "Yes, sir Coach!" I thought to myself, *How am I going to score five touchdowns for my dad in the fullback position? I don't get to run the ball in this position much. My primary job is to block for the tailback who lines up behind me and is the primary ball handler.*

We kicked the ball off to Wind River. They were playing very tough, and we couldn't stop their offense, and our offense couldn't move the ball. It was half time. The score was Wind River 16, Greybull 0. We all ran into the locker room with our heads hung down. We are a better team than they are. How could we be losing? The head coach came into the locker room pissed off and kicked a chair across the locker room, picked up the garbage can, and threw it into the shower area across the locker room. He yelled at us and called us a bunch of pussies. The coach yelled, "WE ARE GOING TO MAKE SOME CHANGES IN THE SECOND HALF! WERBELOW, YOU ARE GOING TO TAILBACK. KOTTER, YOU ARE GOING TO THE FULLBACK POSITION! NOW GET YOUR ASSES OUT THERE AND PLAY SOME DAMN FOOTBALL!" I thought to myself, *Here is my chance to score five touchdowns for my father.*

Wind River kicked off. I received the ball on the two-yard line and ran it to the thirty-yard line. Our quarterback formed the huddle and called the play. The ball would be handed off to me right up the middle. I looked at ten other players in the huddle and said, "You guys want a touchdown! Just block your man, do your damn job, and I will run the ball for a touchdown!"

I heard the quarterback say "HUT, HUT." The ball was handed off to me, and the line had opened up a hole for me big enough to drive a truck through. Nobody touched me. I ran seventy yards for a touchdown. All the players ran to the end zone with me and piled on top of me, congratulating me. I handled the ball twice that drive and went ninety-eight yards for a touchdown. We were soon on defense, and I hit a guy so hard that he fumbled the ball, and we recovered it. I got back in the huddle and yelled at all the players, "YOU WANT ANOTHER TOUCHDOWN? BLOCK YOUR MAN, AND I WILL GET IT DONE!" I broke another touchdown for thirty yards.

The score was now 16–14 Wind River. I later scored three more touchdowns, and Greybull would win the game 35–16. I not only scored 5 touchdowns for my dad but also scored them all in the second half. This was simply amazing. My coach awarded me Player of the Week that week, and gifted me a football that had the player's signature and jersey number written with a Sharpie marker. I would cherish that football forever. Nobody on the team ever knew who I was playing for that night.

My father died the next day at forty after being diagnosed with cirrhosis of the liver. I was very sad when my father died, but I knew he was with me that night and that he would always be with me for the rest of my life.

I also knew there must be a God, and my father was with him. I never told this story to very many people over the years because it would make me cry every time I told it. I later told my football coach this story nearly eleven years later. He was speechless. He just hugged me, and we both sobbed. There is a power of God, and sometimes you just can't explain it. I miss my father every day, even though we didn't have a real close relationship when I was young. My father loved me dearly. He just never knew how to express himself, and neither did I. He is still with me every day.

RIP William Werbelow

It took about six months for me to realize that the long-distance relationship with my girlfriend in California was not working well for me. It just seemed we grew further and further apart each month we were away from each other. We would talk on the phone several nights a week, but it seemed we had less and less to talk about with each phone call. I was frustrated that I couldn't be with her every day. The cute neighborhood girl who had helped me doctor my horse Daisy was now going to high school her senior year. She had been homeschooled until her senior year. Now she was riding the same bus to school each morning and would sit next to me on the school bus. Her name was Lana. She never talked except that day she helped me doctor my horse Daisy. And I was so embarrassed that day that I wasn't sure I ever wanted to talk to her again either. Something always intrigued me about Lana. I'm not sure what that was ever all about.

Her parents owned a beautiful ranch next to our ranch, and I would occasionally see her ride her horse by the house at White Creek wearing only a bikini. She had long dark hair and a slender build with nice muscle tone in her arms and legs. She played basketball her senior year and was a very good athlete. She later received an award from her basketball coach for Defensive Player of the Year, and she later became valedictorian of her class. The school would not give her this award because she only attended school her senior year. I was probably most intrigued by her because I had been going to school with all the other girls since the first grade, and they all seemed like my sister by now, plus I had dated several, and that never seemed to work out.

For entertainment in my life, we would gather up several friends on a Friday or Saturday night and go out late at night and chase jackrabbits on our snow machines. How I didn't kill myself some of those nights I will never know. We would ride our snow machines from my parents' house in Shell through the hills to White Creek Ranch and chase jackrabbits out in the hay fields late at night. This activity usually involved drinking alcohol and running over all of Martin's gated irrigation pipe buried underneath the snow.

By the end of the night, our snow machines would be torn up from jumping irrigation ditches, hitting rocks, and sometimes running through a barbed-wire fence. We would work on the snow machines all week in shop class and get them running again for the next weekend. My friends and I would always sit on the bus each Monday morning headed to school and talk about all the crazy fun we had chasing jackrabbits in the dark on our snow machines.

One Monday morning on the school bus, my friends and I were talking about how much fun we had over the weekend riding our snow machines. The neighborhood girl Lana overheard our conversation and asked me if I would take her with me next Friday night to chase jackrabbits. I couldn't believe what I was hearing. Was she asking me out on a date? She already knew I had a girlfriend in California. I smiled and said, "Sure, I will pick you up Friday night at your house around seven." This was the first time that she talked to me since the day that she had helped me doctor my mare Daisy. I thought to myself, *What in the hell did I just do? I really didn't want or need another girlfriend! Oh well, just because we go out and chase rabbits on a snow machine doesn't mean we have to be dating. We can just be friends.*

The next Friday one of my best friends came over to spend the night with me. His older brother had bought us a bottle of whiskey and a bottle of Schnapps. We were going to have a great time that night chasing rabbits on our snow machines that we had spent all week repairing. We left the house in Shell about 6:00 p.m. and headed over to White Creek Ranch.

Man, rabbits were running everywhere, and we had about eight inches of fresh new powder to play in. We had the time of our lives that night; and after chasing rabbits in the fields, we decided to head up Black Mountain because the snow was deep enough for us to ride up there without hitting too many rocks. We went clear to the top of the mountain, shut our machines off, and gazed at the beautiful stars overhead. My buddy said, "Man, what a night. Have a snort of this." He then handed me a bottle of peppermint Schnapps. I took a healthy swig and shouted, "SHIT, I was supposed to pick the neighborhood girl up tonight at seven. WHAT TIME IS IT?"

My buddy looked at his watch and said, "About nine thirty."

I said, "SHIT, WE HAVE TO GO RIGHT NOW!"

We hauled ass off the mountain and pulled into the driveway of the neighborhood girl's house at about 10:00 p.m. I was drunk and late for the date. The lights were still on in the house. Maybe she was still awake. Should I knock on the door this late at night? What would her parents think? I finally mustered up enough confidence to bang on the front door of the house. I had heard her parents were religious. What would they think of me picking their daughter up on a snow machine drunk at 10:00 p.m.? I was standing on their front porch of their house with my snow machine suit and helmet on. Here it goes. *BANG, BANG, BANG!* I knocked on the front door.

Her parents greeted me and my buddy at the front door. They were very cheerful and invited us in for a hot chocolate and some ice cream. We took our helmets off and introduced ourselves. The ice cream tasted good because I had the munchies from drinking alcohol all night! The next thing I knew, I was telling her dad dirty jokes, and he would laugh so hard after each joke I told. We were bonding! And my buddy sat on the couch and kept looking over at me like "I can't believe you just told that dirty joke." His daughter Lana came walking into the front room. She was dressed very nicely, and I could tell she had prepared herself for this date because this was the first time I had seen her put on eyeliner. She looked very beautiful and smelled of nice perfume. I felt horrible that I had forgotten to come to pick her up at 7:00 p.m.

She walked into the front room and said, "Well, there you are! I thought you had forgotten about me tonight."

I said, "Sorry we are late. We were having so much fun in the new powder that we decided to go up the Black Mountain road and lost track of time."

She said, "Well, let me get my warm clothes on, and we can go for a short ride tonight."

I said, "That would be awesome, if it's all right with your parents."

Her dad said, "Sure, go have some fun, and we will wait up for you guys to return home shortly." This told me that her dad was concerned about me taking his daughter for a snow machine ride, and he wanted her home quickly.

We went for a short ride and chased jackrabbits around the fields out back but never caught up with any of them because I didn't want to drive too crazy and fast with Lana riding on the back of my snow machine. I brought her back home within an hour and was again invited to her house for another cup of hot chocolate with her parents. We didn't stay long and were soon headed back home to Shell through the hills. We got back home, and my buddy smiled and said, "I didn't know you and Lana were dating."

I said, "We are not dating. She is just a friend of mine who helped me doctor my horse one day and wanted to go riding with us some night. Besides that, I have a girlfriend, and she lived in California."

Over the next several weeks, Lana would talk more on our bus ride to town each morning. She would even sit next to me during school lunch in the cafeteria. I'm sure others were talking about us and probably thought we were dating. I had purchased a couple of airline tickets to fly out to California with my brother, Wade, over Christmas to see my girlfriend. Wade would be home from college, and I thought that would be a fun vacation for both of us to get away and spend some time in the sunshine down south.

My feelings for Lana would get stronger and stronger over the next several weeks. She was a nice girl, and I liked her. But how would I deal with my girlfriend in California? I loved her and was flying out to see her in a few weeks! Lana knew I had a girlfriend. She also knew that I was flying down to California over Christmas to be with her. This really bothered Lana, even though we were not officially dating. Lana later wrote me a letter one day and gave it on the bus. The letter said she had strong feelings for me and that if she and I would ever be together, I would have to break up with my girlfriend in California.

My brother and I were on the plane headed for California, and this was weighing heavily on my heart. I loved my girlfriend, but the long-distance relationship was not fair to either of us. Hell, we were young and would only see each other maybe two or three times a year. We finally made it to California, and I spent a week with my girlfriend at her parents' house. We had a great time together, but she knew things were different between us. The last day I was at her house she opened a letter she had just received from her best friend from Greybull. I read the letter over my girlfriend's shoulder.

The letter read, "Scott and Lana are having a secret love affair. I see them eating lunch together every day in the school cafeteria." My girlfriend confronted me with this news, and I told her that Lana and I were good friends and that I liked her parents and that they owned a ranch next to my parents' ranch. I told her that, yes, we did eat lunch together; and, yes, we did go snow machining together chasing jackrabbits.

My girlfriend became very sad and cried. I could not break up with her. I loved her so much. She then gave Wade and me a ride to the airport. We said our goodbyes and boarded the plane. It was raining that day. I wiped the fog off the small round airplane window and looked down at the ground below the plane. My girlfriend had run out to the plane and blew me a kiss as she sobbed heavily. This broke my heart. Would I ever see her again? The plane took off, and she was still standing in the heavy rain by herself, sobbing with her head down as the large jet left the pavement and headed for Wyoming.

Once back in Wyoming, Lana called me one night and asked me if I would like to go to a drive-in movie with her in Basin. Her dad just had a brand-new four-door Toyota truck, and she was dying to take it for a ride somewhere. I agreed to go with her, and she picked me up at my parents' house in Shell. She looked nice, and I was excited to see her. She didn't seem excited to see me and actually didn't say a word all the way to Basin. We were just pulling into the small town of Basin, and Lana said, "Can I ask you a question?"

I said, "NOPE."

She said, "Well, I'm going to ask you anyways. Did you break up with your girlfriend while you were in California?"

I said, "NOPE!"

She said, "I have very strong feelings for you, and my parents will not allow me to date you if you already have a girlfriend."

I told Lana I still loved my girlfriend and could not break up with her, especially while I was living in the same house with her and her parents for the week. The movie was long, and the trip home was even longer because Lana would not say another word that day. She dropped me off at my parents' house in the brand-new truck she was driving and gave me a look that said, "Shit or get off the POT!" Lana and I quit talking for several weeks after that conversation.

I had several more phone conversations with my girlfriend in California. It seemed things were never the same again. I even suspected that she might have found another boyfriend and moved on herself. We broke up one night over the phone. That would be the last time I ever talked to her, and my heart still hurts when I think about that final kiss she blew on that rainy day at the airport in California.

She was such a sweet girl, and I loved her much. Circumstances just pulled us apart. I later ended up dating Lana. I picked her up at her house one night on my snow machine, and we climbed up Black Mountain. I shut the snow machine off and looked at all the beautiful bright stars above. I was nervous and not very good at this stuff with women. I took a swig of peppermint Schnapps, leaned over, and stole a kiss from Lana. She never even kissed me back, but I got the first one out of the way.

Brother Wade returned home from college one weekend after Christmas. We jumped on our snow machines and went for a ride. We were headed back home and raced each other up our steep driveway to the house. The hill was steep and had several blind curves in the road. Wade got ahead of me, and I would try to pass him on the inside of a blind corner going up the hill. I was taking the corner just as fast as I could to get around him on the inside, but he was still just ahead of me. Once I got around the corner, I looked up and noticed a 1970 K-5 Chevy Blazer coming right toward me with its front tires locked up sliding right toward me. I didn't even have time to say shit. I was going too fast and would hit this Chevy Blazer head-on. I quickly stood up on my running boards and sprung off my snow machine as hard as I could to my left. My body hit long ways across the front grill of this Blazer. The Blazer hit me so hard that it pitched my body on the bank to my left about twenty feet.

It knocked me unconscious, but I remember hearing a loud smashing noise before I was knocked out. This was the noise of my snow machine crashing into the Blazer. When I came to, several people were looking over me and talking. I could hear them yelling as they smacked the side of my helmet with their hands, "OH MY GOD, ARE YOU ALL RIGHT? ARE YOU ALL RIGHT?" I could feel warm blood running down my face and my neck. My right eye and face hurt badly. The guy driving the Blazer helped me to my feet. I was dizzy and walked down the steep embankment toward the Blazer and my wrecked snow machine. My right hip hurt badly. I could barely lift my left leg to take a step.

The next thing I remembered was helping this guy jack up the front of his Blazer so we could pull my snow machine out from under his transmission. The snow machine had hit the front of that Chevy Blazer so hard that it went completely under the Blazer and lifted both front tires of the Blazer off the ground. We finally got the snow machine pulled out from underneath the Blazer with the help of my brother. My brother was very shaken up because he went around that blind corner first and nearly hit the Blazer himself. He knew I was right behind him, so he quickly jumped off his snow machine to stop the man driving the Blazer, knowing I was coming around the corner right behind him at a high rate of speed. My brother waved his arms frantically to tell the guy to stop. That's why the guy had stomped on his brakes and locked up the front tires of the Blazer before me coming around the sharp corner on the ice-packed road.

My brother looked at me and said, "Oh my god, you broke another helmet. Take your helmet off and look at it" I took my helmet off and looked at it. The whole right side of my helmet was cracked; the large crack ran from the front of the helmet all the way around to the back. My brother said, "Holy shit, isn't that like the fourth helmet that you have broken now?" My brother was correct. That was the fourth helmet I had broken before the age of eighteen. I rarely ever wore a helmet but seemed to always be wearing one on the days I had bad accidents. I'm sure someone was always looking over me. We quickly hooked a chain to my mangled 1969 Puma 440, and the driver of the Blazer dragged it up the hill to our house.

We had company that afternoon. Martin had cooked a prime rib, and everybody was enjoying a nice game of pinochle when the Blazer pulled into the front yard dragging my mangled snow machine behind it. My mother looked out the large picture window and screamed, "OH MY GOD! Scotty has been in a terrible accident. Look at his snow machine!" Wade gave me a ride up to the house on the back of his machine. I could barely walk. My right eye had swollen shut and was very black and blue. My mother met me out in the driveway, screaming, "ARE YOU ALL RIGHT? OH MY GOD, ARE YOU ALL RIGHT?" Tears ran down her face.

I said, "I'm all right, Mom, but I may need to go to the hospital and get some stitches in my right eye, and my hip hurts really badly." My mom thanked the nice man for dragging my snow machine back up the hill and dropping it off. I looked at the front of the Blazer as the man was turning around. The Blazer had a very heavy-duty, custom-made grill guard on the front of it. My hip had hit the grill guard, and my head had broken out his passenger-side headlight. I told my brother, "Look at the size of that snow machine catcher mounted on the front of that damn Blazer!"

My brother looked at me and said, "You big dumbass!"

I was embarrassed to walk into the house with all our company over. I had now disrupted the pinochle game and prime rib dinner. I didn't want everyone to see the injury to my face because it looked horrible. It reminded me of what my dad looked like when he fell into the brick wall and smashed his face. My mother called the sheriff's office to report the accident. The deputy told her he would be right up to talk and fill out an accident report. The deputy soon showed up. Shit, it was the same deputy I had to deal with when I shot the damn dog named Spot. The deputy walked into our house, shook my hand, and sat down on the couch. He had a smile on his face, and he looked at me and said, "What did you do to your eye, scope yourself with a rifle shooting another damn pet dog?"

I was embarrassed, got the accident report filled out, and Mom hauled me to the hospital for some stitches. I hauled my snow machine to school to repair it in shop class. After several days of trying to repair it, I realized that it was irreparable. That was the end of the 1969 Puma 440 Arctic Cat snowmobile.

In my senior year, I excelled in football and loved to play the game. During my final home game, I had scored five touchdowns and had run the ball to the one-yard line. My coach pulled me out and said, "How many touchdowns do you have this year?"

I replied, "Coach, I have eighteen!"

He said, "How many touchdowns did your brother, Wade, have his senior year?"

I replied, "I think he also had eighteen."

Coach then said, "We will leave it at that. Take a seat and relax for a while!"

My coach didn't want me to outdo my brother. I thought that was pretty neat of him. He yelled, "NOEL, get in there and score a touchdown!" Noel was a third-string running back and never got much playing time. They handed the ball off to Noel up the middle. The next thing I saw was Noel come flying about five yards back out of the line of scrimmage. He got hit so hard he lost about five yards and fumbled the ball. That was Noel's first and last play of the game.

Our football team ended up with a record of 6–2 that year. I ended up with over 1,200 yards rushing and 18 total touchdowns for the year. I also learned that some coaches from other colleges had been down watching some of my games. At the end of my last game my senior year, a man came up and shook my hand. He said, "Great game, young man. My name is Coach Turner. I coach the Chadron Eagles in Chadron, Nebraska. I know your brother very well and I would like you to consider coming to Chadron to play football for us next year!" I was honored to hear this, but I was not going to college. He then said, "Come on and try us out. If you prove yourself the first year, I will get you a scholarship to play football for the Chadron Eagles!" He smacked me on the butt and said, "Great game, son. Please consider my offer!"

I did very well my senior year in wrestling. I lost only two matches all year, and one loss would be in a hard-fought match during the state championship with a guy from Kemmerer, Wyoming. I had never beaten this guy before and gone several overtime matches with him over the years. He was six feet and four inches tall and a very good leg wrestler. I was in the best shape of my life and trained hard to beat him because I knew I would wrestle him in the state championship match my senior year. This same guy beat me earlier in the year by one point in an overtime match. I lifted weights and ran nearly ten miles a day to get in shape for this match. I was much stronger than him, but he was a very good wrestler with a technique much better than I had. I had no other competition my senior year and pinned most of my opponents in the first period.

I would practice a double-leg takedown repeatedly. I had decided this would be the takedown that I would use in my state championship match I went home one night all excited that I would be using this takedown in my state championship match and wanted to show the move to my stepfather, Martin. We were in the basement, and I told him I wanted to practice the move on him and show him how good I was at it. I told him to stand still and I would show him the move. I would only do the move half speed. I shot in on Martin's legs and picked him up in the air over my head. He slumped off my shoulder, and I dropped him on the tile floor next to the woodstove. He lay in excruciating pain and couldn't get back up. We later hauled him to the hospital with a broken shoulder. Sorry about that, Martin. Most young wrestlers hang on tight when they are in the air.

I had decided that I was stronger than my opponent from Kemmerer, so I would just go out on the mat and wrestle my match, not his. Just before the match, he walked over to me and shook my hand and said, "Well, here we are again. MAN, I hate wrestling you. Good luck."

I shook his hand and said, "Best of luck to you as well!" The butterflies in my stomach were horrible because I had never beaten this guy before and known what he was capable of. We shook hands on the mat, and the whistle blew.

I tapped him on the head with my hand to block his vision and shot in for a beautiful double-leg takedown. I wrapped both my arms tightly around his legs and picked him up over my head. While he was in the air, I put a half-nelson on him and gently put him down on the mat on his back. He was on his back the entire first period, and I thought I had him pinned twice, but the referee would not call it. The score at the end of the first period was 7–0. He would take me down in the second period. I should have lain on my belly and stalled because I had the lead and he was not strong enough to do anything with me. But I thought, *No, I will wrestle my match.* I went to stand up, and he quickly threw me in a standing cradle and pulled me over backward to my back for three points.

I wasn't smart enough to learn from that, so I tried to stand up again; and again, he threw me in the same move and got three more points. I still wasn't smart enough to learn from that, and I tried standing up a third time; and he put me on my back again in a standing cradle for another three points. At the end of the second period, he was leading 11–7. He started in the down position during the third period, and he finally escaped with a switch during the end of the third period for another two points. The score was now 13–7. I jumped thinking we had another period to wrestle, and the referee grabbed his hand and raised it in the air and said to the winner, "Congratulations, nice match!"

What the hell had just happened? I thought to myself as the referee raised his arm for the win while the crowd cheered for him. That entire match seemed it lasted only a couple of minutes. I was sure we had another period to wrestle. But no, I had just lost the state championship match I had trained so hard for all year long. My record for the year would be 28–2, with both losses going to the same guy. I would never forget this match my entire life. I wanted so bad to get one more chance to beat this guy, but it was over just like that.

The year was 1986. The Greybull Buffs wrestling team would win yet another state championship. It was an exciting bus ride home from Casper to Greybull that night. All the wrestlers were happy. They would laugh out loud and sing, "We are the champions. We are the CHAMPIONS OF THE WORLD!" It was hard for me to join in on the celebration because I was very upset with myself for losing the championship match. I just wanted to be alone and sleep on the way home.

The cheerleaders were also on the bus that night. Everyone was having a great time. So, Coach, if you are reading this book, I will give you the answer to your question you asked me years ago. Yes, there was alcohol on the school bus that night on the way home from the state wrestling trip from Casper to Greybull. And yes, the cheerleaders snuck the alcohol on the bus, and at least one of them lost their virginity in the backseat of the bus on that beautiful night.

About one week later, after winning our fourth state wrestling championship in a row, we had a party out in the hills. We found a secluded spot we could have a huge bonfire and not be found by the deputy sheriff. We hauled about twenty wooden pallets to burn for firewood out to the area the day before the party. This would be a huge party, and we wrestlers would celebrate and do it right. The bonfire was huge. Most wrestlers drank copious amounts of alcohol and did some reminiscing about school and the wrestling season. One wrestler became very drunk and built a cross out of wood. He caught the cross on fire and hiked to the top of a large nearby hill. Once on the top, he held the burning cross over his head and yelled, "I'M THE CHAMPION OF THE WORLD!" This wrestler had won his state championship match in the 185-weight class and was very proud of himself.

I got drunk that night—too drunk to drive home. I slept on the ground next to the warm fire with several other friends by my side. The next morning the sun came up. I woke up with a screaming headache. My eyes were bloodshot, and they hurt. It felt like I had a headache behind each eye. My face and hands were dirty and covered in charcoal from lying in the dirt and handling wood all night. My hair was uncombed and standing on end. One of my best friends woke up and said shit as he looked at his watch. I said, "What?"

He said, "We need to hurry up and drive to Basin and take the ACT at 9:00 a.m."

I said, "What the hell is the ACT?"

He said, "The all-college test, you dumbass!"

I said, "What the hell is that?"

He said, "It's a test you have to take if you ever want to get accepted into a college."

I thought to myself, *Well, sucks to be you, because I'm not going to college. The last damn thing I want to do right now is drive over an hour to take a goddamn test.*

My friend then said, "Hurry up. We have to go. I rode to the party with you! You are going to have to give me a ride because I need to take the test as I plan to attend Chadron Nebraska College and play football on a football scholarship! This is the last chance I will have to take this test before college starts next spring."

I looked at my other buddy and said, "Are you going to take that silly test as well?"

He said, "Yeah, I probably better. My dad told me to take it!"

I thought to myself, *How come I never heard about this test before if it's so damn important?* I said, "All RIGHT, get loaded up, and we will go!" We jumped in the Datsun B210 and hauled ass for Basin. Hell, I was still feeling drunk, and my head was pounding.

On the way to town, I thought to myself, *If this test is so important, maybe I should take it if I go to college on a football scholarship.* I would need a scholarship because I was flat broke, and so were my parents. We had just filed bankruptcy and lost both ranches. My parents had no money, and they never mentioned that I should ever go to college. I had about an hour to think about it on the way to Basin. I finally decided, *Oh, what the hell, maybe I better take this test.*

I walked through the front door of the testing room hungover and my hair standing on end. This chubby girl was sitting at the front registration desk. She looked up at me and said, "Driver's license and $10 please." Shit, I didn't have either. My two buddies each loaned me $5, and she told me I could send a copy of my driver's license to her once I got back home. I sat down and took the long exam with my bloodshot eyes and a pounding headache. This was one of the worst days of my life. I wasn't even sure why I was taking the damn exam.

I did actually end up with a high school diploma and graduated from Greybull High School in 1986. I was proud of myself for graduating. There were times I wasn't sure I would ever see that day. Lana and I were still dating, and I would need to figure out what I would do for a living.

Chapter 11

COLLEGE

I stayed very busy laying moss rock on other people's houses that summer of eighty-six. I laid moss rock on retaining walls, basement foundations, and fireplaces. I even painted some houses and did small remodeling jobs to earn much money. The more skills I learned, the more money I could make. My brother, Wade, called me again one night and asked me if I would go to college. I told him no, I hated school and was making good money. He said, "You really should come down to Chadron and play football with me. It's really fun. I have a nice room in the men's dorm. We could even room together!" He then said, "Besides that, there are plenty of pretty girls to look at down here." I told him I would think about it, but that would be a huge change for me, and I didn't feel good about it. I thought to myself, Am I even good enough to play college football?

Shortly after that conversation, I received a letter in the mail one day from Coach Turner. It was a letter of intent to sign if I was interested in playing football. My best friend Pat was also going to Chadron to play football. Pat and I had been best friends since the third grade. We chewed tobacco together and sat out on the roof of our old lambing shed at night telling each other stories. We played sports together all the way through high school. He was also the one who told our wrestling coach that wrestling was more important than his girlfriend. He was so full of shit he was head over hills in love with that girlfriend.

Pat and my brother, Wade, would be playing football. Maybe it would be fun to go play football in Chadron, I thought to myself. I asked my mother what she would think if I wanted to go to college and play football. She said, "I hope you have a bunch of money because we sure as hell don't have any right now." I thought to myself, *How will I ever pay for college? Will I ever get a football scholarship? If I did get a scholarship, how much would it be worth? What is the cost to go to college anyhow?* I did some research and found I could apply for a Pell Grant. This grant was available to low-income families and would help pay for my college. I applied and succeeded in getting money to help out with the cost. Between what I made that summer and this grant, I could pay for one year of college. If I could go out and prove myself on the field, maybe I would get a scholarship next year.

The next thing that I knew, I was signed up to go to Chadron State College to play football. Wade and I loaded up the Datsun B210 and headed for Chadron, Nebraska. We had that car loaded to the gills. If we hit a small bump on the highway, the leaf springs would drag on the highway and make a horrible sound. I told Wade it was a good thing I installed the four-inch lift kit, or we would be bottomed out. The speed limit was fifty-five miles per hour. If we were loaded with a Casper headwind, that little car wouldn't even do fifty-five miles per hour. We would have two weeks of fall training with the football team before school would begin. We weren't allowed to check into our dorm room until school started, so we would have to stay in a different building with all the football players for two weeks.

I showed up for my first day of football practice. I was nervous, and I had never seen so many big guys in all my life. These guys had huge muscles. It was very evident that many of these guys spent a great deal of time in the weight room and might have been taking steroids as well. The first week was very intense. We did many agility drills so coaches could figure out which players were the fastest, the strongest, and best suited for each position. I set a new college record and did 148 sit-ups in two minutes. I also excelled at push-ups and pull-ups and outdid my competitors in both these physical tests of strength. I soon discovered that the big guys couldn't do hardly any pull-ups. I also realized quickly that I was not near as fast at running compared to most of those trying out for the running-back positions. We would not suit up in pads and do any hitting until week two. This was a good week to get to know all the players. We became close to one another because we spent so much time together during those two weeks. We ate together, played together, went to meetings together, and all slept in the same barracks together.

We padded up the next week and met on the football field. The coach yelled for all the fullbacks to line up next to him. My brother and I both played the fullback position and stood in line together. Once all the fullbacks were in line, I counted nine, and four were African American. They were from California, Illinois, and Texas. After all my accomplishments in high school football, I felt I was a stud at that level in Greybull, Wyoming. Now I'm standing in line with nine fullbacks from all over the country, and most were much bigger and faster than me. I felt I had gone from hero to zero in two seconds. I weighed only 170 pounds!

On our first drill, the coaches stood up a wooden door on the playing field. They positioned a line of linebackers on one side of the door and a line of fullbacks on the other side of the door. The coach would blow his whistle, and the linebacker would come flying around one side of the door or the other. The fullback never knew which side of the door the blitzing linebacker would be coming from, but our job was to block them and protect the quarterback. I stood in line eagerly awaiting my turn as this would be the first physical contact or hitting that we had done. And I was very eager to hit someone.

As I stood in line, I noticed the seniors and juniors were cutting in front of the freshmen and would not allow them to have their turn. Quickly, I was next in line to go, and a senior grabbed me from behind and pulled me out of line and cut in front of me. He never said a word, just cut in front of me. This pissed me off. This was my chance to prove myself, and he was taking that away from me. I grabbed him by the collar on his shoulder pads (horse collar) from behind and quickly jerked him to the ground quickly and hard. When he hit the ground, I put my shoe with cleats on his throat and held him to the ground. I calmly said, "Don't ever cut in front of me again. Do you understand?" He lay with his eyes bulging out and said with a squeak in his voice, "I'M SORRY!" I gave him a hand and helped him up.

My adrenaline was pumping at this point, and I was next to block the blitzing linebacker. The linebacker came at me from the right side of the door, and I quickly met him head-on. *BAM!* The noise was loud as our helmets made contact. It hurt badly, and I didn't want to get up, but I did and soon noticed the linebacker I had hit was knocked unconscious. The coaches came running out to assist this guy and make sure he was all right. I got up and walked back to stand in line. I glared at the senior who had cut in front of me in line as I walked past him. My glare said, "Don't mess with me, or I will knock your ass out as well." That day, I developed respect from the running backs, and I felt I was part of the team.

Football practice was hard, and it consumed all of my time. If we weren't practicing, we were attending meetings at night to watch plays and study other teams we would soon play. It seemed I didn't have time for anything else. It was very time-consuming, and I wasn't even getting "paid" to play like most others on the team. But I was determined to do my best and try to earn a scholarship next year. After the first two weeks, Wade and I would move into our dorm room and room together. We ended up in Andrew's Hall room 148.

It was Monday morning. Wade woke up and said, "Dummy, you need to register for classes today!"

I said, "What do you mean register for classes?"

He said, "You have to go to school!"

I said, "What do you mean go to school? I came here to play football!"

He said, "Yeah, you came here to play football, but you also have to go to school and major in something."

I said, "What do you mean *major* in something?" I honestly thought I was going to school to just play football. I didn't know you needed to take classes and shit like that.

Wade then said, "If you are not sure what you want to major in, just take some GEs the first semester."

I said, "What the hell is a GE?"

"GENERAL ELECTIVE, YOU DUMBASS!" my brother shouted. He then explained these will be classes like math, reading, English, physical science, social studies, etc.

I said, "What the hell do I have to take those classes for? I just took all those classes in high school."

My brother just looked at me and said, "You have a lot to learn, dummy!"

So I got dressed and headed down to the business office to sign up for classes. This was also when I learned that you have to pay for those classes as well. I had to write them a check, and I spent every last dime I had saved in my checking account. My room and board and meals had been paid for with the grant money I had received. Wade and I had gotten a room in the men's dorm versus living in a house off-campus. This way, our utility bill would be paid up for the year and we could turn the thermostat on the heater and leave it on high all day if we wanted. Hell, we didn't even have to worry about shutting off the lights if we didn't want to as the bill was already paid. Three meals a day were also paid for Monday to Friday. I signed up for English I, physical science, algebra, Intro to Humanities, and a couple of other stupid classes.

I left the business hall thinking to myself, *What in the hell have I just done? I'm broke. I just signed up for classes I know absolutely nothing about, and how will I ever become a game warden taking those classes?* I got my class schedule and learned that I had classes only on Mondays, Wednesdays, and Fridays. I thought, *Hell, that's cool. I can take Tuesdays and Thursdays off.* I knew I would need to find a job, so I might work on those days I didn't have school. This might be cool because in high school you had to go to class Monday through Friday from 8:00 a.m. to 3:30 p.m.. I looked for a part-time job. Jobs were hard to find because every college student was looking for part-time work to help pay the bills.

I quickly learned that the college itself had certain work-study jobs you could apply for. I looked over the list of available jobs. There were only a few jobs still available. Some jobs looked pretty fun, but those positions had been filled. The only job left on the sheet was titled library aide. I thought to myself, *Library aide. The only two times I had ever been in a library were the day I checked out three encyclopedias and the day I returned three overdue encyclopedias full of deer hair and blood from when I had hit that damn deer on my motorcycle.* Since that was the only job left, I applied for it and all be damned if they didn't offer the job. The job paid $3.46 an hour, and I could work up to twenty hours per week. This would be perfect for my schedule with two days off from classes each week.

I would soon work nights at the library, and my job was to restock the shelves with books that students had returned. I knew absolutely nothing about the library or its shelving system with all the complicated numbers on the books and the shelves. I would walk around all night with a large cart full of books and try to find the correct location for each book to be shelved again. Some nights I would look for nearly an hour just to put one book back in place. A cute lady from Cody, Wyoming, would help me learn the stocking system. I took several weeks to figure everything out as the library was three floors and contained thousands of books. I would have to wait two weeks to get my first paycheck for $138.40 before taxes. Hopefully, this would be enough for me to eat on weekends and pay for fuel to travel back home every couple of weeks to see my girlfriend Lana.

Lana had attended Northwest Community College in Powell her first semester. She would major in equestrian science. She had a strong love for training and riding horses. Lana was not happy unless she was riding a horse seven days a week. Apparently, she had bought back my crazy mare named Daisy from the ole boy I had sold her to earlier in the sale barn for $55. He said she was crazy as hell and needed an experienced rider. Lana paid the ole boy $50 for the mare and broke and train her while she was attending horse training classes in Powell. The ole boy only lost $5 on that deal but probably ended up in the hospital with broken bones after trying to rider her.

Lana called me one night laughing. She said, "You won't believe what Daisy did today. I crawled on her in the indoor riding arena, and she blew up and went bucking across the arena. She was headed for the wall of the arena, so I jumped off. I looked up, and Daisy ran right through the green fiberglass wall of the arena and took off bucking down the streets of Powell!"

I laughed and said, "Hope you are all right. You can't break a horse that has been traumatized from being pulled behind a three-wheeler at thirty miles per hour."

She laughed and said, "Yeah, I guess Daisy hit a car in the parking lot and flew over the hood of the car and landed on her side. Some cowboy from my class saw this happen and quickly caught Daisy before she could run off again."

I said, "Well, be careful and good luck with that one!"

I knew it would be tough to be separated from Lana while going to school in separate colleges. Wade and I didn't have enough money to pay for phone service in our room, and cell phones had not yet been invented. We would pay our RA (resident advisor) $10 a month so we could borrow his phone and call our girlfriends back home once a week. Sometimes Lana would call the RA's phone, and he would have to run down the hall and get me so I could talk to her. We didn't talk long because we got charged by the minute to visit.

It would be a long time before my first paycheck; and I still had to purchase school supplies such as tablets, pens, pencils, calculator, etc. I went down to Safeway and bought all my school supplies. I shopped carefully because I simply had no money to speak of. I loaded my cart with supplies and went through the checkout line. A handsome young boy was the checker, and he smiled and said, "How are you today? Looks like you are attending college in Chadron with all the school supplies that you are buying."

I said, "Yes, I am attending school, and I'm flat broke until I get my first paycheck."

He smiled and said, "No worries. I will help you out with your school supplies!" He grabbed a couple of items out of my cart and rang them up. He smiled and said, "That will be $2.50!" He then smiled and loaded all the other supplies in a bag and said, "Have a great day. If you need any leftovers from Taco John's, come by at eleven tonight because I will be working there and will take care of you."

I can't believe he had just done that. He probably just saved me about $30 in school supplies. After that day, my brother and I became huge supporters of Safeway and Taco John's. We would only shop when this kid was working. He would check us out each time and charge us pennies on the dollar for everything that we bought. We never asked for any favors. He just did it. It's like he understood what it was like to be flat broke. We would go to Taco John's about three times a week for leftovers after 11:00 p.m. We had more tacos, nachos, and burritos than we could ever eat. We had so many leftovers that we would invite other friends to our room each night to help us eat all the leftover Mexican food. My best buddy Pat lived in a dorm room right above us on the second floor, and he would come over nightly and fill up on the leftovers. And man, could Pat eat. He was a lineman for the Chadron Eagles football team and weighed well over three hundred pounds.

I soon learned I would have to make some extra money somehow. I discovered that the garbage cans in the men's and women's dorms were full of aluminum beer cans every Saturday and Sunday morning. I would fill huge Glad bags with aluminum cans and sell the cans for money downtown at a scrapyard. I also discovered that Chadron, Nebraska, had huge nightcrawlers; and if you went outside at night with a flashlight after a heavy rain, you could collect dozens of nightcrawlers. Back home in Shell, they didn't have nightcrawlers, and the stores sold regular worms for $1.50 per dozen. I bought some worm bedding at the local pet store, and the school cafeteria gave me hundreds of little Styrofoam cups with lids on them. I would soon start a worm farm and keep them under my bed in the men's dorm.

My worm farm grew and grew. Finally, I had eighty dozen nightcrawlers stored underneath my bed. I counted twelve nightcrawlers and put them in the small Styrofoam containers. I hauled the containers back to Shell, and the lovely lady at the Shell store would give me $1.50 per dozen and buy everything that I had. I left with $120 cash in my pocket. This was a hot commodity because you couldn't find nightcrawlers, and fishermen loved to use them for bait!

Once my worm business started taking off, a friend told me an easier way to collect nightcrawlers. He told me to take an extension cord and split the wires and solder a kitchen fork to each wire, stick the forks in the ground about three feet apart, and plug into an electrical outlet. I tried this several times, but no worms ever came up. I wasn't sure it was working, but a house cat did walk nearby and jumped about four feet in the air one day. So apparently, the electrical shock was working. This little trick never worked for me getting worms out of the ground. But my brother and I learned that if you plug a fork into each end of a raw hot dog and plug it into the wall, it will cook a raw hotdog in about two to three seconds.

My buddy Pat and I had physical science class together. This would be the first class I attended in college. The instructor told us we would all need to purchase a book at the bookstore for $50. I looked at Pat and whispered, "FIFTY DOLLARS! Do you have $50?"

He said, "HELL NO!"

I said, "How come we have to purchase our books? They gave them to us for free in high school! We will just come to class every day, take good notes, and pay good attention, and we will be fine." Pat agreed.

We showed up on Friday. The instructor said, "All right, everyone. Take out your books. We have an open-book test today." He also told us we would be having an open-book test every Friday. I looked at Pat and said, "HOLY SHIT, what are we going to do now?"

He shrugged his shoulders as if to say, "HELL if I know." Pat and I placed our names on that exam and never answered a single question on the test. After class, I told Pat we needed to get our asses down to the bookstore and purchase a book before next Friday.

Pat agreed, but not only did we not have $50 for the book, but the library had also sold all their books and they were on back order. We couldn't even share a book because of the open-book exam each Friday. We each ordered a book and prayed that they would be in by next Friday. Next Friday came and still no books. Pat and I sat in class and again miserably failed another exam. On the third Friday, both Pat and I would have to ask the instructor if we could miss test day as we would be traveling at an away game with the football team. The instructor said that would be fine and that we could make the exam up on Monday morning. We were relieved as we still hadn't received our physical science book yet.

On Monday morning the book still had not yet shown up. Here we were in class, getting ready to take another exam. The instructor seemed irritated when he stood up and said, "Everybody who needs to make up the exam, come with me." We followed him down the hall. He placed all of us in a small cold room with very poor lighting. He yelled, "When you are done with the exam, bring it back to class and place it on my desk." He then slammed the door, and the room became even darker. I looked at the questions on the entire exam and could not correctly answer a single question. I thought to myself, *What in the hell is this?* I have been attending class, taking good notes, and paying attention; and I can't even answer a single question on this damn exam. This would be the third exam in a row I had failed. I was very mad. I jumped out of my desk, grabbed my exam, and marched out of the quiet room, slamming the door as I exited. I marched down the hall, walked into the classroom, and slammed my exam on the instructor's desk as he was giving a lecture to other students in the class. I looked at the instructor with glaring eyes and shouted, "WHAT IN THE HELL IS THIS?"

The instructor calmly walked over to me and whispered, "Come test day, there were sixteen students absent from my class! Quite frankly, Scott, that pissed me off, so I made up my exam that was much more difficult than the other students' exam who attended the class on Friday."

I stated very firmly, "THAT IS BULLSHIT. I'M HAVING A TOUGH-ENOUGH TIME PASSING YOUR CLASS AS IT IS!"

The instructor responded, "I have been meaning to visit with you about this. Meet me in my office after class."

I said, "Yes, SIR!"

I met with the instructor after class down the hall in his office. He asked me a couple of questions about the table of elements chart we had been studying. I was surprised that I answered his questions correctly. He then said, "See, Scott, you understand all this. How come you can't pass one of my exams?"

I said, "I'm sorry, sir, I don't have a book for the open-book tests every Friday."

He said, "Oh, I'm sorry, Scott. Why don't you have a book?"

I lied and said, "I had a book, and someone stole it. I went down to the bookstore to buy another one, and they were sold out."

He said, "Oh my god, someone stole your book? Why didn't you say something earlier? Take my book. Don't drop this class. If you work with me, I will work with you!"

I thanked him for the book and told him I would return it just when my new book came in. Boy, was Pat going to be upset with me. I had a book now, and it didn't cost me a dime.

The instructor then asked me what I was good at in life. I told him I really never excelled in school at anything except sports, PE class, woods, and welding. He said, "We here at Chadron State College have a state-of-the-arts industrial technology program! I suggest you go and talk to Dr. Miller across the street, and he can tell you about their program!"

I thanked my instructor and shook his hand and said, "I will pass the next exam. I promise you that, sir!"

I went across the street to talk with Dr. Miller. Dr. Miller was an older gentleman who dressed very nicely and sat behind a big oak desk wearing a suit and tie. I was very nervous to walk into his office and talk with him. Dr. Miller greeted me at the door. He shook my hand as he introduced himself and asked me to sit down at a large table in his office.

After visiting with Dr. Miller for a few minutes, I felt at ease while talking to him. He was a smooth talker and seemed very confident with everything that he said. He was a good listener and asked a lot of questions about me. He finally said, "Scott, what do you want to do for a living for the next thirty years of your life?"

I responded, "Dr. Miller, I would really like to become a game warden for the Wyoming Game & Fish Department someday!"

He sat back in his chair and rubbed his fingers through his thin hair and said, "Scott, I'm going to be very truthful with you. The Wyoming Game & Fish Department is not hiring right now. They have no retirements, and therefore, they have no open positions for a game warden. You could spend the next four to five years getting a wildlife management degree and then spend another four to five years working temporary jobs for no benefits and low pay before you ever land a permanent job as a Wyoming game warden."

I thought to myself, *Man, I didn't know it would be that difficult to get a job as a Wyoming game warden.* This news crushed me. I will never forget those strong words. I didn't want to go to college for four to five years and then work four to five years in temporary positions to finally get a permanent job. He then said, "Scott, they have an extremely competitive exam that you must first pass. There will be hundreds of applicants who will take the exam. If you are lucky enough to pass, you will then go through a rigorous background check, take a polygraph test, go through oral interviews, and take a psychological exam. The whole process is very competitive, and if you are one of the lucky few to make it through the whole process, there are no jobs available." He then told me they had a very great industrial technology program with state-of-the-art equipment, and they placed over 92 percent of their teachers within the first year after graduation. This sounded good, and I felt it might be something that I was very good at and would enjoy. I still wanted to be a game warden, but this information had taken the wind out of my sails.

I ended up passing my next physical science exam with a C. The instructor gave me a D for a final grade that semester. I did all right in the other classes, except English. I had to read and write a book report for my final exam in English. I got the book report back after the instructor had graded it. I had never seen so much red ink in my entire life. He wrote a large F across the entire front page with a note that read, "This is absolutely horrible! Please consider taking a fourth-grade remedial English class in writing before pursuing any other classes related to English." His penmanship was sloppy. I could tell he was pissed when he wrote his comments. This hurt my feelings; but when you misspell every other word in a book report, you'll have that. We didn't have spellcheck back then. I would end up with a 1.97 GPA at the end of my first semester. The D in physical science helped a little, but at least he passed me considering I had only received a C on one exam, and that's because he loaned me his book.

I learned a great deal about how the school worked after the first semester. Things would be smoother the second semester. I signed up for classes in the industrial technology program to see if I would not only like it better but also excel at it. I hated my job at the library and discovered that the college was looking for a poolroom supervisor. This was not swimming but a billiards pool. I loved to shoot pool, and this job would be my calling in life. There were many applicants for this job, but I prevailed and landed the job. I was so excited. My boss said I could work nights and weekends, and I could work up to forty hours a week if I wanted to.

This job would beat the hell out of shelving books for a living in the library. I took the job and loved it. When it was slow, I could shoot pool myself. I soon learned who the pool sharks were on campus, and we would shoot pool for hours on end. I became so good at the pool I never once worried about losing a game to anyone. I was good enough I would purposely leave myself with a bank shot for the next shot and make it nearly all the time. I was getting paid to play, so to speak. I was not only getting paid to play but also soon played my opponents for money. We would generally play for $1 per game but sometimes $5 per game.

You can play a lot of games over an eight- or even a four-hour work shift. When we tired of playing pool, sometimes we would fire up a poker game on my supervisor's desk in the poolroom. We always played for money. I soon learned that I was supplementing my income with the money I had won from playing pool and poker. I had also met a neat lady who cooked pizza next door, and she would send me home with a free large meat lover's pizza each night at the end of my shift. Wade and I had so much free food in our room we would have four to five friends come over each night and watch *Cheers* at ten thirty-five each night and eat pizza and leftover Taco John's food mixed with Milwaukee's Best beer.

The second semester I signed up for seven classes worth eighteen elective credits. They were all classes in the industrial technology major. I decided that for the first time in my life, I would actually apply myself and study, do my homework, and just do the best I could do. I soon learned that if I would go back to my room after classes each day and complete my homework, I could have my weekends off from doing schoolwork. I learned how to take good notes and how to study for an exam the night before.

Soon I would be getting As on most of my exams. At the end of the semester, I couldn't believe my eyes when I looked at my report card. I had received six As and one B. I was so excited. This was the first time in my life I had actually applied myself, and I received mostly all As. I was having fun now. I looked in the mirror with a smile on my face and said, *You can do this, Scott. Great job!* This gave me the confidence to keep plugging forward. Dr. Miller had put me on the right path to success, and my physical science teacher had recommended me to Dr. Miller all because I had never purchased a book and couldn't pass his exams. Sometimes things happen for a reason.

I survived my first year of college, went back home to Shell, and worked hard all summer. I would again lay moss rock on houses, paint houses, and do small remodeling jobs. I was now majoring in industrial technology and wanted to get more experience learning how to build houses. I had earned enough money to pay for my second year of college, but there was little money left once all the bills were paid. I was excited that I might be getting a football scholarship for my second year playing football. Lana and I were still dating, and she had decided that she would attend school with me at Chadron State College.

Once back at Chadron for my second year of college, I received word that the head football coach had either been fired or retired. We now had a new football coach. I went out for football my second year and was told by my new head coach there was no funding available for a scholarship; but if I again went out and proved myself, I could earn a scholarship the next year. I again went out for football and practiced hard that year. Football took up all my spare time. I would again fill my schedule with classes that went toward my major and again worked as the supervisor of the poolroom. Lana signed up for general elective classes and lived in the high-rise girls' dormitory or, as some men called it, "the hog rise."

My brother and I continued to room together in room 148 in Andrews Hall. We never had much patience with other students who would party into the wee hours of the night and play loud music. Typically, these dorm parties would start at about 2:00 a.m. and continue through the night with sounds of loud music and girls laughing. One night at about two, my brother, Wade, and I were lying in bed and our room suites who shared our bathroom and lived in the room next door had a loud party. My brother got out of bed and knocked on their door. Some guy opened the door and said, "What do you want?"

My brother said, "Could you please turn your stereo down so that my brother and I can get some sleep tonight?"

The drunk man responded by slamming the door in my brother's face.

My brother went back to his bed and lay down for a couple of minutes. Quickly, someone in the other room turned the stereo up even louder. My brother looked over at me while lying in bed and said, "Dummy, I'm losing my patience!" Wade lay there in bed for a couple more minutes, then very calmly got out of bed, and grabbed his ten-inch stainless-steel .44 magnum Ruger Redhawk revolver out of the dresser drawer. He walked through the bathroom wearing only his white underwear and carrying his long-barreled stainless-steel pistol. He kicked the door open, cocked his long-barreled pistol as he aimed it at their stereo, and yelled, "I SAID TURN DOWN THE FUCKING STEREO NOW!" The girls in the room screamed, and everybody in the room left immediately. Wade walked over and turned off the stereo and shut their light off. These two roommates moved out the next day and never returned. So Wade and I now had another dorm room to ourselves for the rest of the semester.

After a few of those kinds of moments, my brother and I had a reputation in Andrew Hall from others who lived in the same dorm. They called us those "crazy-ass brothers who lived in room 148 in Andrews Hall." If you were being drunk and disorderly after hours, my brother and I would escort you out of the building. If you need an "ass-whooping," my brother and I would gladly give you one. Soon, nobody would ever live in the room next to us, and we would have a spare room every semester to ourselves.

We later turned this room into our reloading room. I'm not sure that you were supposed to have firearms in your dorm room, but we damn sure did and plenty of them. We loaded up a rock tumbler with miniature rice. We would then dump all our empty brass into the tumbler and let it run all day and night to shine our brass for reloading ammunition. Other students would walk down the hall and stop and listen on the outside of the door to figure out what that noise was. Once our brass was polished, we would invite a couple of friends over to drink Old Milwaukee beer and reload shells all night long. When we were too drunk to reload, we would start a card game called pitch. We would play pitch until the wee hours of the morning or until our case of Old Milwaukee beer was gone, whichever came first.

I would continue to supervise the poolroom and shoot as much pool as I could. I loved the game and became very good at it. On Friday nights, I would play snooker for about four to five hours on an eight-foot table. The balls and pockets were smaller, so you would have to be very accurate to make a shot. Once I was practiced up on that table, I would head down to the bars on Friday night and play for money and drinks.

The pool tables I would be playing on were only six-foot tables and had much bigger pockets to put the balls in than the snooker table at college. These smaller tables made the game of pool seem easy after playing on the eight-foot snooker table all afternoon. I would generally shoot pool from about 8:00 p.m. until closing time around 2:00 a.m. I rarely would lose a game and drink for free all night long. Back then, we played for $1 a game and an occasional drink. Over time, the players who got to know me well would no longer gamble with me on a game of pool. I would bring my winnings home each night and shove my dollar bills in an empty shoebox in the closet. At the end of that semester, I discovered that I had won $1,578 from the shooting pool for $1 per game.

At the end of my second year of college, I made the dean's list with my grades. I actually liked school more and more. I had more freedom from my parents, I developed some good friends, and I was still enjoying playing football. I learned early on to do all my homework during the week. That way, the weekends were mine to do whatever I wanted to do. I also learned how to take good notes during class and how to study before an exam. I learned to go over my notes several times at night before bed. The next morning all the information was crystal clear in my head during test time.

Lana and I took a history class together that semester. We had to pick a book and read it and write a book report for our final grade. We picked the same book except I never got time to read mine. The morning of test day, I asked Lana to explain the book as I had not read mine. She was not impressed and did not want to give me any information on the book. I think she wanted to see me fail. She loved to read, and I didn't. I finally pried a few facts about the book out of her so I could write a final report. When the smoke cleared, she got a B on her book report, and I got an A. She was mad and said, "That just goes to show what a BULLSHITTER you really are!"

I just smiled and said, "That's Mr. Bullshitter to you, ma'am!"

During that semester, I had stopped by to see my grandma Peggy in Greybull. We discussed everyone in the family for several hours. She told me things about my family I didn't know before. It seemed she wanted to make sure that she had told me everything about our family. We visited for about four hours. She gave me a hug and $10 for gas money to get back to college. Little did I know this would be the last time I ever got to talk to my grandma Peggy ever again. She soon became very sick after that visit and was diagnosed with pancreatic cancer. My mother called me at college and told me I needed to come home quickly as Grandma Peggy was in the hospital and not doing well.

Wade and I made a quick trip from Chadron, Nebraska, to Powell, Wyoming, to visit my grandma Peggy in the hospital. When we arrived, everyone was standing in the waiting room sobbing. My grandma Peggy had just passed away. I felt horrible. I never even got to say goodbye. The last time I had talked to her, she was doing fine. What had happened to her so quickly? Is this why she shared all the family stories with me that one day? I'll never forget that day as it was Mother's Day.

I remember driving back home to Shell that night in an absolute blizzard. It must have snowed nearly two feet that night—very rare for this storm in May! Was it my grandma Peggy saying her last goodbye to the world? I felt very heartbroken. Both of my grandparents had now passed away. When I cleaned out her top dresser drawer, I found the first arrowhead I had ever found nearly twelve years ago. She had kept it in a safe place for me and wrapped it in a small white cloth. This made me cry thinking of all the memories I had with my grandparents—arrowhead hunting, fishing, and camping—as a young child over the years. I was pretty blessed to have had them as my grandparents.

I returned home to Shell that summer and worked hard laying moss rock and painting houses. My business started to take off. I stayed as busy as I wanted to be. I would again earn enough money to pay for another year of college. Lana had decided that she wanted to finish her associate's degree in equestrian science at Northwest Community College in Powell. I again went out for college football under our new head coach. This would be my third year playing football. The head coach apologized and said, "Scott, I'm sorry we have no scholarship money again this year, but if you keep proving yourself, I will see that you get a scholarship." My heart sank. I had been working so hard for this scholarship, and football was taking up a huge amount of my time I could be working and making additional money.

I was about halfway through the football season that year. It was a hot day. The coach put me on the service team. The service team was the third-string offense running plays against the first-string defense. I was a running back and would run the ball often. It soon dawned on me that the third-string offense simply couldn't block the first-string defense. And as a ball-handler, I was getting *killed* almost every play. The second I would get the ball, about four to five large defensive players would hit me hard. Each time I got hit, it would take me longer and longer to get back up. Finally, a linebacker came blitzing through the line untouched and hit my shin bone head-on with his helmet. He blew both my legs out from underneath me. I lay there on the field in excruciating pain. I looked down at my shin bone. I had a knot about the size of a baseball on my shin with blood trickling out all the way around the wound.

It hurt so badly I just wanted to scream. I slowly got up and limped back to the huddle. I reached the huddle and listened to the next play called by the quarterback. DAMMIT, they were handing the ball off to me again to run right up the middle. I hadn't even recovered from the previous play, and nobody gave a shit about my injury. I turned and walked out of the huddle toward the locker room. I had had it. I was done. I was quitting football. It finally dawned on me, *What in the hell am I doing out here day after day getting the shit knocked out of me? I'm getting no scholarship, I'm not starting, and I have no time for anything else in my life.* I started crying. I had never quit anything in my life. Was I making the right decision? What would my brother, Wade, my best friend Pat, and my parents think of me now?

What would Lana think of me? What would her parents think of me? What would all my friends back home think of me? And what would my father up in heaven think of me? I had let everybody down! I knew what they would think of me—I'm a goddamn pussy! A quitter! I threw my helmet across the locker room and sat down on the bench and bawled. Quickly, I felt someone put their hand on my shoulder. I looked up, and it was my coach. He said, "What's wrong, Scott?"

I said, "COACH, I QUIT. I HAVE FINALLY HAD IT!"

The coach calmly said, "Scott, I really like you, and I really would like you to reconsider your decision. You are a very good player. Your day will soon come on the playing field."

I said, "Thanks, Coach. I really appreciate that, but I'm done!!" He padded my shoulder with his hand and turned and walked away. I just sat there and bawled. This was the first thing in my life I had ever quit. My mother always taught me, if you start something, you better damn sure finish it. I was not sure how I would tell my mother or my brother the news I had quit football.

I'm sure I let many people down with my decision that day including myself. I soon realized that I actually had more time to myself. I could actually study after school or go to my room and just take a nap before I had to work in the pool hall. I felt like a huge weight had been lifted off my shoulders. I could even go hunting and fishing after class. That was a hell of a lot more fun than getting the shit kicked out of me every day out on the football field! Once football had ended for me, I spent more time studying and getting my homework done after each class. I started to actually enjoy school and my classes. My classes would continue to get tougher and more involved with professional-level teaching classes.

The next semester Lana quit calling me as often. She seemed distracted when we did talk on the phone. She would be quiet on the phone as if she was no longer interested in me or what I had to say. At the end of the conversation, I would say, "I love you, honey!"

She would reply, "Good night!"

This was breaking my heart. Was my girlfriend seeing someone else? Was she no longer interested in me? What was wrong with her? All these thoughts went through my head. I would try to call her every night instead of just on weekends. Some nights she would answer the phone; other nights she wouldn't. When we did talk, she was quiet. She eventually quit calling me altogether. Something was wrong. The more that I tried, the worse our relationship became. Finally, I lost my patience and told her I had tried everything in my power to make the relationship happen and that I could no longer do it anymore. I yelled at her on the phone and said, "I'M DONE!" I slammed the phone down.

I cried and went for a long walk that night on campus. My life seemed like it was in turmoil. I had quit football, lost my girlfriend, and probably let my whole family down. Maybe Lana lost interest in me because I had quit football? Was Lana seeing someone else? Is it the cowboy who caught her horse Daisy out in the parking lot that day that her horse ran through the wall of the indoor riding arena? Whatever it was, my heart was broken. I had never felt this down in my entire life! I would focus my time on working more hours at the poolroom. I also drank more than normal and participated in all-night poker games with a handful of college wrestlers.

These wrestlers were tough and crazy and took their poker games very seriously. If you were new to the table and winning their money, they wouldn't let you leave the table. Sometimes if you were ahead in the game, they would order pizza and beer and make whoever was winning pay the bill. You didn't dare argue with them or the leader, who was named Bob, or he would kick your ass and you would never be invited back to play with them. Bob was tough. He loved to box. He was an exceptionally good college wrestler, and he loved to fight. Plus, he was very hotheaded.

Once I figured out how they operated, I would have to sneak money into my pockets while we were playing so they didn't notice winning. At the end of the night, Bob would go around the table and ask how much you won or how much you lost. I would say, "I think I broke even!"

He would say, "Well, where in the hell did all the money go if you broke even?"

I slowly got up and walked away from the table with my shirt untucked and hanging over my pockets. When I got back to my room that night, I pulled $48 in quarters out of my back pockets of my jeans. I didn't pay for pizza or beer, and I got out of there alive. They were tough as hell but not very smart!

One night, while I was supervising the poolroom, a Native American walked and said, "I hear you are pretty good. Rack them up!"

I said, "I am pretty good. Why don't you rack 'em up?"

He racked up the balls. I broke them with the cue ball and quickly ran all the balls off the table. The next game I gave him a shot, and he ran the table on me. We would play for hours that night. This guy was an exceptional pool shooter. If he couldn't run the table, I could! I never knew his name. I just called him Indian. He would show up several times a week, and we would battle it out. If I missed a shot, he would run the table almost every time. I thought to myself, *Man, this guy can shoot pool. If we team up and go downtown to the bars at night, we could hustle people for some serious cash.* I asked him if he was interested in the idea, and he said, "You betcha, man!" He shook my hand.

The Indian took his pool very seriously. He once told me that the game of pool was like a jungle: if you make one mistake, you are dead. We later teamed up and went downtown to the bars. Nobody could beat us, and we made good money. We would have to let our opponents win sometimes. Then we would up the bet and barely win the next game. One thing I learned quickly: when you add alcohol and money to a game of pool, fights broke out often. The Indian was a talker. He would talk smack the entire game, get the opponent flustered, and then run the table. This would not only piss off the opponent. They would want to play another game and up the ante. One Friday night, we would soon meet our match down at the bar.

Two guys were playing on a table. They had owned the table all night. Nobody could beat them. One guy was built and wore a tank top with bulging muscles and tattoos. He looked like he was on steroids, and he was very hotheaded and cocky. His partner was short and very skinny and had a chain attached to his wallet in his back pocket. He wore a cap with a sharp bend in the brim. The brim looked like he had been sticking his head in a mailbox looking for his government subsidy check every day. The cap was black and read *Peterbilt.* He had a lot of energy and was very cocky as he wheeled around the table, making a bank shot after bank shot. The Indian looked at me and said, "Here is where we will make our money tonight. Put your quarters on the table and let's play them next."

I placed my quarters on the table, and we were soon playing them. They told us if we wanted to play them, it would be $10 per player. This would be high stakes for what we were used to playing. We would lose the first three games, and it would cost us $30 apiece. We were not hustling.

They were just flat-out shooting us. In the fourth game, the Indian said, "You guys think you are so good. Let's play for $100 per player." I couldn't believe what I was hearing. I didn't have this money, and neither did he. They both agreed to $100 per player, and we shook hands.

They broke first and ran the table down to the eight ball. The big guy had a short and "straight in" shot at the eight ball. The Indian bent over as he was taking the shot and said, "Hey, man, whatever you do, don't miss that straight-in shot!"

The big guy got pissed and took his eye off the ball as he looked at the Indian and shot the ball hard. The big guy looked at the Indian as he took the shot and said, "Fuck you!" He missed the shot!

The Indian said, "Man, you shouldn't have done that. Thanks for the victory!" The Indian quickly ran all the balls off the table and sank the eight ball. Holy shit, we had just won the game for $100 apiece. "Time to pay up, boys!" the Indian said.

The big guy walked up to me and said, "We have a small problem. My partner thought I had the money, and I thought he had the money. We have been buying drinks all night, and we don't have the cash!"

I said, "That's bullshit. You don't make a bet if you don't have the money!"

He said, "What are you going to do about it?"

I said, "I'm going to kick your ass."

The fight was on. He took a swing at me. I ducked and pushed him backward over a table with drinks on it. I quickly jumped on top of him and was trying to punch him when bar security personnel pulled me off the top of him and told us to leave the bar. The big guy said, "I'll leave the bar and go out in my car and get my checkbook if you want paid!"

I said, "Good idea. You should have done that a few minutes ago!"

He left the bar and soon returned with his checkbook. He opened up the checkbook and shoved it in my face and said, "Look here. I'm out of checks. Isn't that just too bad?"

By now, my brother, Wade, had come over to see what all the racket was about. I said, "Yeah, that is too bad," and I took a swing at him. I missed with my punch. The security personnel again intervened and kicked us out of the bar. We got into an argument outside of the bar. Finally, the big guy yelled, "If you want paid, come to my house at 221 Pine Street!" He then took off running and jumped into his car and sped off, leaving black marks on the pavement.

My brother said, "Shit, we should have kicked their asses while we were in the bar!"

The Indian said, "Shit, man, this is getting too crazy for me. If you can collect my money, you can have it. I'm out of here!"

My brother said, "Get in the truck. Let's follow them to their house!"

We soon found their address, and the big guy's car was parked out front of the house in the street. There were no lights on in the house or on the front porch. I told my brother to wait in the car. I would go bang on the front door of their house. My brother said, "Be careful. I have my pistol, and I have your backside!" I walked onto the dark porch and banged on the front door. The big guy answered the door and yelled, "IF YOU WANT PAID, GET YOUR ASS IN THE HOUSE WHILE I SEARCH FOR MY CHECKBOOK!"

I said, "You have had plenty of time to find your checkbook. Go find it and bring me a check for $200!"

He said, "If you won't come in, you'll be waiting out there a long damn time for your check!" He slammed the door in my face. I stood there for about five minutes and banged hard on the door again. *BANG, BANG, BANG!*

The door quickly opened. The big guy reached out of the door, grabbed me around the neck with both hands, and tried to pull me into the house! I was expecting something and quickly pulled back and got away from his tight grip. He slammed the door in my face. Wade yelled, "GET YOUR ASS OUT OF THERE!" I ran for the car and turned my head back toward the house to see what was going on. There was a long skinny window on each side of the door with a light curtain that hung over the window from the inside of the house. They had turned on the kitchen light in the house so you could now see into the house through the light curtain. Standing next to the window on the left side of the front door was the skinny dude holding a shotgun. I could clearly see the silhouette of his body and the shotgun. I ran to our car and jumped in quickly. I told my brother, "Screw this. They just tried to pull me into their damn house and shoot me over $200!"

My brother said, "Dammit, we should have kicked their asses while we were in the bar!"

We went back to our dorm room. It was 2:00 a.m. We both crawled into bed. I lay there awake thinking to myself, *I almost just got shot tonight over $200, not to mention I was in a fight with a person who was bigger and possibly stronger than me and was probably on drugs.* My brother lay in bed for a while and quickly jumped out of bed. I said, "What are you doing?"

He said, "I'm pissed. I'm going to drive down there, kick their asses, and get your money!"

I said, "No, don't do it. They are on drugs and will shoot your ass!"

Out the door went my brother, Wade. He was mad, and I was worried about him. He came back about two hours later and said, "You were right. They are both still standing on each side of the door holding shotguns in their hands." I never did see that couple again. The Indian and I never did get paid.

Lana and I would end up getting back together after a couple of weeks. I'm not sure what happened there, but I suspect her roommate was trying to talk her out of having a long-distance relationship with me when there were plenty of other cowboys to chase around campus. I would finish my junior year of college again with good grades. I also had a reputation as being a very good arm wrestler. I would have wrestlers and large linemen from the football team wanting to arm wrestle me. It didn't matter how big or how strong they were. I could easily beat them. I would beat them so fast that they would often say, "Shit, do that again. I wasn't ready!" At this point in my life, I had never lost an arm-wrestling match. It would upset my buddy Pat and my brother, Wade, they couldn't beat me after all the hours they had spent in the weight room lifting weights. Back then, I always believed that if you were good at shooting pool, arm wrestling, and playing poker, you could always earn extra money to survive. But if you weren't careful and took it too far, you could also end up broke or even shot.

That summer Lana would race her horse in a one-hundred-mile horse race in the Bighorn Mountains. She loved riding horses and had always wanted to enter this race. They would leave the start line at 5:00 a.m. and race up the Bighorn Mountains and across the top and back down to the starting area. If you were good enough to even finish the race, you would end up at the finishing line after 8:00 p.m. The race was held in July, and the weather was warm, reaching temperatures of one hundred degrees. This race was very strenuous on the horse and the rider.

She would lead seventy-five miles into the race. She stopped to water her horse when the gal in second place came running up behind her horse. This sudden activity spooked her horse. Her horse reared up in the air while drinking out of the small creek. The horse came down hard and landed its front foot on a sharp rock in the creek. This caused her horse to become lame, and Lana could no longer ride her horse to finish the race. She was so determined to finish the race she took off jogging and leading the injured horse for the next twenty-five miles. Lana finished the race in second place that year. The next week she became very sick and was throwing up every day. She was very cranky to be around and didn't feel good at all. I asked her if she had drunk any water from the mountain streams while running in the horse race. She said she had drunk a bunch of water while running the last twenty-five miles of the race. I said, "Maybe you should go to the doctor and get tested for *Giardia.*"

She went to the doctor the next day and called me from her parents' house that afternoon. She said, "We need to talk. I went to the doctor today."

I said, "Oh, what is wrong with you?"

She said, "I'M PREGNANT!"

I couldn't respond. My life flashed in front of me. What about college? How will we be able to pay for this and raise a child? Will I have to quit school and find a real job? Before I could respond, she said, "My mother already knows, but you will need to tell your parents and my father!" I told her I loved her and that I would come over later and visit with her and her father. This would not be an easy conversation as her father was a strong Christian and didn't believe in having a sexual relationship unless you were married. I waited for my parents to come home from work. They both walked in the door together. I wasn't sure what to say to them as they came through the front door of our house.

I looked at my mother and said, "Well, are you ready to retire?"

She said, "Why? Did I win the lottery?"

I said, "No, you are going to be a grandma!"

Martin looked at me and said, "Let me grab us a beer, and we can talk about this." They both hugged me and supported me. I thought they might be mad at me, but they were both happy for both of us. They didn't ask many questions. I told them I needed to tell Lana's father the news. This would be very difficult for me to do as I didn't feel like I had a very good relationship with her father.

Would he yell at me and be mad? Would he support us? Would he be naive enough to think that his daughter had not had sex with me? I drove the five miles with butterflies in my stomach. What would I say to him? How would I start the conversation? When I pulled into the driveway, he was mowing the grass in the front yard. He shut the lawnmower off and came walking over to me. He was wearing a white T-shirt and a red bandana around his head. The day was hot, and he had sweat dripping off his forehead and down his cheeks. He walked over to me and extended his arms to give me a big hug. We hugged to where I almost cried. It was difficult for me to hug another man. It just felt uncomfortable. He never said a word and went back to mowing the lawn. He didn't need to say anything that day. I knew that he knew, and he just let me know that he loved and supported both of us with the big hug he gave me that day.

I had always planned on marrying Lana someday. I just hadn't thought much about it until this time in my life, and we had never discussed it before. We had big decisions to make. Should we get married right away? Should we get married over Christmas break when I would be home from college on break? We discussed our options and got married at the end of August right before I would go back to college to finish my senior year. The only problem was it was already the beginning of August, and I had booked a caribou hunt in Alaska for two weeks in August and wouldn't be returning home until the twenty-fifth of August. It was decided that we would get married on August 26 and that I would travel to college on 27 and begin my senior year on August 28. So much for having any time for a honeymoon.

There were times during the caribou hunt I wasn't sure I would survive to make it back home and get married between the crazy bush pilots and getting lost out in the tundra while hunting. But I survived and returned home on August 25. My buddies from college had shown up at my house in Shell and wanted to have a bachelor's party for me that very night. So we moved into a vacant house trailer on our property and drank copious amounts of alcohol and played poker until the sun came up the next morning. I would not recommend this to anyone the day before your marriage. The next thing I knew, my best buddy Pat was helping me get fit into a white tuxedo. He gave me a fist full of Aleve and said, "Hurry up. We need to get going before we are late."

The wedding would be held at Lana's parents' ranch at the base of the Bighorn Mountains. This was a beautiful location right along Shell Creek, with all the cottonwood trees showing their fall colors along the creek. The men that would be standing by my side at the wedding were my brother, Wade, my best friend Pat, and my little brother, Dan. Everyone looked nicely dressed in their white tuxedos. Apparently, I was to ride my dirt bike to the wedding and show up as everyone was seated. Lana was to come riding in on her horse and be greeted by her father just before he walked her down the flowered aisle. The wedding was nice and well attended. Lana looked beautiful in her wedding dress.

Our preacher would be the bus driver I had as a kid at Bear Creek Ranch, the man who taught Wade and me how to trap. The ceremony was nice. I kissed Lana and walked her down the aisle. Once at the end of the aisle, I jumped on my motorcycle and rode off into the sunset, pulling a wheelie. Lana jumped on her black mare named Dusty and galloped off the other direction on her horse with her wedding dress flapping in the wind behind her horse. Thank god, I didn't go over backward on my motorcycle that day while riding a wheelie. I would have ruined my rented tuxedo and had to pay for it. The day went fast, and the night went faster. Soon the next morning, I would be headed for college.

My senior year at college was very stressful. I had several tough classes that semester, and I needed to do well and hopefully get selected to do my student teaching at a high school somewhere in Wyoming later in the spring that year. Would I actually graduate from college with a teaching degree? Where would I be doing my student teaching? Was I good enough to be a teacher in the industrial technology field? Did I make the correct decision to not pursue my career as a game warden? These were all the questions that ran through my mind daily. Plus, I had just got married and would soon become a father. Lana had stayed home at the ranch to be close to her parents and work on the ranch that summer and fall. This was a stressful time for me to be away from Lana and have to take upper-level classes to graduate from college.

I continued playing poker with the wrestlers and shooting pool with the Indian to make any extra money I could. My nightcrawlers under my bed caught a disease, and all died. Boy, did that smell good. I would do well in all my classes that semester and again made the A honor roll. I was also selected to do my student teaching at the high school in Douglas, Wyoming, for three months in the spring. I would need to find a place to live while in Douglas, and I had little money. I tried to think of anybody I knew who lived in Douglas and could help me out with a place to live for three months. I finally remembered that I had an aunt and uncle who lived in Douglas, and my uncle had a good-paying job in the oil field and a nice two-story log home. Wade and I had stayed with them in their beautiful log home nearly ten years ago. I remembered little about it, but they were the first people I knew who actually had HBO and could afford it. I might get their phone number from my mother and call them up to see if they had an extra bed for me to sleep in for three months.

I eventually got ahold of my aunt. She was a sweet lady. She was so excited that I had called her. I told her I had been selected to do my student teaching in Douglas and was looking for a place to stay for about three months. She said, "Oh, please come stay with us. We would love to have you. We will clean out the little office and make a bedroom for you to stay in. Oh, I'm so excited. We have three kids, and you guys will have so much fun together!" She gave me her address and told me to keep in touch. "I AM SO EXCITED TO SEE YOU!" she screeched.

The day came. I loaded up all my personal belongings and headed for Douglas, Wyoming. While searching for my aunt's address, I was on the south side of the railroad tracks in the poor part of town. This didn't look familiar. The last time I stayed with my aunt and uncle, they had a nice log home out in the country. Now, I was driving through a low-income housing complex filled with single-wide trailers that had truck tires on the roof to hold down the metal roofing to keep it from blowing off during high winds. I had finally found the correct address and couldn't believe what I was seeing. They no longer had a beautiful two-story log home. They were living in a single-wide trailer house with tires on the roof. My aunt came running out of the trailer and greeted me with a big hug. She said, "I'm so glad to see you. Please grab your stuff and come in and make yourself at home."

She took me down the hall and showed me my bedroom. It was a small room with a single-wide bed and a small desk. The room was about eight feet by ten feet and had no windows. She said, "Here is your bedroom. Please make yourself at home." I felt very grateful to have a place to stay, but I thought to myself, *What have I just got myself into?* She told me that my uncle would be gone for several weeks, and she introduced me to her kids. She had three boys. Two were high school age, and the youngest was in fifth grade. They seemed excited to see me, but I could sense that something was wrong. They soon disappeared into their bedrooms to play video games. I visited with my aunt for a while and got caught up on some family stories before going to bed. I crawled into my small bed and turned off the light. I thought to myself, *She never did mention anything about my uncle. I wonder why.* I had butterflies in my stomach. I would be getting up early in the morning and head for the high school to begin three months of student teaching.

I had a difficult time falling asleep that night with the sound of the heavy wind blowing the metal roofing. The small bedroom didn't have a heater and became very cold quickly once I closed the bedroom door for privacy. I felt alone. I had left all my friends at college and my warm dorm room. I had been married for about six months and had only seen my wife a few times. Lana was pregnant and would be due in a few short weeks. Where was my life headed? What was I doing here in Douglas, Wyoming, right now?

Morning came early, and I soon realized that they had only one bathroom in the trailer. All the kids were taking showers. If I waited for them all to shower, I would be late for my first day of teaching. I was hungry, but nobody was eating any breakfast, and I had bought no groceries yet.

I felt terrible. I would start my first day of teaching without a clean shave and a shower. I stopped at a gas station and purchased a breakfast burrito. I had my newly purchased suit and tie on and even purchased a leather briefcase. I was flat broke again but would need to purchase groceries after school and bring them to the trailer house. I would also have to figure out a shower schedule with the three boys by tomorrow morning. I met all the teachers in the industrial technology program that day. What a great bunch of highly trained staff with one of the best state-of-the-art equipment in the entire state. I would work on lesson plans and take over teaching in each class. I taught mechanical drafting, auto mechanics, advanced welding, and woods class. The kids were highly trained and motivated to learn and work hard.

I couldn't weld better than the kids in my class. They would enter welding and automotive competitions with other high schools and win them all. Kids would earn scholarships at tech schools and auto mechanic schools for winning competitions. It was an excellent program. Kids excelled to do well, which made teaching them easy. Douglas High School was known across Wyoming for having one of the best industrial technology programs in the state. It was a smooth transition for me, and I enjoyed working with all the instructors. I got to where I actually looked forward to teaching every day, and I knew that I would be successful in this school and their program.

A couple of weeks had gone by, and things were going smooth back home at the trailer. We figured out a shower schedule, and the oldest boy worked nights at Pizza Hut. He would bring home pizza and breadsticks every night after work. I would learn to eat pizza for dinner and breakfast each morning. I offered to give my aunt money to help pay the bills, but she would not take any. I still hadn't seen my uncle, and the family never talked about him. I thought to myself, *They must have made a bunch of money during the oil boom to afford their nice log home and then something went wrong financially, causing them to lose or sell their nice home and end up in the trailer house.* I did not judge them for this. My aunt was a very special and nice lady. I crawled in bed one night and again lay there listening to the metal roof flap in the wind. I heard the phone ring down the hall at about 10:30 p.m. My aunt rushed back to my bedroom and said, "Scott, it's your wife. She sounds upset!"

I jumped out of bed and ran down the hall to the kitchen, thinking, *Oh my god, is she going into labor?* I answered the phone. Lana's voice sounded weak when she said, "You need to hurry home. I think I'm going into labor!"

I said, "Hang in there, honey. I'm on my way!"

She said, "Drive carefully. We are having a nasty blizzard here right now!"

I quickly got dressed and grabbed a change of clothes. I told the boys to tell my instructors at school in the morning I had to rush home in the night and be with my wife for a few days. I ran out the front door of the trailer and soon discovered that we were having a huge blizzard. It was snowing hard, and visibility was very poor. Thank god, I was driving Lana's four-wheel-drive Toyota truck. As I got through town and approached the interstate, I noticed a bunch of flashing amber lights in front of me. It looked like something was blocking the road, but I couldn't see well because of the heavy snowflakes hitting my windshield. I thought to myself, *SHIT, THE ROAD IS CLOSED!*

I had driven in many snowstorms in my life, and I'll be dammed if I would let this snowstorm prevent me from being with my wife while our first child was born. I sat in front of the closed gate for about five minutes trying to think what I should do. This would be a five-hour drive if I had to go to the hospital in Powell, and the roads might be slick the entire way. Plus, visibility could be from poor to horrible. I couldn't imagine my wife being in labor without me. I put the Toyota in four-wheel high and blew around the closed gate. The roads were horrible all the way. There were times I had to pull over and wait awhile just to see the next delineator post. I never met another vehicle on the highway all the way home. I made it home at 4:00 a.m. My wife was sleeping peacefully and had not yet gone to the hospital.

We would drive to Powell the next day. We knew we were close but didn't know just how close as the contractions would come and go. We went to dinner and a movie. The movie was *Look Who's Talking*. At the end of the movie, Lana would have strong contractions. She looked at me and said, "I think it's time to go." We left the movie early and went to the hospital. The time was 11:00 p.m. I asked Lana if she thought she was ready to check into the hospital as we stood out in the front entrance. She said, "I'm in a great deal of pain, but if we check in before midnight, they will charge us for another day."

I said, "Well, just say the word, and we will check in." We sat in the Toyota truck with the heater on for one more hour and checked into the hospital at 12:01 a.m.

The day would be the afternoon of March 9, 1990. Lana would give birth to a healthy baby boy. He was a beautiful baby boy who weighed over nine pounds and measured over twenty-one inches in length. The delivery went about as smooth as it could have, but it was difficult for me to see someone I loved so much be in so much pain. Both of our parents were there to provide support for us. Lana and I had narrowed it down to three names if we had a baby boy. The final three names would be Bo, Cody, or Wesley. We could not decide. We would be checking out of the hospital the next day, and they wouldn't let us leave the hospital until we had a name. We put the three names in a hat. I drew the name Wesley Scott Werbelow. We were very proud parents and headed back home to Shell, thankful that we had a healthy baby boy.

Life didn't seem fair. I had to rush back to Douglas the next day and continue my student teaching. I felt bad I had missed three days of teaching, but I needed to be there for my wife and the birth of my son. I was feeling I was not close to my wife because we simply had spent little time together in the past six months. But I was determined to graduate from college with a degree, something that few people in my family had ever achieved.

I returned to my aunt's trailer late that night. The trailer was dark inside. I soon discovered nobody was home. Maybe they had all gone somewhere together and would be home later that night. I woke up the next morning, and nobody was in the trailer. This seemed very odd. I ate breakfast and went to school. Once I arrived at school, one instructor called me into his office. He asked me how the delivery went, and we discussed that for a few minutes.

He then said, "Scott, there is something that I need to tell you. That family that you are living with is having some serious problems!" He said that my uncle was an alcoholic and had been going through rehab for the past several weeks. He told me that my uncle was not doing well and might not survive his drinking problems. He then said, "Your aunt was admitted into a mental institute yesterday. She had a mental breakdown. The kids have been turned over to the Department of Family Services."

I didn't know what to say. I told him, "Those are good kids, and I will take care of them for the next two months."

He said, "Are you sure you want to take on that level of responsibility?"

I said, "Hell yes!"

So there I was getting the three boys up in the morning, cooking them breakfast, and getting them off to school each morning. I would cook them dinner at night, or we would eat pizza from Pizza Hut. We became close, and I would play video games with them or watch a movie in the evenings. My aunt was such a sweet person I would not let her down by taking care of her kids. The middle child was in trouble at school all the time. I would have to meet with the principal several times to keep him in school. The oldest child hated school and wanted to quit. I would have to give him pep talks each evening to keep him in school. The youngest child just needed his mother, and I couldn't substitute that.

This went on for almost two months. Their mother finally returned home one day. She thanked me for all my help taking care of her kids and apologized for what had happened. I told her it was not a problem, and I enjoyed taking care of her kids. I would complete my student teaching, and all my instructors gave me an A for my efforts. All my instructors wrote me letters of recommendation and said very kind words about me. I would return to college and graduate in May with a bachelor's of science degree in industrial technology with coaching endorsements in football and wrestling. I ended up with a cumulative GPA of 3.87. That was one of the happiest days of my life! I had done it. I said I would never attend college, and now I was graduating at the top of my class. I was so proud of myself. I got a score of 14 on my ACT, and that was Chadron's cutoff score to accept students into their college. Not bad for being hungover when I took the exam.

I would return home to Shell to be with my family again. But now, I was a father and needed to provide for my family. Lana and I would soon rent a small cabin in the town of Shell for $250 a month plus utilities. The logs of the cabin weren't sealed well, and Wesley's bedroom would have a small snowdrift across the floor during the winter months when the wind blew hard and it snowed all night. Could my son now be repeating my childhood? I would end up substitute teaching in Greybull for grades K–12 for two years and coaching high school football as an assistant coach. I would continue laying moss rock, painting houses, and performing remodeling jobs on houses. After two years of substitute teaching, I was not sure that I wanted to be a teacher anymore. Had I made a huge mistake in my life?

Chapter 12

THE BEGINNING OF THE REST OF MY LIFE

After graduating from college, Lana and I would move off the ranch and rent a small cabin in the town of Shell with our newly born son, Wesley. Lana continued working for her father on the guest ranch as a wrangler, and I continued substitute teaching in grades K–12. I also had a side business that included remodeling houses, painting houses, laying moss rock, and coaching high school football as an assistant coach. I soon learned that if I would ever be a permanent teacher, it would have to be high-school-aged kids. I didn't have the patience for elementary kids, and middle school kids were just flat mean to one another. I hadn't applied for any teaching jobs yet as the high school shop teacher was near retirement, and I was hoping that someday I could land that job and stay in Greybull. I got along well with all the teaching and coaching staff in the Greybull school system, and maybe that would help me land the shop teaching job someday when it came open.

Lana would get pregnant with our second child. Wendy Nicole Werbelow was born in Powell, Wyoming, on May 18, 1992. She was a healthy, beautiful baby girl weighing almost nine pounds. I was now a young father trying to raise a family the best I knew how. I would take every odd job I could find just to keep up with all the bills coming in every month. I never felt like we ever went without, but we lived from paycheck to paycheck. Lana's mother was our full-time babysitter with both kids while Lana continued working as the head wrangler for her father at the family's guest ranch.

I would paint the Lutheran Church in my small hometown of Emblem that summer. I submitted a very reasonable bid, and the church board selected me for the job. I did a very good job at a reasonable rate. The next thing I knew, I couldn't keep up with all the little ole ladies in Emblem who wanted me to paint their houses. I got to where I could scrape, prime, and paint a house by myself in less than a week. I would charge between $800 and $1,200 per house depending on how big they were and how much work would be required. At the end of that summer, I had put on over three hundred gallons of paint by hand by myself. I was making good money but didn't care for painting that much.

My stepfather, Martin, was busy taking care of cattle and sheep and working on White Creek Ranch. He was still working long hard hours every day and wasn't getting any younger. Martin always had a dream of having a log-made lodge in the Bighorn Mountains on his property near Snowshoe Pass. He worked a deal with a guy who was a logger and built log homes and lodges. Martin would trade this man standing timber on his private mountain ground in trade for a lodge to be built at Snowshoe Pass. Martin never had a floor plan. What started as a single-story lodge would quickly develop into a three-story lodge that stood over thirty feet tall. Every time I would drive up the mountain to visit Martin, he was adding another floor to the lodge with huge cathedral ceilings and large picture windows. This lodge would be beautiful when completed. I couldn't wait to see the final product.

Martin called me one summer day and told me that a mountain lion had got into his sheep last night and killed nine lambs up on Shell Rim. He told me that the Greybull game warden named Bob Trebelcock would be headed up the mountain to look at the dead lambs and try to confirm what had killed them. I quickly hung up the phone with Martin and called Bob at his game warden station in Greybull. Bob answered the phone and I told him who I was. He had remembered me from Bear Creek Ranch when he visited with me years ago about shooting all those damn pigeons and someone stealing my trap. We visited for a short period when Bob asked me, "What can I do for you today, Scott?"

I said, "Oh, not much, I just got off the phone with Martin, and he said you were headed up to look at some dead lambs on Shell Rim."

Bob said, "Yes, as a matter of fact, I was just putting my boots on and headed out the door when you called!"

I said, "Would you mind if I rode along with you today?"

238

Bob said, "I would be honored to have you ride with me today. Would you like me to pick you up in Shell?"

I said, "Yes, that would be awesome. Just pick me up at the guest ranch that Lana's parents own."

He said, "Perfect, I will see you in about thirty minutes!"

I don't know why, but I was very excited to go with Bob that day. The last time I had spoken to Bob, he had snuck up on me one night while I was spotlighting jackrabbits on White Creek Ranch. I wasn't doing anything illegal, but he didn't know who I was or what I was doing until he checked up on me. The time before that, he had pulled me over late at night on top of the Bighorn Mountains as I was headed home from sitting on my bear bait until nearly ten that night. Bob always suspected that I was up to no good, but I guess that's what makes a good game warden. I was just a very avid hunter and fisherman and was always out and about doing something. If it wasn't hunting or fishing, I would generally be out somewhere searching for arrowheads or buffalo heads in sometimes very remote areas on my motorcycle.

Bob soon showed up at the guest ranch and picked me up. His patrol truck was bright and shiny and had all the cool gadgets. I was excited that I would get to ride with the local game warden in his patrol truck. I thought to myself, *This is pretty cool. I get to ride in a game warden's truck, and I'm not even in trouble.* I was a little nervous around Bob because I didn't know him well. Plus, my father had been a poacher for many years but was now deceased. I jumped in Bob's truck and shook his hand and thanked him for letting me ride with him for the day. He said, "No problem at all, but you better buckle up. State law, ya know!" We took off and headed up Shell canyon.

As we were going around the first sharp switchback in Shell canyon, we noticed a man walking toward us on the right-hand side of the highway. The man had a stringer full of rainbow trout. It looked like he had at least six fish on the stringer if not more. The limit on trout was six fish. Bob waved at the man as we went around the sharp corner, and the man waved back. Bob said, "We should probably stop and check his fishing license."

I said, "Yeah, and if he had an overlimit of fish, he probably just tossed them over the guard rail down into the steep canyon below."

Bob grabbed the steering wheel and whipped the truck hard to the left as we were going around the right-hand corner. The truck's tires squealed as we made the quick U-turn on the highway. Bob about threw me out of the passenger-side door when he turned so hard and fast. Good thing I had my seatbelt on. Bob romped on the throttle, and we soon caught up with the fisherman. The fisherman had his license and his legal limit of six fish. I thought that was pretty cool to get to see a game warden in action.

We headed back up the mountain. Soon Bob and I would be telling stories and discussing many topics. I was enjoying my time with Bob. I had now seen a side of Bob I hadn't seen before. He was actually a real person and knew how to joke and laugh and have a good time. I had only seen the serious and professional side of him before. As we got higher on the mountain, the two-track road had become rough. There were a couple of times that my head had hit the roof of his truck from bouncing over large rocks in the road. I looked over at Bob and noticed that his seat would gently go up and down with each large bump in the road. I asked Bob what kind of special seat he had installed in his truck. He looked over at me with a smirk on his face while chewing on his toothpick and said, "It's an air seat, buddy, and I highly recommend it."

We finally reached the area where the lambs had been killed. I noticed there were two other green game-and-fish trucks parked off the rough road. I jumped out of the truck, and Bob introduced me to the wildlife biologist for the area. He said, "Scott, have you met our wildlife biologist Tom Easterly?"

I said, "No, it's my pleasure to meet you, Tom!"

Bob then introduced me to the other guy standing there. He said, "Scott, this is Seth Knore. He is our damage technician for the area!"

I said, "Pleased to meet you, Seth!" and shook his hand with a firm grip.

Bob then said, "All right, let's get started skinning these dead lambs and see if we can confirm what may have killed them."

It was a gruesome sight. Dead lambs were lying everywhere. Some lambs had bloated up, and the flies had found them. Bob skinned the first lamb out while we all watched. Bob explained the characteristics of how a mountain lion would generally kill sheep. He removed the skin from the neck area of the lamb and pointed his knife at two large puncture holes on one side of the lamb's neck. He then stretched the lamb's hide out and pointed at the two large canine puncture holes in the hide. He said, "Look here at these canine puncture holes in the hide and on the side of the lamb's neck. This is consistent with how a mountain lion kills sheep. They typically bite them on the side of the neck or in the throat area when they kill." He then pulled out his tape measure and measured the distance between the puncture wounds on the lamb's hide. The distance between the canine puncture wounds measured three inches.

Bob said, "The distance between the canine puncture wounds is approximately three inches. This is also consistent with that of a mountain lion." Bob then said, "Let's skin the rest of these lambs out and see what we can determine." I stood there and watched Bob skin the second lamb. I knew what he was doing and what he was looking for. I also noticed the other two guys were just standing around watching Bob skin the second lamb. I thought to myself, *I wonder why these guys aren't helping Bob skin lambs. We have eight more to skin, and this is going to take a while.* I asked Bob if he would like me to help him skin some lambs. He said, "Sure, I'll take whatever help I can get." I pulled out my sharp pocket knife and skinned the third lamb out. This was nothing new because I used to skin lambs when I was a young kid to draft the dead lamb's hide to a live bum lamb and try to get the mother to take it as her own.

We finally got all the lambs skinned out and determined that they had all been bitten in the side of the neck except for one lamb. We could find nothing on the one lamb indicating that a mountain lion had killed it. Bob said, "All right, I'm certain that a mountain lion was responsible for the death of eight lambs!" He then said, "Generally, a mountain lion will drag off a lamb and bury it somewhere. We call this the stash pile. If we can find the stash pile, there is about a 98 percent chance this lion will return tonight and feed on the dead lamb. Let's all spread out and see if we can find the stash pile. We are on the top of the Bighorn Mountains with a huge canyon on two sides of us. This lion could have dragged one lamb off anywhere, and we may never find it."

I stood there for a moment and used some common-sense thinking. I thought to myself, *These lambs weigh nearly one hundred pounds. If the mountain lion killed a lamb in the same area as the other lambs, it will simply drag it downhill to the nearest cover away from the open ridge and two-track road.* I looked down the hill below where I was standing and noticed a large single pine tree with low-hanging bows. I thought to myself, *That is the closest cover for that lion and it's down out of sight from the road.* I walked down the hill toward the lone tree and noticed the tall yellow grass had been lain over by something walking through it. You could only see these tracks in the grass if you looked directly into the sun to highlight the small blades of grass being bent over. A sheepherder had taught me this when I was a kid. That same sheepherder had also shown me how to use the sun to find arrowheads.

I followed the tracks in the grass down off the long hill for about two hundred yards and came to a barbed-wire fence. I looked at the top wire on the fence and noticed a small tuff of sheep wool stuck to the barb on the wire. This lion wasn't dragging this dead lamb. It was carrying it in its mouth, and it tried to jump the fence with the dead lamb. As it went over the fence, the lamb's wool snagged the barbed wire and left a small tuff. I knew I was on track because it would be rare for a sheep to jump that fence. I headed on down the hill and looked under the large pine tree, and sure enough, there was the stash pile. I had only been gone from the pickup for less than five minutes and had found the dead lamb buried underneath the tree. I yelled up at Bob, "I found it. It's down here!"

Bob quickly came down the hill and said, "Good job, Scott. I have searched for hours for these stash piles sometimes and never do find them!" He then said, "I'm pretty excited about this. I think we can catch this lion. I wish I had some traps with me right now. We could set them and catch this damn lion tonight!" I told Bob I had some 114 new house traps at my home in Shell and that we could drive off the mountain and grab them quickly and come back up the mountain and set them. Bob said, "That sounds like a good idea. Let's get going so we can get back before dark and get them set." We jumped in Bob's truck and headed off the mountain.

Bob and I had a great visit while driving off the mountain. Bob asked me what I was doing for a living. I told him I was substitute teaching and doing some remodeling jobs on houses in Greybull. I then asked Bob, "Just what exactly does a damage technician do for the department?"

Bob said, "It's a brand-new position, and they just take care of all our damage-related work such as deer in hay fields, antelope in bean fields, and stuff like we dealt with today with the mountain lion killing sheep."

I said, "No offense, Bob, but that guy didn't do a damn thing today except stand around with his hands in his pockets. He never even helped you skin any lambs out."

Bob said, "He is brand-new and from Illinois and doesn't know much about the job yet."

I asked Bob many other questions about the job, and he explained the position the best he could. I said, "Man, that sounds like an awesome job. I would love to do something like that someday."

Bob said, "I thought you were into the teaching profession. Isn't that what you went to college for?"

I said, "Yes, but I don't have a full-time job yet, and I would love to do something like the damage technician job. That would be much more up my alley."

Bob said, "OH REALLY? Actually, that job doesn't pay much. There are no benefits, it's seasonal, and quite frankly it's probably one of the worst damn jobs in the department." Bob said that dealing with wildlife damage was one of the more frustrating parts of the job that game wardens didn't much care for. He then said, "That is why we created the damage technician position in the Cody region so that game wardens could spend more time trying to catch poachers instead of dealing with wildlife damage to crops all the time!"

I said, "Well, I obviously don't know much about the job but sounds pretty dang cool to me."

We picked up the traps at my house in Shell and headed back up the mountain. This gave Bob and me more time to spend together, and we discussed many topics. Bob enjoyed talking and getting my perspective on things growing up as a ranch child. I'm sure he picked my brain on who I thought all the local poachers were. I enjoyed visiting with Bob and greatly respected the man. Besides that, who would have ever thought I was riding in a game warden's truck getting ready to set traps to catch a sheep-killing mountain lion? It got no more exciting than that for me. We soon arrived back at the tree where the mountain lion had stashed and buried the dead lamb.

We carried my traps down the hill. We had tied drags on the traps rather than securely fastening the trap to the ground. Bob was very meticulous when he set his first trap. He explained how far the trap should be set away from the dead lamb for the lion to step in the trap. He then dug a hole and placed the trap in the hole and sprinkled light dirt over the trap to hide the trap and make everything look natural. He also made sharp stepping sticks and placed them in the ground in front of and behind his trap. He explained that mountain lions do not differ from house cats and don't like to step on anything sharp if they can avoid it. Setting traps was not new, but I had never set a trap to catch a mountain lion as it was illegal to trap mountain lions. I asked Bob if it would be all right with him for me to set the second trap we had with us. He said, "Sure, show me how to do it, buddy!"

I went around on the other side of the large pine tree and made a dirt-hole set similar to Bob's, except my trap was set closer to the dead lamb. It was just getting dark as we returned to Bob's truck. He gave me a ride home and asked me if I wanted to jump in with him in the morning to go back up and check the traps. I said, "Heck yeah! What time do you want me ready?"

He said, "I'll be right here at 5:30 a.m. See you bright and early."

I was on cloud nine. This had been one of the best days of my life, and I would get to do it all over again in the morning. I couldn't sleep that night. I was so excited at the thought of us having a mountain lion in our trap in the morning. If we caught that lion the first night, Martin would be so proud of us because he wouldn't lose any more lambs to that mountain lion.

Bob arrived at 5:30 a.m. sharp. I grabbed my lunch and thermos full of coffee and jumped in his truck. Bob said, "Good morning, buddy. Make sure you buckle up. State law, ya know!" I smiled and said good morning back as I buckled up. We had another nice visit about many topics as we drove back up the mountain. We enjoyed each other's conversations. We arrived at the trap location and walked down the long steep hill to the lone pine tree. As we approached the tree, something just didn't look right. The lion had shown up in the night and reached over Bob's trap and had pulled the dead lamb into Bob's trap. The trap went off and caught the dead lamb, preventing the lion from dragging the dead lamb out of the area. The lion then ate the dead lamb and all that Bob had in his trap was a giant wad of sheep wool. I went around the back side of the tree to check my trap. HOLY SHIT, the trap and drag were gone! I had caught that damn mountain lion. I was so proud of myself. The first mountain lion I had ever tried to catch and I got it.

But where did he go? I positioned myself to look into the morning sun just rising over a distant mountaintop. I could faintly see drag marks in the grass and dirt from the metal drag I had attached to the trap. This metal drag was a chunk of railroad track about three feet long and heavy to carry. I slowly followed the drag marks downhill into a steep canyon. Quickly I looked about twenty yards in front of me and noticed the trap and drag lying on the ground in front of me. It didn't have a mountain lion in it, but it had something in the trap. As I approached the trap, I noticed a yellow-bellied marmot (rock chuck) in my damn trap. Apparently, before the mountain lion showing up that night, I had caught a rock chuck in my trap. The lion later showed up, set off Bob's trap, and ate the lamb. He then looked over and dragged the rock chuck off and bury it for another meal for another time. The mountain lion tired of dragging the rock chuck attached to the trap and the heavy drag, so it just ate the rock chuck in the trap. That's right. All I had was the hide of a rock chuck stuck in my trap.

I was a little embarrassed as I had thought I had caught that damn mountain lion and Bob would be so proud of me. We both just stood there and laughed. Bob said, "Well, all be god damned." He chuckled.

I told Bob I had a friend who owned some hound dogs, and we should try to get ahold of him and have his dogs try to tree this lion. I wanted to meet this lion that had just outsmarted both of us. Bob thought that was a good idea, so we went back to the truck and used Bob's mobile truck radio to call dispatch. Bob got on the radio, keyed his radio mic, and said, "Greybull GF-30." A cute female's voice came back on the radio and said, "GF 30, go ahead with your traffic!" Bob asked her to call the houndman at his home to see if he could meet us up on the mountain ASAP to try to tree this mountain lion. Pretty quickly, I heard, "GF-30, SALECS!"

Bob keyed the mic and said, "Go ahead, SALECS!"

The cute voice on the other end said, "I was able to get ahold of the gentleman with the hounds, and he will be 10-76 to your location immediately!"

Bob responded, "10-4, thank you for your help!"

I didn't know what this radio talk was all about, but I was impressed that we didn't have to travel all the way back down the mountain to get ahold of my friend who owned the hound dogs.

As we were sitting in the truck waiting for the houndman to show up, I asked Bob, "What does SALECS stand for, and what does 10-76 stand for on the mobile radio?"

Bob said, "All law enforcement people use a 10 code to communicate because there are many folks out there with police scanners, and we don't want them to know what we are talking about. 10-76 means that they are en route to our location. SALECS stands for state agency law enforcement communications system." He then showed me a large white card attached to his sunvisor that had all the ten-codes from 10-0 through 10-99. I quickly read through them all and thought to myself, *My god, how could you ever memorize all them damn codes?* About two hours later, the houndman showed up with his three blue-tick hound dogs.

The dogs were barking and eager to chase a mountain lion. We took my friend and his dogs down to where we had last found the trap with the rock chuck hide in the trap. We were hoping that the dogs could pick up on the scent of the lion track and follow it until they eventually chased the lion up a tree so we could shoot it. The dogs took off on the scent of the track and were all barking loudly as they headed down the steep heavily timbered canyon. It didn't take long, and the dogs were way ahead of us. We were having a tough time keeping up with the dogs because of all the heavy downfall timber and steep slopes we had to climb. I was in good condition at that age but couldn't keep up with them. All I could do was follow the sounds of the dogs barking as there was no snow on the ground to track anything.

I finally had caught up with the barking dogs. They had the large male mountain lion treed in a large pine tree. The pine tree was about forty feet tall and huge in diameter. As I approached the tree, I soon saw the mountain lion standing out on a large branch about twenty feet high in the tree. This large branch was hanging out near a rock cliff face straight up and down. As the dogs were barking, Bob and my friend were coming up the hill. I watched the mountain lion leap from the pine branch over to the cliff face and race straight up the cliff face and over the top of the mountain out of sight. The dogs could not climb the cliff wall, and neither could we. My heart sank as I stood there and watched the mountain lion run over the top of the cliff wall and out of sight. The dogs were going nuts as they still thought the lion was up in the tree, but nope, the lion was long gone. It had outsmarted us all again. We never did catch that lion, but it sure wasn't from lack of trying. We thanked the houndman, and he gathered up his dogs and went home.

Bob and I again had a good visit while we traveled off the mountain toward home that evening. It had been a long day as he pulled into my driveway at about 8:00 p.m. He thanked me for all my help over the past two days and said, "Sometimes the lion wins." As I exited the truck, Bob said, "Hey, I'm not sure if you would ever be interested in that damage technician job, but if Seth doesn't return next spring, I would sure give you a good recommendation to the regional wildlife supervisor in Cody if you are interested."

I said, "Thank you, Bob. You don't know how much I would appreciate that!"

Bob said, "You betcha, buddy. Thanks for all your good help and good night."

I said, "No, thank you for having me. I just had the best time of my life over the past two days. Good night."

I went into the house tired and hungry and happily told my wife, Lana, about the exciting day I had just had with Bob. I was so excited, but I didn't want to get my hopes up as Seth might come back next spring and it was possible this job would never come open for a long time. This was only July, and I wouldn't even know anything until next April if the position would be open or not and if I even would qualify for it since I didn't have a wildlife management degree. Again, I couldn't sleep that night because I was so excited about the prospect of possibly working for the Wyoming Game & Fish Department someday.

Week and months would soon go by. There was not a day I didn't think about the damage technician position. The spring of 1993 finally came. I would call Bob weekly to see if he had heard if the previous damage technician was coming back to work for the department or not. Bob would say, "Sorry, I haven't heard a word, but I will let you know if I hear anything."

Finally, the call came one day. Bob said, "It doesn't look like Seth will be coming back this spring. If you are still interested in the job, I will give you my recommendation to the Cody regional wildlife supervisor."

I told Bob I was still *very* interested in the job and thanked him for all his help and support. He recommended that I drive over to Cody and pick up a state application at the regional office and try to meet with the regional wildlife supervisor named Gary Brown. I was so excited. I told Bob I would head to Cody in the morning and thanked him again.

I drove to Cody the next morning and pulled into the public parking area of the regional office. I had butterflies in my stomach. I thought to myself, *Who is Gary Brown? He must be very important if he is the supervisor of the whole Cody region.* I wondered if Gary had ever chased my ole man around back in his day when he was doing all his poaching. I wondered if Gary would recognize my last name and ask me about my father. As I walked through the front door of the regional office, I became very nervous. I was soon greeted by a very nice woman named Bonnie. She jumped out of her chair and said, "How may I help you today, young man?"

I said, "I'm here to pick up a state application and possibly meet with Mr. Gary Brown if he is in the office today."

She smiled and said, "Yes, he is. Let me take you down the hall to his office, and I will find that application while the two of you visit." She then led me through a waist-high spring-loaded door with a sign that read

Employees Only. Now I was nervous, and the butterflies in my stomach were working overtime.

We got to the end of the hall, and Mr. Brown's office door was closed with a sign that read Please Don't Disturb hanging in the center of the door about eye level. Bonnie tapped lightly on the door and cracked open the door. She said, "Excuse me, Mr. Brown, but I have a young gentleman here who would like to visit with you if you have a minute."

Mr. Brown had a deep voice, and I overheard him say, "WHO IS IT?"

Bonnie responded, "I'm sorry I didn't get his name, but he is picking up a state application and wanted to visit with you, if you have time."

Mr. Brown said, "I don't have much time but send him in!"

Bonnie turned around and smiled at me and said, "Okay, here he is!"

I walked into Mr. Brown's office and said, "Hello, Mr. Brown, my name is Scott Werbelow!" I shook his hand firmly, and our eyes locked. Mr. Brown did not hold eye contact with me long. He had a deep voice and a nervous laugh.

He said, "Yes, Scott Werbelow, come in and sit down." He closed his door. He then told me that he had heard my name through Bob Trebelcock, the Greybull game warden.

I told Mr. Brown that, yes, I knew Bob pretty well and had helped him try to catch a mountain lion in the Bighorn Mountains last summer. I didn't tell him the whole story because catching a rock chuck instead of a mountain lion was embarrassing for me. We had a nice visit. Mr. Brown asked me why I was interested in the damage technician position, my education, and where I lived. I explained to him I had always wanted to be a game warden someday but had heard there were no jobs and getting hired would be very difficult. He said, "Well, what you heard is 100 percent correct. We don't have many permanent wardens retiring at this point, and it's a very competitive process to get a permanent position as a warden." I then told him I left college with a BS degree in industrial technology and had been substitute teaching in Greybull for the past two years. I also told him I lived in Shell, Wyoming.

We only visited for about ten minutes. I felt that Mr. Brown was a straightforward and serious supervisor. He meant business when he talked, but he was also very difficult for me to talk to as he rarely would make eye contact with me. This was the middle of February. He told me they were hoping to have the position filled by April 1. I felt our conversation was slowing down, so I stood up and shook his hand and told him it was a pleasure to finally meet him. He stood up, shook my hand, and said, "Likewise. Grab an application at the front office on your way out."

I said, "Yes, sir, I will."

I headed down the long hallway and took a deep breath of relief. I had just met the big boss, and he told me to fill out an application. As I approached the front desk, Bonnie got out of her chair and said with a smile, "Here you go, sweetie. You can fill it out right now or take it home with you and mail it back to us!"

I was so excited I filled it out right there at her front desk and proudly handed the application back to her. I said, "Please make sure this application gets back to Mr. Brown."

Bonnie said, "I will take it down to him right now."

I thanked her and left the office with a feeling of relief and a big smile on my face. I had possibly just made my first step to becoming a game warden someday!

Days and weeks went by. I had not yet heard a word from anybody. I called Bob weekly to see if he had heard anything from Mr. Brown, and he had not. I had my hopes up so high. I thought to myself, *What if I don't get this job? I'm really not enjoying teaching and painting houses anymore. What will my future hold? Will they hire me for this position with no wildlife management degree?*

One morning at about nine, I was standing in our kitchen cleaning up breakfast dishes when the phone on the wall rang. I quickly picked up the phone, and I heard a voice say, "Hello, Scott, this is Gary Brown. Do you have time to stop by my office and discuss this damage technician job?"

I said, "Yes, sir, I can be there in about two hours if that works for you."

He said, "That will work for me. I'll see you then."

I was so excited that I yelled yes at the top of my lungs. I wanted to tell Lana the exciting news, but she was out riding her horse somewhere. I quickly jumped in the shower, jumped in my Bronco, and headed for Cody.

On the way to Cody, I became very nervous again and asked myself questions: is this going to be an interview for the position, or is he going to offer me the position? I wonder how many other people put in for the position. What if I don't get the job? I walked through the front door of the regional office. Bonnie jumped out of her chair with a smile and said, "Hi, sweetie, follow me back to Mr. Brown's office!" She again tapped on Mr. Brown's closed door and opened it slowly. "I have a visitor here to see you, Mr. Brown," Bonnie whispered through the crack in the door. I walked into Mr. Brown's office and again shook his hand. He closed the door and invited me to sit down.

He explained all the responsibilities of the damage technician position. When he was done explaining the position, he looked at me and said, "The job is yours if you are interested."

I said, "Yes, sir, thank you very much!" I did not do a cartwheel right in his office.

He then said, "But, Scott, I want to be honest with you. This job is only a temporary nine-month position with no benefits, and it will not be a stepping stone to becoming a game warden someday. It's just a temporary job. That's it!"

Those words hit me hard that day, and I never forgot them. He stood up, shook my hand, and told me to stop by the front desk. Bonnie would have a packet of paperwork for me to complete. He also handed me the keys to the new truck I would be driving and told me where it was parked in the compound. His last words were "Get all the paperwork completed, fill out a uniform allowance form, and order you a couple of red shirts and a few hats, Then get with Bob Trebelcock, and he will teach you everything that you need to know about your new job."

I'm not sure there was another human in the entire world that was as excited as I was at that moment. I filled out the mounds of paperwork and headed out the back door to go check out my new game-and-fish truck. About that time, Mr. Brown stepped out of his office and said, "Oh, by the way, here is a box of stuff that you will need for the job!" I grabbed the box and set it on a nearby table to look through it. It had a very beat-up spotting scope, a pair of even more beat-up binoculars, a sawed-off shotgun, and several boxes of cracker shells. Cracker shells are shot through the 12-gauge shotgun and travel about fifty yards before making a loud bang in the air. They are used to scare wildlife out of producers' fields. There were also other boxes of devices you shoot out of a revolver pistol, and they make loud screaming noises as they go through the air for about seventy-five yards. Man, was I going to have fun with all these pyrotechnics.

I went outside and found my new truck. It was a shiny game-warden green 1992 Ford Ranger with chrome alloy wheels and a chrome toolbox in the back. It had to be the only game-and-fish truck in the entire agency that had chrome alloy wheels! Back then, our administration wouldn't let us have anything fancy because they were all worried about public perception. I'm not sure how this truck got approved and delivered with chrome alloy wheels, but it looked badass. It had very tall deep-lugged tires to give it additional clearance. It also had a spotlight mounted in the driver's-side door post and another spotlight mounted in the center of the roof overhead. The truck had a large box-style mobile radio mounted to the floorboard in the center of the truck with many buttons that said PL Tower 1-8. I was assigned a call number of GF-125.

I was on cloud nine as I jumped into that little Ford Ranger. I put my seatbelt on because I was now an official state employee, and Bob told me too. I never used to wear one before. I found a brown gas card in the middle console and noticed that I was low on fuel, so I headed to Cody to fuel the truck up. I didn't know how to use the gas card, but the cute gal at the Maverick showed me I needed to fuel up first and then bring the card in and she would run it through her machine. It took all her strength to run the card reader over the top of the credit card, and it made a loud noise as she swiped the handle over the card. She then had me sign a duplicate receipt, and it was that simple. I stopped at Taco John's on the way back to Greybull because that was my favorite place to eat. The meal was $3.50. I was so excited about just getting hired that I gave the young gal $10 and told her to keep the change. It felt so good to be happy and help someone else out while doing so.

About one hour later, I reached Greybull and stopped at Bob's house to tell him the good news. Bob was very happy for me and congratulated me. He said, "Funny how life works. You used to cuss them red-shirted sons a bitches, and now you are one!"

I got a chuckle out of that and thought to myself, *My dad is probably rolling over in his grave right now.*

Bob then said, "Well, congratulations, why don't you plan on meeting me here at the warden station at 8:00 a.m. and I will show you what your job is all about?"

I rode around with Bob all day that day, and he taught me so much about everything in the department while we were checking fishermen for licenses. He taught me how to read maps, do my monthly reports, and code all my time each day I worked. It was a very complicated process with hundreds of codes to use each month for each different activity you spent time on each day. Thankfully, my job didn't have many activity codes to keep track of daily as his did. He showed me I would have to code my vehicle mileage every day and break each day down at the end of the month and code the proper mileage for each activity I worked. I wasn't liking all this paperwork, but that was part of the job. After a long day of checking fishermen, Bob said, "Let's get some dinner. Then I will take you out tonight and show you some ranches that have deer on them causing damage to crops."

We drove out north of Shell onto a large ranch that had hundreds of acres of alfalfa planted. The plants were just popping through the ground, and the deer were eating the plant heads off as they grew. The landowner was very upset with the Game & Fish Department because all the deer were eating him out of his house. He hated the deer, and he hated game wardens.

Bob turned on his spotlight, and I couldn't believe what I was seeing. There must have been 1,500 to 2,000 deer that lit up in the spotlight. Bob said, "Normally, we would just count them so we can pay for damages later, but I think we should try to move them tonight because the face of the mountain is starting to green up, and maybe the deer will stay out of the alfalfa fields if we hit them hard tonight." Bob then set me up with his shotgun, cracker shells, and bird bombs. The bird bombs would be shot out of a small pistol, and they would make a loud whistling noise as they screamed through the air for about seventy-five yards. Bob got me all set up and looked at me with his toothpick hanging out of one side of his mouth and said, "Are you ready?"

I said, "Yes, sir," not knowing what was about to happen.

Bob turned on his sirens, romped on the throttle, and turned his red-and-blue lights on. The sirens were loud. He had his overhead spotlight shining on the deer as we chased them from behind. He yelled at me over the noise of the sirens, "GET TO SHOOTING!" I fired cracker shells, bird-bomb whistlers, and cherry bombs just as fast as I could load and shoot. It looked like the Fourth of July out there and sounded even better. We had hundreds of deer running for the nearby mountain in front of us. We drove every road on the ranch and chased every single deer we saw off the hay fields and into the hills toward the mountains. We finally came to a stop. My ears were ringing from the sounds of the loud sirens and cracker shells going off.

I couldn't even focus my eyes on all the bright flashes in the night from the cherry bombs and cracker shells going off in the night. Bob looked over at me while he was wearing his earmuffs for hearing protection and yelled, "WELL, WHAT DO YOU THINK OF YOUR NEW JOB?"

I yelled back, "IT'S BETTER THAN SEX!"

He said, "WHAT DID YOU SAY?"

I yelled back, "IT'S THE BEST!"

Bob laughed and said, "I thought that's what you said."

At that moment in my life, I could not believe that I was going to actually get paid each month to have this much fun. Bob had told me it was a crappy job. I thought, *I'll show him a crappy job. This is going to be fun.*

Bob would take me out over the next several weeks and show me where all the ranches were located that were having spring deer damage. My primary job was to either count every animal on the fields or run them off once the mountain had spring green up with grass. All my damage technician work would begin late at night as that is when I would get the best counts on deer, elk or antelope, or whatever species of wildlife was causing the damage. I would need to document the number of animals each night so the department could accurately pay the landowners if they submitted a damage claim" each year. The department is bound by state statute to pay for damages to crops from any animal classified as a big game. The department is also liable to pay for any damages to livestock caused by any trophy game—which is a black bear, mountain lion, grizzly bear, and wolf—if the department personnel can verify what killed the livestock.

My job became very busy as I handled all damage-related calls in nine game-warden districts in the Bighorn Basin. I dealt with sandhill crane, Canadian goose, and sage grouse damage to crops. I dealt with antelope in beans, deer in corn, elk in alfalfa, and grizzly bears in beehives. You name the damage, I dealt with it. That was my job. I had a passion for game-warden work and would ride with Bob much to learn more about what game wardens do daily. Bob was a great investigator. His investigations of wildlife poachings were very thorough and complete, and his interview skills with suspects caught poaching were also very good. I was so fascinated with game-warden work I was working seventy to eighty hours a week. I would spend all day with Bob learning game-warden skills and work all night dealing with damage situations. I loved my job and wouldn't trade it for anything. The department only paid me for forty hours per week. My first paycheck was $960. I couldn't believe that I actually got paid for having so much fun!

Once that fall came, damage work slowed down, so I would have time to check hunters in the field while they were hunting. I would work from daylight until well after sunset checking hunters and recording harvests of big and trophy game animals. I was not a "commissioned" law enforcement officer who could carry a firearm or issue citations for wildlife violations. But if I came across a violation, I could report it to the nearest game warden; and they would show up and deal with the violation. Bob enjoyed having me for backup on many occasions. Bob owned a German shepherd police dog I fell in love with. I got myself a German shepherd puppy, so I too had a companion to travel with. I got a male full-blooded German shepherd puppy. I named this dog Sarge. This was one of the best dogs I ever owned.

The dog was well disciplined and would do whatever I asked him to do. If I wanted him to track a hunter, he would track the hunter. If I wanted him to find a wounded or dead animal in the field, he would find it. All I had to do was get him on the scent of a human track or wildlife track and tell him to "go find them," and he would take off on the track until he found whatever we were looking for. As he got older, he became very protective of me and my truck. If a hunter was giving me a bad time while checking licenses in their hunting camp, I would yell, "SARGE!" and he would stand up in the back of my truck and growl at them. This was my backup if I ever needed it, and hunters respected him.

Sarge, when he was a puppy

As Bob and I got to know each other better, he would nickname me Hollywood because I always had a brand-new $5 pair of sunglasses. I couldn't keep track of sunglasses, so I was always buying a new pair every other week. Bob and I would soon become good friends and spend almost every day doing something together. We went on pack trips together checking fishermen in the high-country lakes, we went hunting and fishing together, and some nights we spent all night chasing spot lighters around the hills and river bottoms. We had a great deal of fun with everything we did together. After working with Bob daily, I wanted to become a game warden so bad I could taste it. This is the first time in my life I felt strongly about what I wanted to do for the next thirty years of my life.

Bob and I getting ready for a pack trip into Shell Lakes to check fishermen

Bob and I packing out my bull elk from our hunt together that fall

My nine-month job went by quickly. The next thing I knew, it was January and I would be out of work with the Game & Fish Department. I would again substitute teach grades K–12 through the winter months to pay the bills. I would return to the Cody regional office that spring to meet with Mr. Brown and discuss if I would have a job again as a damage technician. Mr. Brown was a man of few words. When he spoke, you listened carefully. Mr. Brown said nothing about my performance the previous nine months of employment. But what he did say was "Scott, the agency is going through budget shortfalls right now. Cuts are being made monthly. You do have a job this summer, but your position has been cut from nine months to eight months." That was not very good news when I had a wife and two kids to support, but I was just thankful to still have a job and was much looking forward to getting back to work with the department.

Chapter 13

DO YOU HAVE WHAT IT TAKES TO BECOME A WYOMING GAME WARDEN?

I was looking forward to getting back to work with the department. My job would become easier because I now knew where most of the damage situations occurred and I had met many landowners in the first nine months of my employment. My job would start working nights and counting deer on hay fields in Shell, Worland, Manderson, Tensleep, and Lovell areas. The majority of my work was in the Shell and Greybull areas. I soon learned there were many landowners in this area that had no tolerance for wildlife on their private properties. Some landowners not only hated wildlife on their property but also hated the local game and fish personnel. I would receive calls from landowners early in the morning and late at night. Some landowners would yell at me on the phone, "COME GET YOUR DAMN DEER OUT OF MY FIELDS!!" They would take it personally and call them *my deer*.

A landowner who lived north of Shell called Bob at three one morning and told him to come to get all the dead elk he had just shot out of his bean field. The man had been drinking that night and came home in the early hours of the morning only to have a heard of elk cross the road in front of him headed for his bean field. The man jumped out of his truck and shot nine elk in his headlights as they were headed toward his bean field. He then went home and called Bob to tell him to come to get "his damn elk" out of his field. The man was later charged with taking elk out of season and convicted for the crime. However, the landowner submitted a claim that year for damage incurred by the elk and was reimbursed by the department for damage that the elk had caused to his beans. I'm sure the damage claim he submitted was higher than the fines he received for poaching the elk. I also think he ran out of bullets that night, or there would have been more dead elk than just nine.

I would spend time at night and day trying to keep this herd of about 150 elk out of this landowner's fields. I would chase them all night in a spotlight while shooting cracker shells and bird bombs in the air, trying to convince the elk to head back up the mountain to the north. I would get them to the base of the Bighorn Mountains at night and hire a fixed-wing airplane in the mornings to take the elk the rest of the way to the top of the mountain. This work cost the department a great deal of money to keep these elk out of the bean fields. But we wanted no more of these elk shot, and we didn't want to pay any more large damage claims.

One night, I was running this large group of elk at night with my Ford Ranger. The elk were running alongside my truck and were trying to cross the road in front of me and get back into the bean fields. If I made one mistake, I would risk losing all these elk back into the fields. If 150 elk run through a bean field in the night, it can cause thousands of dollars in damage to the beans. As the elk were trying to cross the road in front of me, I was traveling a rough two-track road with elk on my right-hand side. I was driving about thirty miles per hour trying to turn the elk to my right and not allow them to cross the road in front of me. I grabbed my sawed-off 12-gauge shotgun and held it out in front of my windshield. I would be shooting a cracker shell across my front windshield to my right to turn the elk while driving thirty miles per hour on a rough road. I pulled the trigger and heard a loud noise. The next thing I knew, my truck radio went fuzzy, and I could no longer see out of my front windshield. The cracker shell had struck my truck antenna and blew it off somewhere out in the sagebrush. The antenna hit the front windshield of my truck and shattered it.

I quickly came to a stop because I could see nothing out of my front windshield. Thank god, the cracker shell hit perfect right in front of the lead cow and turned them back toward the mountain. I grabbed my flashlight and finally found my antenna about thirty yards from the road out in the sagebrush. I had to roll my driver's-side window down and drive home that night with my head sticking out of the window to see. Home was only about thirty miles away. I got home that night and looked at my shattered windshield. I thought to myself, *Oh shit, What would Gary Brown have to say about this?* I went back to the ranch early the next morning and fixed a bunch of fences the elk had torn up while I was chasing them that night. I didn't want the landowner to chew my ass for all the torn-down fence and submit another claim for fence damage I had caused by running the elk.

I spent a great deal of time that summer and fall trying to keep those elk off the bean and alfalfa fields. I would again jump in a fixed-wing airplane and chase the 150-plus elk up the face of the west slope of the Bighorn Mountains. On this day, the elk had held up right underneath the steep rim of rocks near the top of the mountain. They were in a difficult spot to move them with the airplane because of the steep slope of the mountain and heavy timber that the elk were held up in. The awesome pilot took the plane over the top of the mountain, circled back around, dropped the plane into a narrow canyon, and flew the plane down the canyon. He banked the plane hard to the right and stood the plane on its side as he banked around the steep cliff to get the plane above the elk and move them. I reached out the rear window of the plane and shot a loud bird-bomb whistler out of my revolver pistol.

The bird bomb made a loud whistling noise as the plane was banked on its side. The pilot heard the noise and looked in his rearview mirror to see my sawed-off shotgun propped between my legs aimed at the ceiling of the plane behind him. He quickly straightened out the plane and headed for the airport. He got on his radio and yelled, "DID YOU JUST SHOOT A DAMN HOLE IN THE ROOF OF MY PLANE?"

I said, "No, I just fired a bird bomb out of my pistol instead of a cracker shell out of my shotgun."

The pilot said, "Oh, thank god! I just heard that whistling noise and saw your shotgun pointed up between your legs and thought that you accidentally shot a hole in the roof of my plane."

That fall I would check hunters and help Bob with some of his investigations to catch poachers. I loved this work, and we worked well together catching poachers. Bob told me I should take the Wyoming game-wardens exam that fall if I ever wanted to become a game warden. This excited me, but would they ever let me take the exam without a wildlife management degree? Could I even pass the exam if they ever did let me take it? I soon called headquarters in Cheyenne, and they sent me an application and a packet to fill out.

I never made it over to Cody often, but occasionally, we would have a regional wildlife personnel meeting, a firearm's qualifications, and custody and control training. Wardens would have to qualify with all their department-issued firearms twice a year. These qualifications were very stressful because you had to shoot very accurately and fast. If you failed to qualify with any of your department-issued weapons—which included your pistol, shotgun, and rifle—you would have to then shoot the course two consecutive times in a row to qualify. If you failed to qualify, you couldn't be a commissioned game warden. The regional personnel meeting would last all day and sometimes two days depending on if we were setting upcoming hunting seasons or not.

The firearms training and custody and control training would also take a couple of days to complete. I enjoyed participating in the custody and control training because I was young and had a great deal of experience from all my years as a wrestler. I also enjoyed firearms training because the two firearms instructors would allow me to help them set up their rigid training courses. They would also let me shoot their Beretta 9mm pistols to practice with them while trying out the new shooting courses. This was fun to get together with all the wardens and biologists in the district for a few days.

Everyone worked well together and got along well. My favorite moments were sitting around a campfire in the evenings and listening to all the crazy game-warden stories from wardens who had over twenty years of experience working for the department. Some of these old-timers knew how to drink whiskey and tell a hell of a story. It seemed if one warden told a crazy story about catching poachers, another warden would have to outdo the previous story, and the stories just kept getting wilder and wilder as the night went on. It became clear after listening to all the stories that the Wyoming Game & Fish Department was a whole different agency back in the old days.

Campfire at a Game Warden Patrol Cabin in the mountains

Back then, they would occasionally handcuff poachers to the headache rack of their patrol truck and wait for a deputy sheriff to transport them to jail because they had only single-cab trucks and never had enough room to transport poachers because of their dog sitting in the passenger seat. They also took sedated black bears and put them in the front seat or toolbox of their patrol trucks and transported them to remote areas before turning them loose. Sometimes the black bears would come awake before they got to where they wanted to go with them and run around the cab of their trucks, causing them to have to quickly pull over and release the bear out of the cab of their truck. One warden had to release a black bear in a small town because it came awake in the cab of his truck. He then had to get dogs and tree the bear again before sedating it a second time and transporting it out of town.

My eight months of work would soon end again. I received a letter from the head law enforcement coordinator out of Casper. He had received my application to take the Wyoming game-wardens exam. His letter read he would need my college transcripts and credentials before I could take the exam. I quickly sent him everything that I had and soon received a letter back from him stating that I was not qualified to take the exam because I had to have a wildlife management degree. My heart sank. How would I ever become a Wyoming game warden?

I again substitute taught that winter and did odd jobs to pay the bills. My kids were growing up quickly, and this temporary eight-month job with no benefits was not paying the bills no matter how much I enjoyed the work. The state budget was tight, and the agency had just gone through a process called TQM (teaching quality management). The department had contracted with an outside company to take a hard look at all the programs in the Wyoming Game & Fish Department, and make necessary recommendations to cut programs and eliminate personnel to help balance the budget. *After this process, would I even have a job with the agency anymore?* I thought to myself.

Wesley and Scott with pet deer in the front yard

I again showed up at the Cody Regional Office to meet with Gary Brown to see if I still had a job with the department. Mr. Brown was short with me and explained that because of budget shortfalls, my position had been cut to seven months of work. He then explained that after the whole TQM process, I was very lucky to even have a job. Mr. Brown had been assigned to the TQM team and actually resigned from his position as he could not agree to the decisions that the team was making for future cuts to the agency. I left his office thankful that I still had a job but depressed that things weren't getting any better for having a permanent job or becoming a game warden.

I again went out to the large ranch north of Shell to move all the deer off the alfalfa fields. It was about 10:00 p.m., and I was running my sirens and shooting cracker shells off to move the deer. I pulled up to a closed gate and went to open my truck door. As I turned to open the door, I noticed a deer standing up on the side of my truck looking into my window. I had about two thousand deer running ahead of me and needed to quickly get the gate to keep up with them. What the hell, was this deer doing standing up on my truck looking through the window at me? This scared the shit out of me. As I opened my door, I pushed the deer away from my truck with the door. I got out to open the gate, and the deer followed me over to the gate. I soon learned that the deer was the rancher's pet, and he thought he was a dog.

I scratched the deer on the head, and he followed me back to my truck. I took off chasing the two-thousand-plus deer off the fields, and the pet deer followed me all night long like a dog. Every time I put my truck in reverse to back up, I would see the deer standing behind my truck in my backup lights. I was afraid I might run over it, so I dropped my tailgate, and the deer jumped in the back of my truck. We soon became buddies; and each night I would run deer out of the fields, I would load the deer in the back of my truck and take it with me. It was illegal for the landowner to raise the deer, but I said nothing to him or told him that the deer had been going with me every night. The landowner did not like the many deer on his property or game and fish personnel.

A kiss from one of my little buddies

Late one night, I was leaving the ranch after a night of running my sirens, shooting cracker shells, and moving hundreds of deer off the meadows. I was headed home down the county road. I had just driven by the turn-off to the landowner's house when I noticed headlights behind me. The vehicle was traveling fast, and the headlights were right on my tail. Quickly, the vehicle passed me on the left and slid sideways in front of me running me off the road. A half-dressed man got out of a Volkswagen car and quickly ran up to my door of the truck. The man had nothing on but a pair of pants. He yelled at me, "You will cease and desist from running those sirens on this property in the future. Do you understand?"

I calmly said, "Okay, and who are you?"

He said, "I'm the owner's stepson, and you need to leave the property immediately. Do you understand?"

I almost said, "Who is the owner of the property? God! And you must be Jesus!" But I didn't. I just said, "Yes, sir, I would be happy if I never had to return to this property again."

The next morning the landowner called me and apologized for his stepson's behavior. He said, "Sorry about what happened last night. My stepson didn't know that I had authorized you to be on the property chasing deer and running your sirens. Please continue to come back until all the deer are gone!" About two weeks later, I received a call from the landowner's hired hand stating that the "owner's" pet deer had just attacked his two children on their bikes while they were riding them home from the school bus stop on the county road. He stated that the buck deer had knocked both off their bicycles and "pert near kilt both." He said, "Scott, you and I know it's illegal to raise wildlife, and this is a human safety issue with my family."

I told him to call me the next time he had seen the deer and that I would come out and remove the deer from the property and take it up to the mountains away from people. He said, "I appreciate that, Scott, but don't let the owner know that I mentioned this to you, or he will fire me, and me and my family will have to leave the ranch." I knew this deer very well as he had ridden around with me in the back of my pickup truck many nights while I was chasing deer off the owner's property.

Over the next couple of months, I had received many complaints about this buck deer. He had left the ranch and was traveling up and down the creek bottom visiting all his neighbors. Some calls claimed that the buck deer was very aggressive; others claimed that the buck deer was destroying their flowers. By the time I would get to their location, the buck would be gone. This went on for several weeks. One morning, I received a call at six thirty from a little old lady claiming that the buck deer was acting aggressively and destroying her flowers. I told the lady to sit tight. I was on my way. I jumped in my personnel truck and hooked up my personnel four-horse trailer and headed to her address about five miles away. I arrived at her lane and started up the lane with my truck and horse trailer. The old couple was walking down the lane and stopped me on the road. They told me not to drive to the top of the hill, or the deer would see my truck and trailer and run off.

I told them that I planned to lure the deer into my horse trailer with a bucket of grain and take him to a remote location in the Bighorn Mountains where it would cause no more problems. I didn't want to kill this deer as I felt we were buddies. I parked my truck about one hundred yards from their house, just under the hill, so the deer couldn't see my truck and trailer. I grabbed a bucket of grain and walked toward their house when I observed the buck deer eating flowers out of the sweet old lady's flower garden. I quickly stopped and shook the bucket of grain. The four-point buck deer raised its head and came running in my direction fast. I thought to myself, *OH SHIT, this buck is going to take me!* The buck came toward me fast and stopped about ten feet from me. I shook the bucket of grain, and the buck slowly walked toward me. He got close to the bucket of grain. His eyes got large, and he slowly reached out for a bite of the grain. He got just a nibble of grain and quickly took off into the nearby hills. I thought, *Shit, that didn't work.*

I then grabbed my lariat rope out of my horse trailer and tucked it in my waistband with a loop around the bucket of grain. I walked out in the hills off their property and shook the bucket of grain with me. The buck looked up, and here it came at a full run again. I thought to myself, *OH SHIT, here it comes again!* The buck deer came running hard toward me and again stopped right in front of me. I shook the bucket of grain, and the deer slowly approached the bucket for another bite. Its eyes got larger and looked as if they were glazed over as it took a bite of the grain out of the bucket. At the last second, it turned to run back into the hills, and I grabbed the lariat looped around the bucket and tossed it over its head and around its neck. I thought it would run away from me. But holy shit, it ran toward me and was trying to strike out at me with its sharp hooves (reminded me of my horse Daisy). The old couple was sitting on a nearby log laughing their asses off. I took off running for the horse trailer located about one hundred yards away. It was hard to look cool while this deer was trying to kick my ass.

I couldn't outrun the deer, so I waited for the deer to charge me, and I quickly stepped to my left. As the deer went by me, I jerked on the rope and got the deer down on the ground. I quickly jumped on top of the deer and held it to the ground as I tightened the loop on the lariat in an attempt to choke it off. The deer was now making loud sounds that I had never heard before, and it was trying to get up. I held on tight and kept the pressure on the rope. Finally, the deer was nearly choked off and out of air. I jumped up and took off running toward the horse trailer, dragging the choked deer behind me. I would not ever make it to the horse trailer without running out of air and energy.

I finally arrived and still had to open the door on the trailer and keep the deer choked out. While I was opening the trailer door, the deer jumped to its feet and was still in the fight. I jumped in the trailer as the deer charged me. The deer charged me right into the trailer. I zigged and zagged and got around the buck deer and slammed the trailer door shut fast and hard as I exited the trailer. The deer was jumping up and down, hitting its head on top of the trailer and making loud sounds that I had never heard before. I dusted off my hands and looked over at the old couple still sitting on the log laughing at me. The lady yelled, "Good job, Scott!"

I said, "Thank you, ma'am. I'm a trained professional. A lesser man may have just died."

I took the deer back to my house and called wildlife biologist Tom Easterly. I asked Tom if he would bring his department truck and trailer to my house and we could transfer the deer to his department truck and trailer and haul it up to a remote location in the Bighorn Mountains. Tom said he would be there shortly to help me. Tom soon arrived and backed his two-horse trailer up to my four-horse trailer. The buck deer still had the lariat around its neck and was raising all hell in my trailer. I told Tom to crawl up into the front of his two-horse trailer and hold on to the end of the lariat rope. I then told Tom not to ever pull on the rope or the deer would charge him. As soon as Tom was in position, I went through the small door on the side of my trailer and entered.

I got behind the deer. The deer took off and could see some daylight between the two trailers. He jumped in the air and got its head caught between the two trailers. The deer was hanging by its head stuck between the two trailers. I grabbed the deer around the midsection and quickly threw it in the two-horse trailer. I yelled at Tom, "HURRY UP AND PULL THE ROPE!" Tom quickly pulled the rope, and the buck deer jumped into the front of the trailer with Tom. The deer was kicking the shit out of Tom. I yelled, "Hold tight. I have to pull the truck up so that I can close the door on the trailer." This was probably the longest two minutes of Tom's life as that buck had it trapped in the front of the two-horse trailer. I finally got the trailer pulled forward and the door closed. I jumped in the trailer and pulled the deer off Tom and held it down while Tom exited the trailer.

Tom said as he exited the trailer, "Damn, that deer is pretty cantankerous!"

We transported that deer to the top of the Bighorn Mountains and never heard about that deer again.

I would be done with my seven months of employment at the end of October. I worked the fall hunting season checking hunters during October, but that was it. I had applied again to take the Wyoming game warden's exam and was again told no, I was not qualified to take the exam without having a wildlife management degree. I was hoping that three years of experience would give me enough experience to take the exam. I drove over to Cody and turned in my truck and equipment again, hoping that I would be rehired the next spring. I returned home to Shell and struggled to find enough work to pay the bills through the winter months. That winter I received word from Bob that times were tough with the department. He wasn't sure if my position would still be around or not come next spring.

The next spring, I again met in Cody with Gary Brown. He was all doom and gloom and told me he had fought for my position, but there would only be enough money to fund my position for six months. I nearly cried when I heard the news. This whole job with the game and fish department was only getting worse and not better. My wife had told me earlier that I needed to quit screwing around with the department and get a real job that would provide for the family. I grabbed my truck and equipment and headed back home toward Shell. I cried between Cody and Emblem and couldn't believe that I had wasted three years of my life for nothing.

My job was about to go away. They wouldn't let me take the warden's exam, and there was no way I could raise my family on a six-month job that paid little and had no benefits. It didn't matter how much I loved my job. It was time to do something different if things didn't change for the better. I stopped at the Emblem cemetery and prayed over my father's grave. I asked my father to look over me and help me through the tough times. I prayed to my father I wanted to become a game warden someday, and I needed his and God's help! The ground rumbled as I prayed. I'm sure that was my father rolling over in his grave from me standing over him in my red shirt.

I did my usual damage work in the spring, but my enthusiasm was dwindling. Bob called me one night and asked if I was interested in applying for a party antelope hunt with him and the director of the Wyoming Game & Fish Department in the Red Desert. I told him that sounded fun and that I was interested in putting my name in the hat for a Red Desert antelope tag. Back then, the Red Desert had trophy buck antelope, and I loved to hunt trophy antelope. I was depressed that summer. My job would end at the end of September, and I wouldn't even be able to check hunters that fall.

I was also dealing with a very difficult landowner that summer. He had a little deer causing him damage on his alfalfa fields near his house. This man drank heavily, talked loudly, and had a lisp when he talked. He was hard to understand and talked loudly. He was the same cowboy in the Shell bar the night I left Martin and drove his truck home. He was also the same man who offered to buy me a drink in the bar when I was twelve years old.

Now that I wore a red shirt, he cared little for me. I had learned who my real friends were once I wore a red shirt. Rarely was this man sober, and he hated the deer that caused him damage to his alfalfa fields.

I drove out to his place one night at about ten thirty. I shined my spotlight in his field next to his house and turned on my sirens and shot cracker shells to scare off about forty heads of deer on his field. He must have been at his house getting ready for bed when I made all the noise with my sirens. I heard a truck fire up. Quickly, here he came wide open with his ranch truck. He sped by me on the highway and went down the highway about two miles to cross a bridge to take a road on the other side of a creek I had just run the deer across. I saw him go by at a high rate of speed, so I shut my sirens and truck off so I could listen to the sound of his truck in the night. He soon crossed a bridge and got on the other side of the creek where the deer were all headed.

I listened to his truck as he sped down the rough two-track road in the dark. I could hear stuff flying out of the back of his truck as he sped down the road. Quickly, he slammed on his brakes as the deer were crossing the road in front of him in his headlights. I could see him through my binoculars. He was standing in the road in his headlights with a pistol in his hand. He yelled with a lisp, "Get the fuck out of here, you sons a bitches!" and fired his pistol at the deer. I figured I better get over there and shut him down before he had killed all the deer or himself. I was sure that he had been drinking heavily. He might be a handful when I arrived. I pulled up behind him a short time later, and he was still standing in the road reloading his pistol in the headlights of his truck.

I yelled at him, "WHAT THE HELL ARE YOU DOING?"

He yelled back, "I DONT KNOW HOW MANY OF THEM ALFALFA-EATING SONS A BITCHES I JUST HIT, BUT I TRIED TO KILL EVERY ONE OF THEM DIRTY BASTARDS! THEY DON'T STAND AROUND AND LOOK AT ME VERY LONG WHEN THEY HAVE A .44 MAGNUM SHOOTING AT THEIR ASS!"

This guy was very intoxicated and yelling at the top of his lungs at me. His speech was slurred. I'm not sure if it was because he was drunk or because he had a lisp. I told him to go home and get some sleep and I would be out to visit with him in the morning about what had just happened. He cussed at me and asked me if my name was Bob Triple Dick. I said, "No, my name is Scott Werbelow, not Bob Trebelcock."

I showed up at his ranch house early the next morning. I was sure we

269

had dead deer to go look for after all the shots he had fired the previous night. I walked up on his deck and banged on the front door of his house. About that time, a red heeler cow dog shot out from underneath the deck and bit me hard in my lower calf muscle. I felt the dog's canines puncture my skin deep to the bone as the landowner opened his door. The landowner also saw that the dog had just bitten me badly. The landowner opened the front door of his house and yelled, "Jeeezzuss Chrisst! Did that fucking dog just bite you?"

I said, "He damn sure did!"

He responded yelling with a lisp, "I WAS GOING TO PUT THAT WORTHLESS SUMBITCH DOWN, BUT ANY DOG THAT BITES A GODDAMN GAME WARDEN IS A GOOD SUMBITCH IN MY BOOK!"

We both jumped in my truck to go look for some dead deer he might have killed the night before. My leg hurt like hell and bled down my pant leg and onto the floorboard of my truck. I would not show him I was in any pain. We never did find any dead deer, and I told him to knock his shit off, or he would be arrested for an attempt to take deer out of season and without a proper license. We got along well after that morning.

Bob called me one evening to let me know that we had all drawn the Red Desert antelope license. We would need to plan for the trip as it was coming up soon. I was excited to have the opportunity to hunt with Bob and the director of the department. The day soon came, and we would all meet on the Sweetwater River south of Lander. We set up a beautiful camp in the willow bottom next to the river. We grilled steaks that night on an open fire. We then sat around the fire and told stories over a whiskey and a Cuban cigar that the director had brought for Bob and me. The next morning Bob cooked us a fabulous breakfast, and we drank our morning coffee around an open fire. We packed our gear and jumped in my 1982 Chevy short-box truck to go look for a trophy antelope. We flipped a coin to see who had the first shot if we did spot a trophy antelope. The director won the toss and would have the first shot.

That afternoon, the director spotted a nice buck antelope. He took a shot at it and wounded the antelope. Bob and the director took off together, trying to catch up with the wounded antelope. They left me with the truck and told me to come and pick them up somewhere once they caught up with the injured antelope. About an hour had passed, and they both disappeared over the ridge to my north. I thought, *Well, I better get closer to their location as it's getting late in the day.* I fired up my Chevy truck and headed down a rough and narrow two-track road. I was moving along faster than I should have been driving when I noticed a sharp-looking rock sticking out of the bank on the right side of the road. I swerved to miss the rock at the last second but clipped it with my right front tire. I heard a loud noise—*BOOM!* Shit, I had just blown out my right front tire.

I quickly pulled off the road onto a flat spot to change my flat tire. I soon noticed that my lug wrench did not fit the new lug bolts I had just put on my truck with my new chrome wheels. Shit, what was I going to do to change this tire in the middle of nowhere before Bob and the director would find me without the proper lug wrench? I pulled out my toolbox and tried every socket I had, but none were the right size. I found a wrench that was the correct size, but I couldn't get it in there to get a good-enough grip on the lugs without stripping them out. I bent the wrench in half and got three of the lug nuts off. I tried everything I could think of but couldn't get the other two lug nuts off as they were stripping out. It was now almost dark when Bob and the director made it back to my broken-down truck. I was embarrassed that I had a flat tire and could not change it because I was not prepared with having the correct lug wrench to get the lug nuts off.

The director said, "What's the problem here?"

I said, "I got a flat and don't have a lug wrench that fits the new custom wheels that I just bought."

Both Bob and the director assisted me with trying to change the flat tire. It soon became evident that we would not get the final two lug nuts off. The director told us he would take his portable radio to the top of a nearby hill and see if he had enough signal to call SALECS and tell them we were broke down. The director got to the top of the hill and keyed the mic on his portable radio. "LANDER GF-1."

Dispatch quickly answered, "GF-1, go ahead!"

"Lander GF-1, we are broke down in the Little Buffalo"—and the director's portable radio battery went dead. Dispatch now knew that the director was broken down somewhere in the Little Buffalo. We were actually in the "Little Buffalo Basin," but dispatch did not catch the last word of the transmission, so chances of us getting rescued were probably slim to none without a more accurate description of our location.

The director finally returned to my truck, and it was now dark. The director looked at me and said, "Scott, I know you are proud of your new shiny chrome wheels, but we are going to have to drive this truck to the top of a large hill somewhere so that we can flash our headlights if someone comes looking for us tonight. They will never find us down here in this hole. We will probably ruin your new chrome rim, but I will pay for the damages if we ever get out of here." I then drove the truck approximately two miles on a flat tire and climbed to the tallest hill. We sat up on that tall hill during the night and talked about many things going on in the department. I heard things I probably didn't need to know as a young peon damage tech. I learned that several people pretty high up in the department were about to lose their jobs, and they didn't even know it yet. I kept my mouth shut and just listened to the director talk. I think he was needing someone to vent to, and Bob was that guy.

Quickly, it rained harder than I had ever seen it rained before in my life, except maybe the time I was taking care of the sheep when the sheepherder had died in my lap years ago. It then started to thunder and lightning, and the wind blew hard as my truck rocked back and forth from the heavy winds. I looked up in the sky and observed one of the most amazing things I had ever seen in my life. It was a "white-colored" full rainbow that covered the entire sky right in front of us. I don't know how a rainbow can shine bright in the night, but it was there right in front of our eyes. I thought to myself, *Why am I broken down in the middle of nowhere with the director of the Wyoming Game & Fish Department sitting on a tall hill in a storm, and why are we looking at a beautiful, illuminated rainbow right now? Could my father be with me right now? Did God and my father put me in a broken-down truck in the middle of nowhere with Bob and the director? If so, why?*

That thought had just crossed my mind when the director looked over at me and said, "So, Scott, what do you want to do for a living?"

I said, "I want to become a game warden someday, sir!"

He said, "Well, what's holding you back?"

I explained to him that I had left college with a teaching degree because my advisor in college had convinced me that it was nearly impossible to get a permanent job with the Wyoming Game & Fish Department. I told him that I had always wanted to become a game warden since I was a young boy. He interrupted me and said, "How many years have you been working as a damage technician for the department?" I explained to him I had worked for nine months my first year, eight months my second year, seven months my third year, and now my job has been cut to only six months. I then told him I had a wife and two kids and probably wouldn't be able to hang on much longer with temporary work and no benefits. He then asked me if I had taken the Wyoming game warden's exam yet. I told him no, because I kept getting rejected every year. They kept sending me a letter saying I was not qualified. He said, "Who sends you a letter that you are not qualified?"

I said, "The head law enforcement coordinator in Casper!"

The director looked over at me as if he was mad and said, "SCOTT, you send me your application next time, and you will be *qualified* to take the exam."

I couldn't believe what I was hearing, and trust me, I would never forget those words that night underneath that beautiful white rainbow. Could this be true? Would I someday get to take the Wyoming game warden's exam? The director then told me he would see what he could do to get me a job during the winter months feeding elk in western Wyoming. I was excited about that as I had always wanted to feed elk during the winter months on a state-operated feed ground. That seemed like the coolest job in the world at that age and would damn sure be better than feeding sheep or cattle every morning.

It was now about 1:00 a.m., and nobody rescued us yet! The director became agitated and said he would walk back to camp. Bob and I pulled out a map and looked at it in our flashlight. As near as we could tell, we were about fifteen miles from our camp, and it was still raining hard.

We explained to the director it would be a stupid idea to hike to camp because we were fifteen miles away, and it was still raining. He said, "I don't care how far it is to camp. I can't believe I'm stuck in this truck broken down in the middle of nowhere with you two clowns!" I think he was being sarcastic, but I wasn't sure! About that time, we saw headlights on top of a ridge about five miles away to our north. The director shouted, "HURRY UP. Flash your lights. Keep flashing your lights!"

Quickly, the headlights we were looking at flashed their lights back at us. Could someone actually be out trying to rescue us at this time in the early morning hours. The lights soon disappeared. About twenty minutes went by, and the lights were closer to our location and flashing at us. I flashed my headlights back. Someone had found us, and they were on their way to rescue us, thank god!

A deputy sheriff pulled up in a very muddy Ford Bronco. The director stepped out of the truck and walked over to meet the deputy as he got out of his patrol vehicle. The director said, "Holy shit, if there is anyone in the entire world that could find us tonight, it would be you, JD Gardner! How have you been, buddy?"

They shook hands, and JD said, "When dispatch called me and told me that the director was broke down in the Little Buffalo something or another, I knew this area was your old stomping grounds and that I would find you out here somewhere!" Not only did JD find us at two in the morning, but he also had a lug wrench that fit the lug nuts on my truck.

Bob and I quickly changed the flat tire while the director visited with the deputy, and we were soon on our way back to camp. The road was muddy, and I'm thankful that we didn't get another flat tire on the way back to camp that night. Apparently, this deputy had been working in this area for over thirty years and knew the area well. There probably wasn't another person in the world who could have found us that night! What's the odds of the director having just enough signal and battery power left on his portable radio to reach dispatch and tell her we were broke down?

I would enjoy my hunt with the director and Bob over the next few days. I got to know the director much better. We hit it off well and would tell funny stories for hours on end. I even shot a nice buck antelope with the director at my side. I shot the antelope at less than twenty yards from us that day. The antelope had seen us lying on a ridgeline and came running right to us and stopped briefly about twenty yards away. I couldn't pass up that shot.

Buck antelope taken that day with the director

We would soon have to leave our hunting trip and get back to work. The director shook my hand and wished me luck with my future with the game and fish department. My six-month job would end in two weeks. What would I do with my life after that?

My job ended at the end of September. I drove back over to the Cody regional office. This would be a very sad day for me to turn in my truck and all my equipment. I knew in my heart I would not be coming back to work as a damage technician next spring for only a six-month job. I needed to move on with my life and be able to provide for my family. It was time to quit having fun and get serious about a permanent job and figure out what I would do for the rest of my life. The shop teacher in Greybull was getting ready to retire. I wouldn't even qualify for this job without going back to college and taking more classes that dealt with CAD (computer-aided drafting). The technology was moving fast, and I was already getting behind on some classes. I would need to have my teaching credentials up-to-date, or they wouldn't even consider me for the Greybull industrial arts position.

Our local Schwan's man showed up at our house in Shell one day to sell us some ice cream. He told me I should become a Schwan's man because

I had the perfect personality for the job. He said it was an easy job, and he was making $50,000 a year selling ice cream. That was a lot of money back then. Teachers were only making about $28,000 a year. Long story short, he talked me into becoming a Schwan's man. I would have to live in Powell, Wyoming, because that was where their business was located and that was where they had a job opening. I tried this job for two weeks and soon discovered this wasn't the job for me. I worked more hours than a game warden worked. I was lost all the time and would search for frozen food on the truck for hours until my brain would become frozen for having my head stuck in the freezer so long searching for rainbow-flavored push-ups. The job was all based on commission. You would earn 10 percent of your total sales for the day. Some days I would spend all day lost and make only $400 for the day. My commission would be $40 for a fourteen-hour day. I soon quit this job. The next time you meet a Schwan's man on the highway, wave at him because I will guarantee you, he is having a bad day. He is lost, and his brain is frozen.

After the Schwan's-man experience, I went back to college and took more classes to get my teaching credentials updated. I also applied to take the Wyoming game warden's exam again. This time, I sent my application, college transcripts, and credentials to the director of the Wyoming Game & Fish Department. I had never forgotten his words that night we were broke down antelope hunting. About two weeks later, I received a letter from the head law enforcement coordinator in Casper. The letter read, "Thanks for your interest in taking the Wyoming game warden's exam. We have received your application but still need your college transcripts and credentials to determine your qualifications before taking the exam." This was the third time that I had received this letter over the years, and I could recite it word for word because I had read it so many times over the years. I crumpled up the letter and tossed it in the garbage can. Had the director lied to me that night? How come he didn't follow through with what he had told me? I was furious and heartbroken all at the same time.

I was mad enough that I found a phone number for the director's Office and quickly dialed the number. To my amazement, the director actually answered his phone. He recognized my voice and said, "Scott, how have you been?" I told him I had been better and was frustrated that I had received another letter I was not qualified to take the warden's exam. He said, "OH REALLY? I'm sorry about that, Scott. Please send me your stuff again, and I will see to it that you are qualified to take the exam!"

The conversation was short, and I thanked him for his time. I hung up the phone and said to myself, *I can't believe I just called the director of the Wyoming Game & Fish and actually spoke to him. Who in the hell do I think I am?*

About two weeks later, I received a letter in the mail from the Wyoming Game & Fish Department. I was so excited to open the letter I opened it right in the post office. I couldn't even wait to get home and open the letter. Could this be it? Could this be the moment I have waited for and dreamed about for the last four years? I quickly opened the letter, and it read, "Dear Scott, we have recently received your application to take the Wyoming game warden's exam. We have also received your college credentials and college transcripts. Congratulations, you have been qualified to take the Wyoming game warden's exam." The letter went on to tell me when and where the exam would be held. It also gave me a list of references that I could study to prepare me for taking the exam. YEEEEESSSSSSS! I did it! I finally got the go-ahead to take the exam! I immediately drove home and told my wife, Lana, the good news. As soon as we were done talking, I quickly picked up the phone and called Bob to tell him the good news as well. They were both very excited for me and congratulated me.

After all the excitement and the reality of it starting to set in with me, I became very nervous. I thought to myself, *How will I ever pass this very competitive exam? I have never had a single wildlife management class in my entire life. There will be people from all over the country taking this exam who have way more knowledge than I do about wildlife management.* I met with Bob the next day, and he gave me some wildlife management books to read. He told me to know all the scientific names of wildlife in Wyoming and all their gestation periods. He told me to learn how to do doe/fawn ratios, population studies, and mapping. He also gave me a law book that listed all of Wyoming's regulations. He said, "Read this law book and know all the game and fish regulations inside and out." I left his warden station that day with a bag full of books and a brain full of nothing. This process intimidated the hell out of me. How would I learn all this information in such a short amount?

It was wintertime, and Martin was still building his lodge in the Bighorn Mountains. Since I didn't have a winter job, Martin asked me if I would be interested in staying in the lodge all winter and doing the finishing work inside of the lodge. This sounded like an adventure, and

I was looking forward to spending the winter up in the mountains in his newly built lodge. I went to the library and picked up many books that dealt with wildlife management. I loaded up a duffel bag full of books to study, a suitcase full of clothes, and my best German shepherd Sarge and snow machined about seven miles into Martin's lodge at Snowshoe Pass.

Snowshoe Lodge completed

Martin and I and another friend worked long hard days finishing the interior of the lodge that winter. Martin's friend did all the electrical wiring, plumbing, and most of the serious thinking that winter. I put up and finished all the sheetrock on three floors, trimmed windows, and hung kitchen cabinets and doors. Martin would be right at our sides, helping us with whatever we needed. He always cooked us a big breakfast, lunch, and dinner. We ate well but also worked hard. After dinner, we would play a couple of games of three-handed cribbage and drink a whiskey or two. Once everyone went to bed, I would line up for hours in my quiet little bedroom and study for the warden's exam with my dog Sarge lying on the bed next to me.

Every morning as the sun was coming up, I would jump on my snow machine with nothing on but my pants and T-shirt and go climb the steep hill behind the lodge just so I could make the set of tracks in the fresh snow that day and jump the large cornice at the top of the hill. One morning I came across some other guys riding their snow machines up the steep hill. They all rode up to me at the top of the hill and saw me sitting there on my snow machine with nothing on but my blue jeans and a white T-shirt. You should have seen the look on their faces as I sped off and jumped off the cornice. They had to be thinking, who in the hell was that? We would work hard all week and travel home on Friday nights and snow machine back into the lodge on Sunday evenings so we would be ready for an early start of work on Monday mornings.

This was one of the best winters I had ever had. I worked hard all day and studied hard all night. Before I knew it, I had learned every scientific name and the gestation period for every big game, trophy game, small game, and furbearer animal in Wyoming. I knew the scientific names for all the species of fish in Wyoming and if they spawned in the spring or fall. I knew the law book inside and out, and I knew how to read a map well. With my four years of experience working for the agency and all my experience working with Bob, I felt I was finally ready to take the Wyoming game warden's exam.

That day would soon come. I kissed my wife, hugged my kids, and said goodbye as I jumped in my little blue Ford Bronco II and headed for Cheyenne. I would turn the radio off and get quiet with myself and rehearse everything that I had been studying for the past three months. I soon made it to Cheyenne and checked into the La Quinta Motel. I ate a nice dinner at the motel that night and crawled into my bed early because I knew tomorrow would be a big day for me. The exam was scheduled to start at eight the next morning and would be held in the auditorium at the headquarters of the Wyoming Game & Fish Department. This building was huge and very intimidating. I had never been inside of this building before. Were there people working in this building who had chased my ole man around in his poaching days? I wondered. I set my alarm and prayed that it would go off. I could not be late for this exam, and I would have to drive in heavy traffic in the morning, and I wasn't sure I knew how to even find the headquarters!. I didn't sleep well that night worrying that my alarm might not go off. If my alarm didn't go off, everything I had worked so hard for would be gone forever. This was my only chance to pass this exam. I woke up at 5:00 a.m. ready to go.

I found the headquarters all right, but the heavy traffic stressed me out because I had always been a country boy and grew up in small towns my whole life. I finally found a parking spot about one block from the gymnasium. I noticed a long line of people standing in front of the auditorium. I thought to myself, *OH MY GOD, how many people are signed up to take this exam?* The butterflies in my stomach were now working overtime, and I was very nervous. I stood in line and eventually made my way into the large auditorium. The auditorium was packed with people, and I would be sitting in the back row. I had a big guy sitting to my right. I reached out and shook his hand and introduced myself. He said his name was Dan Smith and that he was a permanent game warden from Arizona but was trying to get hired in Wyoming.

I introduced myself to the guy on my left, and he told me he had a master's degree in wildlife management and this was his fourth time taking the exam, but he could not land a job in Wyoming yet. After talking to only two people in this room filled with excellent candidates, I felt very nervous and asked myself, *What in the hell am I doing here today in this room with no wildlife management degree?* I thought about my studying late at night in my small bedroom with my dog Sarge lying on my bed tucked up in the Bighorn Mountains for the winter. Had I studied hard enough?

Once everyone got seated, the room became quiet. The chief game warden Jay Lawson got up and addressed the crowd. He welcomed everyone and told us how competitive this exam would be. He said that 455 people had applied to take the exam, but it was narrowed down to only 153 of the most qualified candidates in the country. He said, "You should feel honored if you are one of those candidates sitting in this room today." He then talked about a game warden's career. He said, "It's not a career. It's a way of life. When you get up each morning and put this red shirt on, you should feel blessed and honored every day that you were one of the few chosen men and women to have this opportunity in your life to protect Wyoming's most treasured resource: our wildlife. You see, being a Wyoming game warden is an honor, and you need to be willing to work three hundred hours a month seven days a week to protect our treasured resources. Men and women have died in this line of duty protecting our wildlife. If you are not willing to make that level of sacrifice, you should get up and leave this room right now."

I will never forget those words as I felt my eyes well up with tears when he gave that speech that morning. He then said there weren't any job openings in the agency, but they wanted to develop a hiring list for future openings. He said his goal was to hire ten temporary game wardens for a four-month appointment performing watercraft enforcement on Wyoming's larger lakes and reservoirs. He explained that five two-man teams would be hired to fill the reservoir crew and would be stationed throughout the state for four months during the spring and summer months. He said, "If you were lucky enough to be selected for the reservoir crew and succeeded at your job, you *may* be selected as one of the state's three trainees and eventually sent through the fourteen-week training course at the WLEA [Wyoming Law Enforcement Academy]. Once graduated from the WLEA, you would become one of the three trainees in the state and would be in line for any job openings that may come up." He then went on to say, "It's a very rigorous and competitive process. Many of you in this room today will not make it through the whole process."

The chief's final words were "If you pass the exam today, you will move on to an oral interview. If you pass the oral interview, you will move on to a psychological assessment. Depending on how well you do on the psychological assessment, you will then move on to a polygraph test and background check. If you pass all that, you will then have one final face-to-face meeting with our psychologist to determine if you are suited to be a Wyoming game warden. Oh, and I forgot, there is also a self-assessment test that you will need to take to see how suitable you are to be a Wyoming game warden compared to other permanent wardens in the state. We have tested all our Wardens in the state, and we know who are good ones are and who are not-so-good ones are. We want you to comparatively test out the same as our good wardens in the state. Just a reminder, no calculators are allowed during the exam, and if you are caught cheating, you will be removed from the room. Good luck to each of you and God bless you!"

This talk made me nervous. An assistant placed the exam facedown on my desk. Once everyone had their exam facedown on their desk, the assistant said, "You may start taking your exam now. You have three hours to finish the exam. If you are not finished in three hours, your exam will be collected anyways." I started the exam and read each question several times and carefully before answering each question. There was a written exam to complete, a slideshow that showed pictures of different species of wildlife in Wyoming you had to identify, and a practical portion of the exam where you had to identify different wildlife parts such as duck wings and various other wildlife parts all laid out on a table.

They also had four rifles lying on a table, and you had to explain what type of action each rifle or shotgun had. Once you were done taking the entire exam, you had to read a scenario and write a brief report on how you would respond to the scenario in real life. This would show wildlife administration how good your writing skills were and your ability to handle difficult situations. The essay question focused on a landowner with deer damage on his private property and had approached you as the local game warden with his problem. The landowner became very upset and ended up threatening you if you didn't leave his property immediately. How would you handle the situation? I had been in this situation several times before and felt I had answered this question well.

The second scenario involved a group of hunters who had poached animals in a very remote location in the mountains. You are the local game warden and come across this camp while riding horseback in the back country. The hunters have been drinking heavily, and they are all armed with guns and knives. You confront them with their multiple violations you have just found in their camp. They become upset with you and get very belligerent. Six surround you near their campfire. How are you going to deal with this situation? The exam had some very good questions that certainly took some thought and experience in the field to answer correctly. I felt that all my time working with Bob in law enforcement situations would help me answer this question.

I looked up, and I was one of the last people still taking the exam. Everyone else had got up and left the room. I had answered all the questions to the best of my ability and wrote two short essays. I was reviewing my exam one last time when the assistant came up and said, "Sorry, sir, your time is up. Please turn in your exam." I looked up, and I was the last person of 153 people left sitting in the room. I had answered all the questions and felt good about how I had done on the exam. I could only think of maybe two questions I might have missed on the entire exam. I was told by the assistant to walk over to the headquarters as the grades for the exam would soon be posted. I felt very relieved and felt I had done well on the exam.

Once I walked over to the headquarters, I was soon standing in line with 152 other people waiting to see their score. The assistants would call your name, and you had to come up front and get your number. Down there, you were a number. They had set up a large bulletin board in front of the room. On one side of the board, they wrote *pass*; and on the other side of the board, they wrote *fail*. Once your exam was graded, an assistant would come out and write your number under *pass* or *fail*. They finally called my name to come up and get my number. I walked up, and the assistant handed me a small white piece of paper folded in half. I walked to the back of the line and peeked at my number. Oh my god, it was number 111, the same number as the hospital room that my dad and grandpa had both passed away in. I thought, *What does this mean? If anything, did this mean that my grandpa and father were with me that day?* I would wait in line for almost two hours. The numbers under *fail* far outweighed the numbers under *pass*. Soon, a very cute assistant came out and neatly wrote the number 111 under *pass*. Thank god! I had finally taken the competitive exam and passed it! I couldn't believe it! I quickly thanked God for blessing me that day and couldn't wait to call my wife and Bob to tell them the wonderful news.

If you can imagine the feeling I was going through at that moment, all the hard work I had done studying for the exam, all the help I had received just to get to take the exam, and all the people headed home with wildlife management degrees who had just failed the exam! I felt blessed, but the day was far from over. I would soon sit at a large table with eight red shirts firing hard-to-answer questions at me. I nervously walked up to the closed door and knocked at my scheduled time. I knocked, and nobody answered the door. I stood in the quiet hallway dressed in my suit and tie.

Finally, the door opened, and I was greeted by the chief game warden Jay Lawson. He laughed hysterically when he saw who I was. He said, "Holy shit, it's Scott Werbelow. We aren't ready for you yet, but come on in and put your number on the board in the corner of the room." I didn't know how to take that comment. I nervously walked into the room and introduced myself to all eight red shirts in the room. I knew a few of them, so that put me somewhat at ease.

They each went around the table, and each asked me a question twice. That was sixteen questions I would have to answer. Some questions were very difficult to answer, but I did the best I could. I looked everyone in the eye when I spoke. I spoke loudly and tried not to act nervous. Once I had answered all the questions, they all thanked me and shook my hand. The chief game warden told me he would tabulate everyone's scores and let me know within an hour if I would advance to the psychological exam. He told me to grab a cup of coffee and wait in the waiting room. I nervously waited in the room with others for almost an hour when a young girl finally stepped in and said, "Scott, Scott Werbelow, congratulations, you have advanced to the psychological exam. Please follow me!" I followed her down the hall and entered a large meeting room. There was only one empty chair left in the room, and I filled it. I was the last person to be selected for the psychological exam.

I counted the number of people sitting in the room that day. The process had narrowed us down to twenty-three people to take the psychological exam. It had been a long day, and I was tired. I was having a hard time focusing. The psychologist's secretary administered the two-thousand-question exam. She said, "All questions are yes or no. Please fill in all the ovals with a black number 2 pencil. Take as much time as you need and be sure to answer all questions on the exam. When you have completed the exam, please place it on my desk."

I read the questions on the exam:

Question #1: Do you love your mother?

Question #2: Have you ever wanted to be a florist?

Question #3: Have you ever had a desire to wear women's panties?

I thought, *WHAT THE HELL IS THIS ALL ABOUT?* Yes, I love my mother; but if I answer yes, does that mean I want to have sex with my mother? I read every question two to three times before answering them. As I went through all the questions, I noticed a pattern. They would ask you the same question three times but would word it differently every time. This was starting to confuse me.

My brain was now going numb. I looked up to see how many people were still taking the exam. It was down to me and a couple of other guys. I looked through my exam, and I still had two more pages of questions to answer. I didn't want to again be the last person taking the exam, so I sped up my reading and read each question only one time. Quickly, I was the last person taking the exam, and I still had over one hundred questions to answer. I finally got to the bottom of the page and was so relieved that I had completed the test. I got up and handed my test in. My brain was fried by now. Between taking the competitive exam, going through the oral interview, and answering two thousand yes-or-no questions, I had had it for the day. I couldn't wait to get back to my motel room and call my wife and Bob and tell them the good news.

I soon arrived at the motel room and cracked open a cold Coors Light beer. I wasn't much of a beer drinker, but man, did that beer taste good. I sat in my chair next to the bed and chugged about half of the can of beer down. About that time, the phone on my desk rang. I thought who in the cornbread hell would be calling me in my motel room right now? I answered the phone, "Hello."

I heard a woman's voice say, "Ah yes, is this Scott Werbelow? Hey, this is Lacey with Dr. Whyme's office. How are you doing?"

I said, "I'm fine, just having a cold one. How are you doing?"

She said, "Hey, is there any reason that you failed to complete the psychological exam?"

I said, "WHAT? I thought that I had completed it."

She said, "No, you still have two hundred more questions to complete."

I said, "Oh crap, I'm sorry. I will be right down to finish completing the exam!" I swigged the rest of my beer down and headed down the interstate in my Ford Bronco II to complete the rest of my psychological exam.

It was well past 5:00 p.m., and the sweet lady had to let me in at the front doors of the Cheyenne Headquarters building. All the lights in the building were off, and the halls were dark. I felt stupid and embarrassed as I followed her down the hall in the dark with the smell of Coors Light beer still on my breath. I even got to meet Dr. Whyme himself as I walked back into the testing room. He glared at me and said, "Why did you fail to complete the exam, Mr. Werbelow?"

I said, "I'm sorry, sir, but I was the last person sitting in the room, and I thought I was done when I got to the end of the page."

He said sharply, "Well, if you would have turned the page, you would have noticed that you had another two hundred questions to answer. Now please get seated and finish taking your exam. It's getting late."

I finished taking the exam as quickly as I could. I was embarrassed. Now I stood out as a real dumbass to Dr. Whyme. He would remember who Scott Werbelow was. Hopefully, he wouldn't give my administration poor feedback because I had failed to complete the exam. I still had never worn women's underwear and thought I would be all right when the dust settled.

That was one of the longest days of my life! I went back to the motel room, drank a few beers, and made a call to my wife and Bob before crashing into bed. They were both very excited for me and congratulated me on a job well done. I would return to Shell the next day and wait for further word from headquarters over the next few weeks to see if I would advance to the final phase of the process to take the self-evaluation exam and meet face-to-face with Dr. Whyme.

I received a letter in the mail two weeks later that read, "Congratulations, you have been selected as a final candidate in the game warden's exam process. Please plan on meeting with Dr. Whyme at the Holiday Inn in Cheyenne, Wyoming, on February 14 at 2:00 p.m. in room 111." I read the

letter several times to make sure that I hadn't miss read it! Room 111—
are you kidding me? I didn't know what this meant, but I felt it meant
something. I felt my father was trying to tell me that he was still with me
through this whole process, not to mention it was my birthday on the day
that I was to meet with Dr. Whyme.

I showed up at Cheyenne headquarters on the morning of the
fourteenth of February. I completed the self-assessment exam and drove
over to the Holiday Inn to meet with Dr. Whyme. I finally found room
111 and noticed there was a note on the door that read, "Please don't
knock until your scheduled time." I waited for my watch to hit 2:00 p.m.
on the nose, and I knocked on the door. I waited for several minutes,
and nobody answered the door, so I knocked louder this time. The door
quickly came open, and Dr. Whyme yelled, "I'm not ready for you yet!"
He then slammed the door in my face. I waited and waited, not knowing if
I should knock on the door again or not. Finally, after about ten minutes,
I knocked on the door again. Dr. Whyme quickly opened the door and
said, "Come in!"

I walked into the large luxurious room with large picture windows
looking out over the city of Cheyenne. I said, "Man, you sure have a nice
office here, Mr. Whyme!"

He quickly replied, "Please sit down. Let's get started!" He then pulled
out a large packet of papers and pulled a single piece of paper out of the
packet and said, "Scott, is there any reason that you didn't fill out this form
last time we met?"

I looked at the form and could remember distinctly filling that form
out. I said, "I remember filling that form out when I filled out all the other
forms that day. I'm not sure why it's not filled out now!"

He said, "Well, you couldn't even finish taking the exam on time,
and now you are telling me you filled out this form!" He turned over the
form and said, "Look here. You signed and dated the form on this side, but
you didn't complete the other side!" I didn't argue with him. I just asked
him if I could please borrow his pen and fill out the form. He said, "You
may!" I think he was purposely trying to get me mad or trying to start an
argument with me.

He read through all his papers and said, "Scott, I see you were spanked
as a child. Tell me about that. What were you spanked with, a garden hose
perhaps?" I laughed and told the doctor that my parents spanked me with
whatever was handy at the time. I told him it might be a Hot Wheels track,

a vacuum cleaner attachment, a wooden spoon, or my ole man's belt. He said, "Oh my god, did they leave bruises on your skin?"

I said, "Sometimes, but the one I remember the most was when my dad spanked me with his leather belt, and it had pictures of wildlife imprinted on his belt. The next day when I went to school, I dropped my drawers in front of the large mirror in the bathroom, and I could see pictures of large mule deer bucks and elk imprinted in my ass cheeks from his belt." I don't think this bit of information impressed him much, but I was being truthful and my parents always told me to be truthful with others.

He then asked me questions about doing drugs and drinking alcohol. I explained to him I had never tried drugs before because I was afraid that I might like them. But I had chewed tobacco since the third grade and even had a spit cup on my desk in the third grade. I told him I drank alcohol in moderation, only consuming a few drinks at night. I didn't tell him those few drinks might equal a half-gallon of Black Velvet whiskey because he just didn't need to know the particulars about that. I told him that my father had died from cirrhosis of the liver at forty and that I was careful with my drinking because I didn't want to end up dead at an early age like my father. He then asked me if my wife and I ever had spats or got into an occasional argument. I told him I got along fine with my wife and that we never argued or fought about anything. He looked at me cross-eyed and said, "Come on now, Scott, we all have an occasional fight with our wife."

I said, "No, sir, women are like horses. You will never find a perfect woman or a perfect horse. You just have to decide what you can put up with."

I felt my visit with the doctor had gone well because I was honest with him and I had nothing to hide from him. Looking back, I might have been a little too honest with him. I was glad to be done with our meeting, and I was glad to be done with the whole process. I headed back home to Shell to be with my family. I couldn't wait to hear the news if I had been selected as one of the ten-reservoir-crew game-warden positions in the state. Several weeks went by, and I had not heard a word from anybody, but I did hear about several others who had been selected and hired on the reservoir crew.

As more time went by, I learned that they had hired all ten reservoir-crew positions, and I was not one of them. I couldn't believe it! This was my only chance, and it didn't happen. I can honestly say I had given it my best shot, and it just didn't happen. My advisor Dr. Miller at Chadron State College had been correct in what he had told me about the Wyoming

Game & Fish Department. Why didn't I listen to him? Why did I waste four years trying to get hired as a game warden? Why did I not listen to Gary Brown when he told me I would never become a game warden? I felt very stupid and frustrated. It was time for me to pursue another career. I was so heartbroken. I just wanted answers to why I wasn't hired. I had worked my butt off for four years, got along with everybody I worked with, passed the game warden's exam and all the other tests, but why didn't they hire me? Did Dr. (Why-me) give the administration a negative report on me? Did he think that I drank too much? Was he mad I never completed the psychological exam on time? What was it?

I was so frustrated that I called a good friend who was a game warden and who also had assisted with proctoring the warden's exams that year. I asked him if he knew how well I had done on the warden's exam. He said, "Between you and me, all I can tell you is you scored in the top three on the exam, and there was rumor floating around that you may have cheated on the exam because you did so well without having a wildlife management degree." This news upset me. They actually thought I might have cheated on the exam because I did so well. Really, how about I just studied my ass off and wanted this more than anybody in the world? This news upset me!

I was so frustrated that I met with the superintendent of Greybull High School. I told him I was very interested in the job in Greybull as the industrial arts teacher if it came open. He thanked me for stopping by and said that he would keep in touch. That summer I learned that two of the wardens hired on the reservoir crew were fired. I knew they probably wouldn't give the warden's exam again just to replace two people. I figured they might go off the current hiring list they had developed when I took the exam. I would have to eat crow and call the head law enforcement coordinator out of Casper. This was the guy who threw my application out every year, and I finally had to go around him and go through the director to get authorization to take the exam.

I soon went home and called him at his Casper office. He answered the phone, and I told him who I was. I simply told him I didn't know where I was on the hiring list, but I wanted him to know that I was still interested and still available. He was short with me and said, "Okay, I will pull your file and put a sticky note on it that says you are available."

I said, "Thank you very much. I would appreciate that!" I heard the phone go *click* on the other end. He had hung up on me. I didn't blame this man for being mad at me. I had gone around him to take the warden's exam, and he didn't appreciate that.

I was sitting at my kitchen table one Friday morning drinking a cup of coffee. The phone rang, and it was the superintendent of Greybull High School. He called to offer me the job of the industrial arts teacher in Greybull. I was very excited but didn't know what to tell him until I had talked with my wife, Lana. I told him to thank you very much and asked him if it would be all right if I gave him an answer on Monday morning. He said, "That will be fine, Scott. I'll talk to you on Monday morning. Have a great weekend!"

I said, "You do the same, sir!" and I hung up the phone. I was very excited, but I was having a hard time letting go of the whole idea of being a game warden someday. I just needed to let go of being a game warden someday because it likely would not happen. I needed to quit living in a dream world and get a real job to support my family for many years to come.

I sat at the kitchen table deep in thought as I finished my cup of coffee. What would I tell the superintendent on Monday morning? Is this what I wanted to do for the rest of my life? About that time, the phone rang again. I answered the phone, and it was the head law enforcement coordinator out of Casper. He said, "Scott, if you are still interested in a reservoir crew position, we have an opening in Casper that starts April 1, if you are still interested."

I said, "Hell yes, I'm interested. Sign me up!"

He said, "All right, congratulations, we will send your paperwork in the mail next week but plan on meeting with your new supervisor Terry Cleveland in Casper before April 1."

I couldn't believe it! I had just accepted a job as a Wyoming game warden in Casper, Wyoming, doing watercraft enforcement for four months. My new boss had a reputation as being one of the toughest supervisors in the entire state. In his earlier days, he had a reputation of being one of the best game wardens ever. People in Greybull and Shell still talked about him and thought he was a legend. I later learned that he was the game warden who chased my ole man around for many years. This was the best day of my life, but what would my wife, Lana, think about living in Casper, Wyoming?

Chapter 14

A Wyoming Game Warden (Finally)

I would tell Lana the good news when she arrived home from work that evening. She was not nearly as excited about the news as I was, especially when she learned that I had turned down a permanent teaching job that had benefits and summers off. She was also not excited about moving to Casper for four months. She said, "The game and fish department is going to move you all over the state with temporary jobs over the next year. When you get a permanent job somewhere, let me know where that is, and I will move with you." Had I made the right decision giving up a permanent job in Greybull and moving to Casper for a four-month temporary position with no benefits? Now I would have to leave my family at home in Shell and be prepared to work long hours. I would have to impress my new boss Terry Cleveland, or I would never get a permanent job with the department. Mr. Cleveland had a reputation as the "battle-ax" in the department. If you didn't perform at a high level, you would be fired. This new job would either go well for me or not well at all.

I soon called my old high school football coach as he and his wife had moved to Casper to teach and coach several years ago. I figured they might have a place I could rent for cheap for four months. I was broke and would either work long hours on the job or travel back home to see my family. So I basically just needed a place to rest my head at night. My coach was excited to talk to me. He and his sweet wife offered me a place to live in their basement while I would be in Casper. I was so thankful for this. They had no idea how much this helped me out at a time in need. I also purchased a cheap and reliable car and got good fuel mileage as I would be traveling a great deal back and forth to home each month. I loaded up my car with some clothes and other personal items and gave my family a kiss and a hug goodbye. I was very nervous about making this trip but very excited thinking about finally becoming a game warden.

I would show up in Casper a couple of days before my April 1 start date and get settled in with the coach and his wife. They had a nice place for me to stay, and it would be fun to get caught up with Coach after not seeing him for over ten years. The heavy traffic in Casper stressed me out as I wasn't used to driving in heavy traffic and I didn't know how to navigate through the city yet. On the morning of April 1, I was driving to the new Casper office. This office was huge compared to what I was used to in Cody. The butterflies in my stomach fluttered as I walked up the two-level stairway into the front office. The atmosphere here differed totally from that at the Cody regional office. All the employees here seemed so serious and busy with their jobs. Employees were darting all over the place, walking at a fast pace and having short and professional conversations in the hallway and the meeting rooms. I could almost sense the tension in the air as I walked through the front doors of the large building.

Three office managers were eagerly waiting to assist me as I walked through the front door. One of them quickly asked me how she could help me. I told her my name and that I was recently hired on the reservoir crew as a game warden and that I needed to meet with Mr. Terry Cleveland. She said, "Oh sure. Follow me, and I will show you where his office is!" She lightly knocked on Mr. Cleveland's door and opened the door slowly. She said, "I have a Scott Werbelow here to see you!" Mr. Cleveland was on the phone, and he told her he would be done talking in a bit.

She said, "Please sit down in the waiting room. Mr. Cleveland will be right with you." I sat down and was becoming very nervous. Mr. Cleveland soon came rushing out of his office toward me. We made eye contact, and I stood up out of my chair. He shook my hand and said with a deep voice, "Well, Well, if it isn't Scott Werbelow!" as he shook my hand firmly.

I said, "Pleasure to meet you, Mr. Cleveland. I have heard a lot about you over the years!"

He said, "I'm sure you have, living in Shell and Greybull, as I used to be the game warden in that country years ago."

I said, "I know, sir. They are still talking about you. Most of them think you are the director of the Wyoming Game & Fish Department."

Mr. Cleveland blushed when I made that comment. He said, "There are some really great people over in that country and some not-so-good people!" He then asked me about a couple of poachers he had chased over the years back in that country. I said, "Yes, they are still alive and still poaching."

He laughed and said, "Some things just never change!" Mr. Cleveland welcomed me to his region in Casper and took me down the hall to show me my new office and meet my new partner. The office was very nice, clean, and well organized. The computer sitting on the main desk had me a little intimidated as I had never used a computer before, and I was hoping I would never have to. Mr. Cleveland soon returned with my partner. He said, "Scott, I would like to introduce you to your new partner Cleeve Coolee!"

Cleeve shook my hand firmly and said, "Nice to meet you, Scott. Look forward to working with you this summer."

I said, "My pleasure, Cleeve. I'm excited as well!"

Mr. Cleveland told Cleeve to take me under his wing and teach me everything that I needed to know to succeed in my new job. Cleeve said, "Yes, sir, I will do, Mr. Cleveland!" After visiting with Cleeve, I learned that he was from Colorado and had been hired on the reservoir crew the summer before, so this would be his second year on the reservoir crew and he would teach me all the ropes. Cleeve had a great attitude and was a high-energy sort of guy. He talked loud and fast and laughed often. His head was shaved nearly bald, and he wore a long mustache that hung down below his chin. He seemed a very direct person who wouldn't take shit off anyone. He also chewed Copenhagen and loved to hunt and fish. I think we would get along just fine. Cleeve was excited to show me around the office and introduce me to other biologists and wardens in the region.

This office made me nervous. The head law enforcement coordinator for the entire department had an office right next to mine. This was the guy who kicked my application back three times to not allow me to take the warden's exam. This was also the guy who had just hired me. I was nervous to meet him for the first time in person. What would he think of me? How would he treat me after I went around him to get qualified to take the warden's exam? This office also had the head law enforcement investigator in the state who also had an office just down the hall from me. There were several top positions in the state housed right in the Casper office. I think that is why I could always feel tension when I was in that office.

Cleeve took me out into the large equipment compound and showed me where all our equipment would be stored. We had a very nice twenty-one-foot Lund patrol boat equipped with a light bar behind the driver's-side seat. The light bar stood up high in the air and had bright red-and-blue lights. The boat also had a two-way mobile radio mounted under the dash and an antenna mounted on the rear of the boat. Cleeve then showed me a jet boat and a pair of Polaris jet skis that we would be using to patrol the North Platte River. I had always wanted to operate a jet ski and a jet boat, so this would be my first time with both.

I now had a smile on my face from ear to ear. This would be an awesome summer. Cleeve then showed me our new patrol truck. It was a brand-new regular cab Chevy equipped with all the bells and whistles. I thought Bob's truck was fancy. His didn't hold a candle to our new patrol truck. Cleeve had done an excellent job setting this truck up. We had a custom-made front bumper with a WARN winch and fancy new red-and-blue lights mounted in the front. We also had a custom-made headache rack mounted on the bed of the truck with a built-in WARN winch, spotlight, and new red-and-blue rear lights. Cleeve got done showing me around and introducing me to everyone and invited me to his house to meet his wife and eat a steak for dinner.

Cleeve was renting a house in Casper from the Casper game warden. This house sat right next to the Casper game warden's station. He invited the Casper game warden over to drink beer and introduce him to me. The Casper game warden showed up at Cleeve's house while we were sitting at the kitchen table drinking a beer. He walked right through the back door of the house without knocking, entered the house, and opened the refrigerator and grabbed a beer without asking. He then sat down at the kitchen table, swigged down a Coors Light beer, belched, and threw the empty can toward the garbage can. The empty can bounced off the wall and landed on the floor. He stood up from the table and said, "Oh, by the way, my name is Ike!" and he held out his hand to shake mine.

I shook his hand and said, "Nice to meet you as well, Ike!"

He then walked across the kitchen floor, kicked the beer can, and headed out the back door. I looked at Cleeve like "Who in the hell was that?" Cleeve said, "Oh, that's just Ike. You just need to get to know him." And I guess he does own this house, so he doesn't need to knock or ask for permission to get a beer out of the refrigerator.

I really liked Cleeve. I felt he and I were going to have a great summer working together as we had a lot in common. I did have to show Cleeve how to cook a real steak later on that summer. Tomorrow would be a big day for me as Mr. Cleveland had asked me if I wanted to ride to headquarters with him to pick up all my law enforcement equipment. I was to meet him at the Casper regional office at 6:00 a.m. I felt honored that he had invited me to ride with him to Cheyenne, and I think Cleeve was a little jealous of the whole idea. Mr. Cleveland had a brand-new 1995 Ford Bronco with small red-and-blue lights in the top-left corner of the rear window and two small red-and-blue lights in the front grill. Back then, all the supervisors had Ford Broncos and not trucks. I'm not sure if this was a status thing or not.

I met Mr. Cleveland sharply at 6:00 a.m. He was wearing his red shirt, green cap, and mirrored aviator sunglasses. This man was the shit, and everyone knew that. We headed down the interstate toward Cheyenne. Mr. Cleveland hadn't said a word all morning, except good morning when I entered his Bronco. He looked over at me and said, "Man, the antelope population in the Emblem area sure increased dramatically when you're ole man died." I was speechless. All I could do was laugh at his comment. This comment alone told me that Mr. Cleveland knew my ole man was a poacher and that he had probably spent time chasing my dad around trying to catch him poaching back in the day.

I replied, "Yeah, I think my ole man was known to occasionally shoot an extra antelope or two now and again."

Mr. Cleveland smiled and said, "Yup, I chased your dad around for years and could never pin anything on him. I knew he was poaching, but I could never catch him." He then told me a story where he had shown up at my ole man's house with a search warrant one day and found a freezer full of dead eagles out in the old shop behind the house. My dad apparently told Mr. Cleveland he did shoot the eagles, but it was prior to the Early Migratory Bird Treaty Act that wasn't enacted until 1973. Mr. Cleveland then said, "I had nothing. I could not prove otherwise, so I just jumped in my truck and left knowing that I had been beat again because before 1973 you could legally shoot eagles."

After Mr. Cleveland told me that story, I did remember seeing eagles in that freezer when I was a young child. I remembered pulling all the feathers off them and sticking them in my waistband and all over my body. I then climbed on top of that old shop and tried to fly off the roof. I landed hard on the gravel road below and damn near died that day. I then hiked over to Grandma Helen's house and stole her umbrella, grabbed two handfuls of eagle feathers, and tried it again. The umbrella quickly collapsed as

I jumped off the roof a second time and pert near killed myself again. I did not tell Mr. Cleveland that story as it was somewhat embarrassing at the time. On the way to Cheyenne that day, Mr. Cleveland also told me a few stories about my stepfather, Martin, I had not heard before. I thought to myself, *Could these stories be true?* I would need to visit with Martin about this at a later time.

We had a great visit that day on the way to headquarters, and I felt relieved that Mr. Cleveland knew who my old man was and knew him better than I had thought. I felt more at ease he knew my dad and held nothing against me because of my dad's previous history with his poaching. We soon arrived at headquarters, and Mr. Cleveland took me back to the office of Jay Lawson, who was the chief game warden. Jay had a box sitting on his desk with my name written across the top in a black marker. I looked into the box and found a duty belt with a 9mm stainless-steel Beretta pistol in a leather holster. The belt also had a baton, OC spray (oleoresin capsicum), handcuffs, and a leather case that held two spare magazines for my 9mm pistol. There was also a bulletproof vest, a pair of beat-up binoculars, beat-up spotting scope, and a beat-up ticket book. This equipment had seen hard miles, but that didn't matter. I was just happy to have it and finally become a Wyoming game warden.

I returned to Casper that evening and would have to spend the next few days in training. I returned to the Casper regional office the next morning and met with Casper game warden Ike to get my 12-gauge shotgun and M-14 rifle out of the safe from downstairs. I would then spend the next two days qualifying with all my department-issued firearms and going through custody and control training. I was nervous that I wouldn't qualify because I had shot none of these firearms before. I would need to shoot fast and accurately with only seconds to draw my firearm, take aim, and deliver three to four shots center mass into the 3D target of the bad guy. I would qualify just fine with all three firearms that day. I was very relieved that I had made it through this training. I would then spend an entire day doing baton strikes into a "blue man." This is a fake dummy full of padding and stands about six feet tall and weighs nearly 150 pounds. After baton strikes, we would practice elbow strikes, knee strikes, and arm-bar take-downs with the blue man. I was so ready for all this training to end. I just wanted to get to work and be a game warden.

As soon as my training was over, my partner Cleeve took me upstairs to our office and showed me how to properly write a citation. There were hundreds of codes to learn; and you had to make sure that you listed the correct court date, time of the court, and correct judge on the citation. You also had to write the correct VC (violation code) and state statute of what you were charging the suspect with. There were over one thousand codes in our laminated cheat sheets. Each ticket had five carbon copies, so that's where the saying "press hard five copies" came from. Once you issued a citation to someone, you would need to take the original copy of the citation to the courthouse in the county that the suspect was charged in. You would then need to get on your computer and fill out a CMS (case management system) report. That's why I had a computer to complete CMS reports and read e-mail.

Cleeve fired up the computer and said, "Let me show you how this damn thing works." He turned on the computer and told me I would have to come up with a password.

I said, "A password? What the hell is that?"

He said, "Just a unique name that you use so that nobody can break into your computer. Pick something easy for you to remember like the first digit of your first name and the first five digits of your last name."

In the password box, I quickly typed *swerbe*. Cleeve looked over my shoulder and said, "*Swerbe*. I like that!" Cleeve called me Swerbe from that day on in April of 1996, and the nickname stuck and is still with me today over twenty-four years later! Over time, it got shortened to Swerb.

I had just spent my first week in Casper going through rigid training and getting all the equipment to be a game warden. Our job that summer was to patrol Alcova Reservoir, Pathfinder Reservoir, Seminole Reservoir, the Miracle Mile, and the North Platte River. We were supposed to work only forty hours per week. I soon learned that it was common practice to work sixty to eighty hours per week and only code forty hours! During my first week of work, I never even got to check a fisherman or take the boat out. I returned to Shell during midweek to see my wife and kids. I missed them badly but would have to hurry back to Casper because we were expected to work Friday to Monday every week while the lakes were busy with fishermen and boaters out recreating. It was easy to work your forty hours in three to four days because we worked long hours each day. While home, I learned that my brother, Wade, had been hired by the Bighorn County Sheriff's office as a deputy sheriff. He would be living in Byron, Wyoming. I thought it was neat that we had both ended up in law enforcement positions.

I returned to Casper on Thursday to spend the night at my coach's house. It was this night I told my coach the story about my dad's last words before he died. I told him that just before my dad passed, he came out of a coma and told me to make five touchdowns for him in my game that night. Coach remembered that game well and said, "Holy cow, that was the game that we were getting beat 16–0 at the half, and I put you in as tailback during halftime, and you scored five touchdowns in the second half of that game, and we won the game 35–16." Tears welled up in his eyes, and he gave me a big hug and said, "I had no idea, Scott!" He then said, "Didn't you get Most Valuable Player that week and an autographed football that was signed by everyone on the team?"

I said, "Yes, Coach, I did, and I still cherish that football that you gave me that day. Thank you very much, Coach!" We both hugged each other and cried again.

I was so excited to meet with my partner that Friday morning we hooked up the boat and headed for Alcova Reservoir to check fishermen and boaters. I would finally get to be an official game warden. I had worked four long years and many hours for this moment. We got to the reservoir, and there were only a few boats on the entire lake. We unloaded the boat and headed toward Fremont Canyon in our cool patrol boat with the red-and-blue light bar sticking up in the air behind the driver's seat. We hadn't been on the lake for two minutes, and the wind blew hard. I looked across the lake and could see white caps and swells four to five feet deep. I had never been in a boat on rough water before, and I became very scared. Cleeve was now standing up, navigating the boat carefully through the deep swells and rough water! I yelled at Cleeve, "I THINK WE NEED TO GET THE HELL OFF THIS LAKE RIGHT NOW!!"

He just smiled and said, "OH, THIS IS NOTHING, SWERBE. IT GETS A LOT ROUGHER THAN THIS!" Apparently, Cleeve was much more experienced with operating a boat on rough water because I was scared to death.

About that time, Cleeve grabbed his new binoculars and looked out across the lake for a second. He said, "Oh my god, someone is floating around in the middle of the lake in a canoe!" I grabbed my shitty binoculars and located someone disappearing in the deep swells paddling frantically to get back to shore.

I said, "Shit, that guy is going to drown here in that self-drowning unit that he is paddling. We better get over there and help him right now!"

Cleeve throttled up the boat and beat through the deep swells to get over to his location. We finally pulled alongside the guy, and Cleeve said, "How are you doing today? Could you hold up a life jacket for me to see please?"

The man was breathing heavily and said, "I'm not doing worth a shit. Got caught out in this damn wind, and I'm just trying to get back to my camp on Black Beach."

Cleeve said, "I see that, but do you have a life jacket?"

The man yelled, "NO, I DO NOT!"

Cleeve looked at me and said, "Grab him one of our spare life jackets, Swerbe, and throw it to him." I quickly threw him a life jacket, and Cleeve said, "Put that life jacket, on and we will follow you back to your camp to make sure you make it safely back!"

The man said, "Yes, sir, thank you!"

It took the man forever to get back to his camp, but we were right on his tail to make sure he made it safely. On the way over, Cleeve looked at me and said, "Get your ticket book out, Swerbe. You are about to write your first ticket to this man for fail to provide a life jacket."

I said okay as I looked for the brown briefcase that I had used during my student teaching. I finally found it and opened it with the combination. This was tough to do because the lake was so rough, and I couldn't stand up in the boat without falling. Cleeve looked at me and laughed as he said, "Oh shit, this guy is in deep shit because Swerbe just pulled out the brown briefcase."

We beached our boat, and Cleeve told me to go write him a citation for failing to provide a life jacket and that he would stay and hold on to the boat. The wind must have been blowing thirty miles per hour. The man thanked me for the life jacket, and I asked him for his driver's license and explained to him I would issue him a $110 citation for not having a life jacket. He became very upset and yelled at me. He said, "Fuck you and your life jacket!" He threw the life jacket back into his canoe. I explained that the law requires everyone operating a boat to have an approved type 3 PFD (personal flotation device) while operating a boat in any waters that belong to the state. I also explained that he should not have been out in that rough water in a canoe especially without a life jacket. I also told him that's a good way to drown yourself. He yelled, "I thought you guys were good guys, and now you are writing me a fucking $110 ticket!" He then shoved me backward with both hands and said, "THAT'S BULLSHIT!"

Before I knew it, Cleeve jumped between us and quickly took the young man to the ground with an arm-bar takedown. Cleeve had his knee in the guy's back and yelled, "YOU NEED TO SETTLE DOWN RIGHT NOW, OR YOU ARE GOING TO JAIL FOR INTERFERENCE!" *Wow, I thought to myself, Cleeve doesn't mess around with this behavior!*

The man agreed to settle down and take his ticket. I sat at a picnic table and tried to write the ticket out while Cleeve stood between me and this very upset man. I took forever to write this ticket out between dealing with the strong winds and just wanting to make sure I wrote my first ticket correctly. I was happy to have Cleeve for backup. Finally, I handed the ticket book to the man and said, "Sign hard five copies!" The man reluctantly signed the citation and gave me my ticket book back. I tore out his pink copy, and it had nothing written on it because I had not put all five copies above the divider in my ticket book. I quickly explained to him what had happened and told him to take care of it by the court date. I then told him the amount he owed and the address and phone number to the courthouse. I was relieved that I had just written my first ticket, even though I screwed it up. I turned to walk back to our boat, and it was gone. Cleeve's knot came untied, and the vessel went out to sea.

The man looked up and said, "Looks like your boat got away from you. Do you need a ride out to your boat? I can take you in my canoe." I looked at Cleeve in disgust. We were in a real pickle. Cleeve said, "Well, go with him. I'm not riding in that damn self-drowning unit!"

I looked at the man and said, "Yes, I would appreciate a ride back out to get our boat."

The canoes and I didn't get along, and this would suck badly with the strong winds still blowing. But we had no choice. We couldn't even call for help because our portable radios were still on the drifting boat. I jumped in the canoe, and we were headed out to sea in the rough water. The man rowing the boat looked at me and smiled and said, "Hey, guess what?"

I said, "WHAT?"

He said, "We are now one life jacket short!" as he held up the life jacket we had loaned him.

I laughed and said, "We damn sure are, and if this canoe tips over, you can have the life jacket!" This was a very humbling experience for me, and yes, I learned from that but still gave him a citation for shoving me and having an attitude. I soon returned to Black Beach in the rough water and picked Cleeve up. I think that's the hardest I have ever seen Cleeve laugh before, and it wasn't funny.

Cleeve taught me how to operate the boat in rough water and let me drive the boat back to the boat dock. I was now feeling more comfortable with our patrol boat and rough water, especially after riding in that damn canoe. I pulled the boat up to the boat ramp and noticed a young man fishing off the boat dock. Cleeve said, "I'll let you handle this contact, Swerbe!" I had some small talk with the young man and then asked him for his fishing license.

He said, "I have one but forgot it in my car. I can run up and grab it really quickly if you would like me to." I explained to him that the law required him to have it in his possession while fishing.

I then said, "Yes, run up and grab it quickly, and I will wait right here for you."

The young man said, "I'm sorry, sir, but I have one, and I will be right back with it in two minutes."

I watched the man run up the boat ramp jump in his car and speed off. Cleeve looked at me and said, "Did you get his driver's license or his fishing pole?"

I said, "HELL NO!"

He smiled and said, "You will learn!"

We got off the lake and went back to the office. We got the jet boat and checked fishermen on the North Platte River where the wind wouldn't be blowing as bad. We grabbed the boat and put it in at Robertson's bridge south of town. Cleeve told me he would operate the boat for a while and teach me how to run it. This boat was awesome. It had 175-horsepower Johnson motor, and man, did it travel up the river nicely. As we were traveling up the river, I thought to myself, *Man, I didn't think being a game warden was such a tough job. I have already screwed up two cases today, and they were the only two people on the whole damn lake.* As we headed upstream, we came to a bridge that crossed the river. It didn't look like it had much clearance to get underneath it. Cleeve idled the boat down, and we went under the bridge. The windshield on the boat only cleared the bridge about six to eight inches, but we made it under the bridge, hitting nothing. Once we got past the bridge, Cleeve said, "You want to give it a try?"

I said, "Hell yes, I do!"

I stood up and started slowly with the throttle. As I became more comfortable with how the boat handled, I idled it up; and we were moving at a good pace up the river. I was having the time of my life operating this jet boat. This boat would go a lot faster than you wanted to drive it. I looked up, and there was a sharp bend in the river coming up with some fast water roaring. I thought to myself, *Watch this shit. I'm going to scare the shit out of Cleeve.* Just as we were about to the corner, I mashed the throttle down wide open and skipped around that blind corner, shooting about a thirty-foot rooster tail of water out the back of the boat, spraying the Russian olive trees on the bank with water as we rounded the corner fast. Cleeve hit the deck and yelled, "WHAT THE HELL ARE YOU DOING?"

I laughed and said, "I had this vessel under complete control!"

He laughed and said, "Yes, you did, but a fisherman was sitting under that Russian olive tree, and you just douched him badly with your thirty-foot rooster tail!"

I said, "OH SHIT, I didn't see the fisherman sitting there. I better turn around and apologize to him."

I quickly flipped the boat around and drifted down the fast water near the Russian olives. A man stood up soaking wet and yelled, "Fuck you!" as he gave me the middle finger. I beached the boat downstream from him and walked over to him. I said, "Sir, please forgive me. I had no idea you were fishing underneath that Russian olive tree, and I apologize for soaking you with my rooster tail as I went by."

He was mad, but he said, "Apology accepted!"

I reached out and shook his hand and said, "While I'm here, could I take a look at your fishing license and conservation stamp, sir?" He grumbled and pulled it out of his wallet and showed it to me. I thanked him and apologized again for soaking him. I'm sure that guy never forgot that day, and neither did I. I jumped back in the boat, and we headed back up the river with Cleeve at the wheel. We went up the river several miles and decided to turn around as there was nobody out fishing.

We headed back down the river and came around a sharp corner. As soon as we made it around the corner, I looked up and observed four black guys fishing on the shoreline. As soon as they saw our red shirts, they all dropped their poles and took off running up the hill toward some trees. Cleeve yelled, "GET THEM! THEY DON'T HAVE ANY FISHING LICENSES!" Cleeve quickly beached the boat, and I took off running after them in my cowboy boots. I knew I would not catch any of them because I had played college football with black running backs, and they could all outrun me.

I quickly ran up the hill until I was out of wind. There was only one guy still in my sight who hadn't made it to the trees yet. I stopped, drew my 9mm pistol, and fired it in the air and yelled, "STOP OR THE NEXT ONE WILL BE AIMED AT YOU!" He quickly stopped and put his hands in the air. I yelled, "COME ON BACK DOWN HERE. I NEED TO TAKE A LOOK AT YOUR FISHING LICENSE!" He came down the hill slowly with his hands in the air. I looked over at Cleeve and winked and said, "Sometimes you just have to outsmart them!" He looked at me as if to say, "You crazy bastard, they taught us not to do this thing at the Law Enforcement Academy. Oh, that's right. You haven't been to the academy yet!"

The man came back down the hill to our boat. He said he didn't have a fishing license, and neither did the other three guys. I told him I would cut him a break and write only one citation to him for fishing without a license. I asked him for his driver's license, and he handed it. He was from Colorado and told me that the other three guys were also from Colorado. I told him that his citation would cost him $110; and since he was from Colorado, he needed to post a bond in the field or go to jail. He said, "Sir, I don't have that kind of money on me."

I said, "Well, maybe you can go find your friends up in the trees, and they can help you pay. If not, you will be arrested and take a boat ride to town with us."

He looked at the boat and said, "On that thing?"

Cleeve said, "Yes, sir, it won't be the first time and probably won't be the last time that we have hauled people to jail for fishing without a license."

I took the man's driver's license and sent him up the hill to find his buddies. I soon learned to get their driver's license first before turning them loose.

The man returned shortly with all his buddies, and they all emptied their pockets on a picnic table. They counted up every last dime they had, and the man handed me $104.65. He said, "I'm sorry, sir, but this is all we have." He handed me two handfuls of change and some cash.

I said, "That will do!" I issued him a citation and checked the little box at the bottom of the citation that read *bond collected*. This citation would end up costing me $5.35, but that's all right. I didn't want to have to arrest four guys and transport all of them to jail on a jet boat. Besides that, Cleeve and I only had two pairs of handcuffs. Sometimes you just have to get what you can get. I jumped back on the boat, and we headed back downstream. Cleeve looked at me and said, "Don't ever fire your pistol in the air again, you crazy farm boy!"

I said, "Well, if I hadn't, they would have all gotten away, and now we have $104.65, and I will guarantee you that ole boy will never forget the day that the game warden fired a shot in the air and ordered him down the hill and issued him a citation."

Cleeve laughed and said, "I promise not to mention this one to anybody, including Mr. Cleveland!"

We headed back down the river, and Cleeve asked me if I wanted to drive the boat for a while. I said, "Sure!" I grabbed the wheel and said, "Hold on, buddy!" I pushed the throttle lever down, and we were sailing down the river at a high rate of speed. I looked up and seen the low-hanging bridge ahead, the one we barely cleared on the way up the river. I yelled at Cleeve, "YOU MIGHT WANT TO DUCK YOUR HEAD."

Cleeve looked up and yelled, "OH SHIT!" He dove on the floor of the boat.

As we got close to the bridge traveling at a high rate of speed, I thought to myself, *HOLY SHIT, WE ARENT GOING TO CLEAR THE BRIDGE.* I quickly pulled the throttle back and hit the floor with Cleeve and put my hands over my head. All I heard was a loud crashing noise. Once we shot out the other side of the bridge, I quickly jumped and grabbed the steering wheel of the boat and noticed that we were missing our entire front windshield. "DAMMIT!" I said. We could have been killed, and I just wrecked the fish division's jet boat.

Cleeve calmly said, "I forgot to tell you that the water levels always rise in the afternoon. I almost did the same thing last year!"

I ordered a new windshield, fixed it, and paid for it myself telling no one. This was becoming an expensive day for me.

We took the damaged boat back to the office and parked it in the storage shed. Cleeve said, "You better get that windshield fixed and put some teak oil on the deck of the boat, or Cleveland will have your ass. Let's grab some groceries and head up to the Miracle Mile and check fishermen this evening. We can stay at the Cortes cabin tonight and cook a steak if you want to."

I said, "Sure, that sounds fun. Let me grab a change of clothes and a couple of steaks, and I will meet you back at the office in an hour."

Cleeve said, "Sounds good. I will grab a couple of cigars and a bottle of whiskey. What kind of whiskey do you drink?"

I said, "I like the cheap stuff. CLC [Canadian Lord Calvert] will work for me."

We reached the Miracle Mile about one hour before sunset. It had been raining, and the weather was cool. We checked several people fly fishing in the Blue Ribbon fishery as we headed for the Cortes patrol cabin. I looked over and observed a camp of people in the trees along the highway. I told Cleeve to pull into their camp, and we could see if they had any fish in camp. As we got near the camp, they had hung a large blue tarp over a campfire; and they were all huddled around the campfire, trying to stay out of the rain. Cleeve pulled up in front of their camp with our patrol truck. I got out and walked over to their campfire. I observed fishing poles leaning on several trees nearby. One pole was still baited with a worm on the hook. I noticed the worm was still wet and alive, indicating that someone had just fished with that pole. I was very friendly with them and asked them how the fishing was. They were all Hispanic, and it looked like there were about six huddled around the campfire. One man approached me as I was standing away from their fire and not under their blue tarp.

The man spoke broken English and said, "We haven't been doing any fishing yet. We are just trying to stay dry and warm."

I said, "Okay, why don't I take a look at your fishing licenses right now so that I don't have to bother you guys later while you are out fishing?"

The man said, "We have not been fishing, and we don't have our licenses yet. We are waiting for it to quit raining before we buy our licenses. If this storm blows over, we plan on driving down the road and purchasing a fishing license at the little store down the road."

I said, "Okay, that is fine, but I see someone has been fishing with that pole right there with the worm on the hook that is still alive." I pointed at the pole leaning on the tree next to their camp. I then said, "It is also illegal to use bait in this stretch of the river as it is artificial flies and lures only in this stretch of the river." I looked over at the men gathered around the fire and made eye contact with the largest guy in the bunch. He was sitting in a blue camp chair next to the fire glaring at me. Our eyes made contact, and it felt he glared right through my soul. I never broke eye contact, and neither did he. It gave me the chills. Something was wrong with this man.

I asked the man if anyone in the camp had a fishing license. He said, "No, they didn't!" I knew several had been fishing, but I couldn't prove it, and the heavyset guy sitting at the campfire was still glaring at me, and it was giving me the creeps. Cleeve and I jumped in the truck and headed for the Cortes cabin. I looked at Cleeve and said, "Lying bastards!"

Cleeve said, "Yup and we will catch them fishing later." We went to the cabin, and I grilled Cleeve a wonderful steak for dinner. The sun peeked out of the clouds just as it was setting behind a large mountain. It was beautiful out. The sunset was gorgeous. I looked at Cleeve and said, "You ready to write a ticket?"

He smiled and said, "Yup, I was thinking the same thing. Those guys won't be able to resist throwing their line in the water while the sun is shining."

We jumped in the truck and pulled up on the highway where we could see their camp from a distance of about one mile. I grabbed my shitty binoculars and could see two people fishing down by the river below their camp. One guy was wearing a blue coat and red hat, so he would be easy to identify later in camp. The other guy I could only see the top of his pole over the willows and the color of his ball cap, which was white. I watched them both cast and reel a few times. About that time, I observed a young Hispanic man running through the willows toward the river. He was wearing a bright-yellow rain slicker. This was their watchdog. The boy had spotted us up on top of the hill about one mile away and quickly ran down and told the other two Hispanic men that the game wardens were watching.

I looked at Cleeve and said, "Well, I have enough evidence. I observed two of them fishing and have their descriptions. Let's get down to their camp." I observed the two men quickly walk back to their camp. When we pulled up to their camp, it was now dark and they were all huddled tight around a large campfire. I exited the truck and walked near their campfire, but again, I didn't walk underneath their blue tarp. I looked at the man in the red cap and said, "Sir, I guess I need to check your fishing license." I called him away from the others, and we were standing in the dark away from the fire alone. He said in broken English, "I was not fishing!"

I said, "Sir, what would you tell me if I told you that I have been sitting up on that hill over there and watched you fish for the last ten minutes?"

He replied, "I didn't fish for ten minutes. I only fished for about five minutes!"

I said, "All right, you fished, and I need to see your license!"

He replied, "I don't have one!"

I told him that I was going to issue him a citation for fishing without a license and that he would need to post a $110 bond in the field since he was from Colorado, or we would have to haul him to jail. He said, "I don't have that much money. Let me check with my friends and see if they can help me out."

He walked back under the blue tarp. I watched him closely because I didn't trust any of them. I noticed the heavyset guy was still sitting in the blue camp chair glaring at me. This made me nervous and was a red flag to me. The man returned with $110 in cash. I jumped in my truck and wrote the citation in the light of my dome light. Cleeve stood outside my truck and protected me while I focused on writing the citation. I soon returned to the campfire and requested the man come over and sign his citation. He came over and signed the citation and was very upset while doing so. The large Hispanic man in the camp chair was still glaring at me. He would not break eyesight if I stared back at him. I then called the man wearing the white ball cap over to me to interview him. I told him I needed to see his fishing license. He also told me he had not been fishing.

I said, "Sir, with all due respect, you are lying to me as I watched you fish for about ten minutes in my binoculars from that hill up there."

He said in broken English, "I was not fishing. I was only practicing my casting."

I said, "Sir, could you please bring me your fishing pole?"

The man walked back under the blue tarp and grabbed his fishing pole and brought it. I observed his fishing line and noticed that he had a lead sinker on his line but he had broken his line and threw away his hook and worm on the way back to camp when the kid notified him that the game wardens were coming. This man was sharp, but he was lying, and I didn't appreciate that.

We were standing about thirty feet from the fire in the dark away from the campfire and the other people. I got in his face and glared into his eyes and said, "SIR, quit lying to me right now!"

About that time, the big, heavyset guy jumped out of his blue lawn chair and grabbed a double-bladed ax and ran toward me. He quickly jumped between me and the other man and held the sharp ax blade between my eyes. He glared into my eyes and said, "You need to get the fuck out of our camp right now!"

I said, "No, you need to sit your ass back down in your chair right now, or you are going to jail."

My partner Cleeve quickly drew his pistol and stepped back into the dark of the night with a tight bead on the man's head. I could feel the warm sensation of blood trickling down my cheeks as the man had cut the center of my forehead with his razor-sharp ax. I thought to myself, *I could die right now. This being a game warden isn't as fun as I once thought, and this is only my first day on the job.*

Stay tuned for my next book "True Stories of the Wyoming Game & Fish Department" or something along those lines. I survived that situation that day and many others over the next twenty-five years. I learned to have faith in God and never show fear as I knew God and my father have always been with me every step of the way on my incredible journey through my life as a Wyoming game warden.

Printed in the United States
by Baker & Taylor Publisher Services